Network Access Control

FOR

DUMMIES®

by Jay Kelley, Rich Campagna, and Denzil Wessels

WILEY

Wiley Publishing, Inc.

Network Access Control For Dummies®
Published by
Wiley Publishing, Inc.
111 River Street
Hoboken, NJ 07030-5774
www.wiley.com

WILEY

About the Authors

Jay Kelley: A Product Marketing Manager at Juniper Networks, Jay Kelley is responsible for driving the messaging and promotion of Juniper's Network Access Control solutions, including Juniper Networks Unified Access Control (UAC), Odyssey Access Client (OAC), and Steel-Belted Radius (SBR). Prior to serving in his current role, Kelley managed the Product Management and Marketing for Endpoint Assurance, a Network Access Control solution from Funk Software, Inc. until the company's acquisition by Juniper in 2005. With more than twenty years of technology marketing experience, Kelley has worked with and for a number of established companies and start-ups. He actively participates in a number of industry groups and consortiums including the Trusted Computing Group (TCG)'s Trusted Network Connect (TNC) workgroup. Kelley holds a Bachelor of Science degree in Business Management from Daniel Webster College.

Rich Campagna: A Senior Product Line Manager at Juniper Networks, Rich Campagna is responsible for defining product requirements and strategy for both the Juniper Networks Secure Access SSL/VPN product family as well as Juniper's NAC product line, Unified Access Control (UAC). Rich's expertise spans the breadth of NAC and remote access control technologies. Prior to joining Juniper Networks, Campagna was a Sales Engineer at Sprint Corporation. Rich has an MBA from the UCLA Anderson School of Management, and a B.S. in Electrical Engineering from Pennsylvania State University.

Denzil Wessels: A Senior Technical Marketing Manager at Juniper Networks, Denzil Wessels is responsible for access control technologies. This includes helping customers architect Network Access Control deployments, evaluating competitive technologies to provide Juniper's sales and marketing teams with the right sales tools and knowledge. In addition to extensive customer interaction at the evaluation and deployment levels, Denzil manages key business development partners, working with partners on interoperability tests or integration to develop leading, joint security solutions from Juniper and its partners. Prior to joining Juniper Networks, Denzil was a Systems Engineer at F5 Networks, responsible for architecture design and implementing customer solutions. He has also been a consultant for Infinisys, designing and implementing comprehensive customer networking solutions.

Dedications

Jay Kelley: To Nadine, for her love, encouragement, understanding, caring, and (most of all) patience.

Rich Campagna: To Stephanie, for supporting me, loving me, and being proud!

Denzil Wessels: To my loving family, who, without their support, this wouldn't have been possible.

Authors' Acknowledgments

The authors wish to thank the many people who helped bring about this book.

To our wives and families, thank you for putting up with the extra time we spent writing while we should have been doing our chores.

To the team at Wiley, thank you for all of your help and assistance. Without your hard work behind the scenes, this book would never have made it to print.

Last, but definitely not least, a big thank you to our in-house (Juniper Networks) editor in chief, Patrick Ames, who was absolutely critical to the completion of this book. Thank you, Patrick, for keeping us on track, ensuring that we met the deadlines, and for bringing us the idea to write this book in the first place!

Publisher's Acknowledgments

We're proud of this book; please send us your comments through our online registration form located at `www.dummies.com/register/`.

Some of the people who helped bring this book to market include the following:

Acquisitions, Editorial, and Media Development

Project Editor: Pat O'Brien

Acquisitions Editor: Katie Feltman

Copy Editor: Laura Miller

Editorial Manager: Kevin Kirschner

Editorial Assistant: Amanda Foxworth

Sr. Editorial Assistant: Cherie Case

Cartoons: Rich Tennant (`www.the5thwave.com`)

Composition Services

Project Coordinator: Lynsey Stanford

Layout and Graphics: Reuben W. Davis, Jennifer Mayberry, Mark Pinto, Christine Williams

Proofreaders: David Faust, Evelyn C. Gibson,

Indexer: Potomac Indexing, LLC

Publishing and Editorial for Technology Dummies

    Richard Swadley, Vice President and Executive Group Publisher

    Andy Cummings, Vice President and Publisher

    Mary Bednarek, Executive Acquisitions Director

    Mary C. Corder, Editorial Director

Publishing for Consumer Dummies

    Diane Graves Steele, Vice President and Publisher

Composition Services

    Debbie Stailey, Director of Composition Services

Contents at a Glance

Table of Contents

Part IV: The Part of Tens................................ 277

Introduction

*W*elcome to *Network Access Control For Dummies.* It's a scary networking world out there, and this book provides you with a working reference for understanding and deploying what type of network access control (NAC) is best suited for your network and you.

Because you're holding this book, you already know that security issues exist out there — and you've probably, maybe frantically, attempted to protect the network you're responsible for from the scenarios that get printed on the front page.

See whether you can identify with any of the follow scenarios:

- **Authentication nightmare:** You just put in a system to authenticate users who log on to your network, and everyone is hissing at you like snakes. They hate it. They hate you. They claim productivity is down, and the VPs are writing vicious e-mails to your boss.

- **VPN for more than VPs:** Everybody wants to work from home once or twice a week, and you have more and more remote employees working from their home offices around the world. Guess what? You're having a really hard time figuring out who's who and what they should have access to. Complaints about missing files and mission-critical info that's available to all have replaced your bagel with your morning coffee.

- **Portable hi-jinks:** You have absolutely no control over what devices people use to log on to your network, and after they log on, you have no control over what storage devices they can use as peripherals, or what they can take away. HR is investigating people who have left the company with complete DVDs full of trade secrets.

- **Breaches:** You've had breaches, but you can't tell how the attackers accessed the network. Malware may be the culprit, but how do you accuse a trusted user who has a company-issued device? And, at lunch, you hear other people talk about what they downloaded for their kids to play with on their laptops.

- **Productivity slippage:** Your management says that 50 percent of employees are spending 15 percent of their time doing personal shopping on the Internet, surfing, or even playing online games. Oddly enough, you're to blame, not them.

✔ **Quarantine quagmire:** You created a great way to monitor network devices and put those that don't comply into quarantine. You just don't have a great way to get them out. Some devices seemingly sit for weeks because their owners don't know how to update and you don't have the time to tweak every laptop in the world.

✔ **Wireless is less:** The employees love the open nature of WLAN access, and wireless access makes meetings more productive. But without the proper credentials, security, and controls in place, you're just a nose hair away from being snooped or having data stolen, even after a trusted user connects to the WLAN.

This book helps you with all these scenarios and a whole lot more. We purposely made this book a fast and easy way to understand, deploy, and use NAC, and we provide benchmarks for you to judge the merits and capabilities of the many NAC solutions that you can find for sale.

Here's the biggest tip in this book — plan! You can't plan enough when deploying a NAC solution for your network and organization. Take it from our combined 30 years of security work and access control. For every hour you spend planning and testing your NAC implementation, you can save days or weeks trying to fix what you hurriedly deployed. Plan it, then plant it.

About This Book

We fly around the world and say the same things about NAC that we say in this book. If you read it, we help you to

✔ Understand what NAC is and what it can do for you.

✔ Realize the breadth and scope of NAC, as well as how to plan and adapt all these facts into a custom solution.

✔ Home in on what makes the best NAC sense for your organization and how to extend it to fit every nook and cranny in your network(s).

✔ Leverage, repurpose, or reuse your organization's existing network infrastructure to deliver NAC.

✔ Save time, money, and labor in selecting and deploying a NAC solution fit for you.

Something You Should Know About This Book

All three authors are employees of Juniper Networks, which actively markets and sells its own NAC solutions (under the UAC acronym, for Unified Access Control). We try to keep the information in this book as straightforward and unbiased as mere people can, but we admit that sometimes we might go into detail about an issue or feature that we know intimately which some vendors of NAC solutions don't have or implement differently. We're not apologizing. Not one iota. It's just something you might want to know.

What You're Not to Read

We place text you don't need to read in self-contained sidebars or clearly mark them with a Technical Stuff icon. You can skip these items if you're in a hurry or don't want to lose your train of thought. You may decide to browse through the book some day during lunch and read up on all the technical details. They're good preparation for a cocktail party with networking engineers.

Foolish Assumptions

When we wrote this book, we made a few assumptions about you:

- ✔ We assume that you're a network professional, although you don't have to be one. Because our objective is to get you up and running, and you might be reading this book in order to understand what your engineers are telling you, we include only a few basics about how it actually implements NAC and try not to discuss the operations in detail.

- ✔ You may design or operate networks.

- ✔ You may be an IT manager, or a manager who supervises IT managers, or a manager who supervises managers who supervise IT managers.

- ✔ You may procure networks or otherwise work with people who plan and manage networks.

- ✔ You may be a student of NAC or even just entering the networking profession.

How This Book Is Organized

This book is divided into four parts.

Part 1: Unlocking the Mysteries of NAC

Imagine Sherlock Holmes examining your network with a magnifying glass. That's NAC. Read this part, and you qualify to be Dr. Watson.

Part 11: NAC in Your Network

This part gets personal and brings in all the variations that can enable a NAC solution to fit your network needs. A NAC solution can really do a lot for you, after you realize the scope of its capabilities.

Part 111: NAC in the Real World

This part reveals what you really need to know about NAC architectures, standards, and extensions. It's like the form you have to fill out for eHarmony before you get to the dating process. Read carefully, or you may waste your time with several dates from hell.

Part 1V: The Part of Tens

This part offers quick references to the top-ten most helpful stuff on the planet about NAC. You can find help on topics ranging from key definitions, to planning your implementation, to where to go for more info.

Icons Used in the Book

We use icons throughout this book to key you into timesaving tips, information you really need to know, and the occasional interesting backgrounder. Look for them throughout these pages.

This icon highlights helpful hints that save you time and make your life easier.

Be careful when you see this icon. It marks information that can keep you out of trouble.

Whenever you see this icon, you know that it highlights key information that you'll use often.

If you're in a hurry or aren't interested in the details, you can skip the text marked by this icon.

Where to Go from Here

It's a big, bad networking world out there, and 99 percent of the people who use your network don't really understand the security concerns. If you do your job right, they don't have to worry about these concerns. That's the point of this book. Browse through the Table of Contents to find a starting point that sounds like you, and then just dip in. Test the NAC waters. You can skip around like a stone on water, or start with Page 1 and read to the end. Just remember that *you can control who's on your network and what they have access to*. This book is about how to do that.

Part I
Unlocking the Mysteries of NAC

The 5th Wave   By Rich Tennant

"Yes, I know how to query information from the program, but what if I just want to leak it instead?"

In this part . . .

Imagine Sherlock Holmes examining your network with a magnifying glass. That's NAC. Read this part, and you qualify to be Dr. Watson.

Chapter 1

Developing a Knack for NAC

In This Chapter

▶ Approaching network access control (NAC)

▶ Selecting the best approach

▶ Using your existing network infrastructure

*B*ecause you're looking at this book, you've probably heard or read all the hoopla about network access control (NAC). You've likely heard or read reports that NAC is the best thing since sliced bread, the be-all-and-end-all solution for network security or access control, and the best solution for network and device security since antivirus software and two-factor authentication.

Have you also heard that NAC isn't all it's cracked up to be? That it's costly, it takes a lot of time and labor to deploy, working with it can be trying, users don't like it, and it doesn't alleviate every network security and access control issue? Or perhaps that NAC doesn't provide you with a good return on your network security and access control investment?

You probably have at least one peer who told you that NAC isn't the only solution for all that ails networks and network security. And maybe you read or heard about the demise of the NAC market or product category — reports which have been greatly exaggerated.

Boy howdy, is this book for you!

In this chapter (and the whole book), you can discover

✔ What network access control (NAC) is — at least, according to many smart people and organizations

✔ The breadth of NAC

✔ How to home in on what makes the best NAC approach for your organization

✔ How some NAC solutions can enable you to leverage, repurpose, or reuse your organization's existing network infrastructure to deliver network access control, saving your organization time, costs, and labor — not to mention stress, sleepless nights, and gray hair!

NAC's Evolving Description

So, what's this network access control thing that you've been hearing and reading about?

First, NAC isn't the cure-all for whatever security or access control issues and challenges confront an organization and their network. But the right NAC solution, deployed appropriately, can deliver significant protection for

✔ Your network, its applications, and sensitive data

✔ Your users and their endpoint devices

The right NAC solution for your organization can protect against many (if not most) dangerous malware, nefarious hackers, and any malcontent users that the fast-paced, always connected, always on(line) networked world can throw at you.

So, NAC controls access to a network. Unfortunately, that simple definition and description is only partially right.

Many pundits, experts, and vendors find defining, or (more correctly) describing, NAC very difficult and elusive. You can find almost as many different descriptions of and meanings for NAC as organizations that have or want to deploy NAC, or vendors who produce or produced a NAC solution. But a definition exists that exactly fits your network needs — you just need to figure out which definition works for you.

To really understand how NAC works, consider this common — albeit painful, for some — metaphor to describe network access control: the airport!

The steps involved in operating network access control are, in many ways, similar to what happens when you go to an airport to board a plane for a trip:

1. You first stop at the ticket counter or self-service kiosk, where you need your confirmation number and a government-approved ID (such as your driver's license or your passport) so that the airline can authenticate your identity and confirm your reservation. You need to confirm who you are and that you're authorized to travel to your destination. A NAC solution does the same basic verification: It authenticates the user or device, and then checks the user's or device's authorization level to see whether that user or device has authorization to access the network. If your ID is valid, you have a confirmed reservation, and your name matches the name on the reservation, you receive a boarding pass, which means that you're authorized to travel on that flight. Similarly, NAC solutions match the user or device ID — such as a login user name

and password, two-factor authentication (which might include a token), or a smart card — to the authentication database or data store on the network to authenticate the user. If the NAC solution authenticates the user or device, that user or device receives the appropriate keys and credentials to access the network. If NAC doesn't authenticate, the user or device isn't allowed onto the network.

2. After the ticket counter, you have to go through a security checkpoint, including an x-ray machine and metal detector, before you're allowed into the secure area of the terminal gates. This is comparable to a NAC solution's endpoint integrity assessment or host check. In the same way that airport security checks you and your carry-ons for forbidden and dangerous items, NAC checks your endpoint device for any dangerous malware and potential vulnerabilities that hackers and other miscreants could exploit. If you or your baggage set off the metal detector at the airport, security may conduct a further search by hand or wand, if necessary. That extra search is like NAC's host checking of an endpoint device. If a NAC solution detects something amiss in the malware protection of your device, or detects an infection, it may instruct the network to quarantine your device until it can assess and address the anomaly or cure the infection. Then, the NAC solution's host checking can reassess your device before it allows or instructs an enforcement point to allow that device network access. Also, at the airport security checkpoint, security rechecks your ID and boarding pass, which is similar to a NAC solution rechecking authentication while it assesses (and, if needed, reassesses) your device's security state and integrity.

3. After you reach the secure zone at the airport, security can recheck you and your baggage for various reasons, including random security checks, if you're behaving strangely, or if you leave your suitcase unattended. Well, NAC solutions operate in the same way. Even after network admission — which is comparable to being allowed into the secure area — NAC can still conduct random assessment checks on you and your device to determine whether you still meet the organization's requirements to be on their network; or the NAC solution can recheck and reassess you or your device if it uncovers a state change in the security of your device while you're on the network. And, just like at the airport, if everything checks out okay, you and your device can remain in the secure area — or on the network. If the check finds something suspicious, then security (or NAC) may eject you from the secure zone (or deny you access to the network), subject to re-examination.

4. If an authority figure at the airport — a police officer, security agent or guard, or airline employee — feels that you're acting strangely or inappropriately, he or she may stop you and request your ID. He or she can even eject you from the secure zone or request a recheck on you and your carry-on luggage. On a NAC-equipped network, some NAC solutions can interoperate with existing network components, such as intrusion

prevention systems (IPSs), intrusion detection systems (IDSs), unified threat management (UTM)-enabled firewalls, or other network security components. And, if these devices deem that you or your device are exhibiting anomalous or bad behavior, they can signal the NAC solution. NAC can force you and your device into quarantine until you or your device stop the behavior, it addresses and solves the issue automatically (using automated remediation), or it is cured manually. NAC can also force you off the network in mid-session, not allowing you back onto the network until it clears you and your device.

5. The last step in your airport sojourn is the final check by an airline representative at the gate leading to the aircraft. The gate attendant checks your boarding pass and, in some cases, rechecks your ID to make sure that you're who you say you are (authentication), that you have a boarding pass (credentials), that your boarding pass matches the flight number and destination (authorization), and that your name on your ID matches the name on your boarding pass. This process is a lot like application access control on a network. Some NAC solutions can deliver applications access control, in which a NAC solution can recertify a user and device before that user and device can gain access to specific applications and servers, ensuring that only the properly authorized users can access certain specific, sensitive applications and data. For example, an air traveler named Adam may be authorized to take a particular flight to New York, but another flyer, Eve, has a boarding pass for a different flight number, so she can't board that particular flight to New York. A NAC solution delivers application access control in a similar way — only the correct users can access the applications and data.

What NAC is and what it does

Vendors, industry experts, and you may have difficulty in coming up with a common definition and description for NAC because a NAC solution has so many different components. Organizations have a tendency to focus on what problems NAC solves for them or why they want to deploy NAC. And the concept of network access control can include many different pieces of a network environment, or touch many different network entities or organizational departments.

When you factor in a network user's, vendor's, organization's, or individual's perspective when describing NAC — not to mention emotions, deployment, needs, and many other aspects — arriving at a commonly accepted definition or description for NAC becomes a jumble.

When you compare the components of NAC in the following sections, you might create a definition of what NAC is by what it does.

Endpoint integrity

One of the common core functions of a NAC solution involves running an *endpoint integrity* or *assessment check,* checking an endpoint device to ensure that endpoint meets a baseline of security and access control policies.

Policies

Policies are at the core of nearly every NAC solution. An organization can predefine their security and access control policies, or an organization can customize and define the policies they want to use. These policies usually focus on the actions and state of endpoint security products and software, such as antivirus, anti-spyware, anti-spam, or other anti-malware offerings; personal firewalls; host-based intrusion prevention systems (IPSs); specific operating-system and application patches and patch management; and other security-related offerings. Some NAC solutions can probe how vulnerable an endpoint device may be to attack or hack.

Assessment checks

The depth and breadth of integrity and assessment checks vary from NAC solution to NAC solution:

✔ Some NAC solutions simply check whether an endpoint device has loaded a specific product, or a certain set of security products or offerings. NAC may also check whether the device has turned on that product.

✔ Other NAC offerings probe much deeper, checking for the product and version name, the last scan time, when the device last updated the security product, whether the user has turned off real-time monitoring or protection, and so on.

Some NAC solutions check the security products of one or two vendors; other solutions check an assortment of vendor offerings and versions.

Extended assessment checks

A number of NAC solutions have extended endpoint device integrity and assessment checks that include operating system checks; checks for machine certificate values, specific applications, files, processes, port usage, registry, Media Access Control (MAC) addresses, Internet Protocol (IP) address; and other similar checks.

Other NAC solutions enable an organization to define and customize their own endpoint device checks that they want to include in their endpoint integrity and assessment check. Some solutions give you the ability to define an assessment check based on a specific industry or open standard. Others allow you to create your own specific endpoint assessment checks and write policies based on those checks.

Pre- and post-admission checks

The timing of an endpoint check can define a NAC solution, differentiating it from other solutions. Most NAC solutions check the integrity of an endpoint device and assess endpoint security before the endpoint device can connect to a network. This kind of check is usually called a pre-admission host or client check. However, some NAC solutions may perform these same checks periodically after an endpoint device gains admission to a network; these checks are called post-admission host or client checks. When using post-admission checks, some NAC solutions enable you to adjust or set the time for your endpoint-device integrity and assessment checks.

Some experts, vendors, organizations, and users define and describe NAC as the act of checking and assessing endpoint device integrity.

AAA

The acronym AAA, which stands for authentication, authorization, and accounting, is a common term in networking.

To authenticate a user or device, a AAA server ensures that the user or device is who he, she, or it says it is; in other words, the network asks, "Who are you?" The user or device has to prove identity.

Users and their devices can be authenticated in many ways, such as

- ✔ User name and password
- ✔ Two-factor authentication
- ✔ Smart cards
- ✔ Tokens
- ✔ Certificates
- ✔ Hardware-based authentication, such as the Trusted Platform Module (TPM), which the Trusted Computing Group (TCG) specified and standardized

The act of authentication is a must in today's networked world. Wherever you go, whatever network you attempt to access, that network needs to authenticate you. The network needs to know who you are *before* it grants you any level or form of network access. So, identity plays a vital role in yet another potential definition of NAC because NAC must keep track of differentiated access for different users.

In many NAC solutions, where and how a user accesses a network and its resources is dictated by that user's identity. In some solutions, NAC can also associate the user's identity with a specific role. That role determines what kind of access the user has to the network and its resources. For example, with some NAC solutions you can give guest users who attempt to connect to a network a different type of access than employees who access the same network. So, although an employee who accesses the network may have access to specific areas of and resources on that network, the guest user may receive access only to the Internet, not to any other region or resource on the network.

Some experts, vendors, and others define NAC by how NAC apportions access. But, access apportionment is only part of the definition of NAC because NAC encompasses so much more.

Control freak

Control is a vital part of network access control. Controlling admission to a network and controlling access while a user is on the network require similar but different capabilities. For instance, controlling admission to a network may be based on authentication, while controlling application access can be based on identity, authorization, and user roles. The ability to control the access of a user while he or she is on the network is a primary component of NAC — and, typically, a defining factor. Some NAC solutions can save you NAC deployment time and cost by allowing you to leverage existing access policies, working with appliances already deployed on the network (such as switches, wireless access points, firewalls, routers, and other equipment deployed as enforcement points within the network), or deploying new appliances to serve as enforcement points within the network environment. The enforcement points enforce the access control policies applied to users and devices, both pre- and post-admission to the network.

Evolving on the job

NAC needs to do more than just *control* network access. While threats evolve, NAC needs to adapt and evolve to protect against them.

For example, NAC solutions need to address application access control. *Application access control* is the ability of an organization to define policies that enable certain network users, and not others, to access specific, protected applications on their network. In effect, you can segment your network by using NAC.

You can base such access policies on user or device identity. Some NAC solutions can grant a specific user access to specific applications on a network based on that user's identity. Other NAC solutions determine where a user can go on a network, what applications that user may have access to, and how he or she can access protected resources based on a user's role. By identity-enabling application access, you can ensure that only the appropriate, approved users can access sensitive, critical applications and data on your network.

You can accomplish application access control by defining and enforcing access policies on the network that a NAC solution distributes, which routers and firewalls enforce to protect the vital network applications and resources. NAC solutions have made a huge evolution by addressing application access, and this evolution now enables organizations to best address regulatory compliance, for example.

NAC solutions also evolve by increasing visibility into, and monitoring of, user access. This extended user (and usage) monitoring and visibility can occur both when a user is attempting to gain network access and while he or she is on the network. Moreover, NAC solutions that include the ability to track users and their usage by user identity (such as user name) or a user's role on the network, are evolving faster than others. NAC solutions can address many situations (including regulatory compliance) if they can track users (particularly by user name or role, rather than simply by IP address), where those users go on the network, and what they use on the network. NAC that can track users by identity can also help address the growing scourge of insider threats by increasing the network visibility and monitoring into users already on the network, so organizations can more easily track users, and what those users are doing, throughout the network.

Your NAC solution needs to continue to evolve and expand its interoperation with other new or existing network security and infrastructure products, such as firewalls, intrusion prevention and detection systems (IPSs/IDSs), secure routers, security information and event management (SIEM) products, and so forth. Some NAC solutions can already interact with these devices, using the devices as access and security policy enforcement points to which the NAC solution pushes access control and security policies. But be sure your NAC definition includes that ability to evolve and expand.

NAC solutions can interact with IPS/IDS appliances, SIEM products, or other products that provide network behavior analysis (NBA) or deliver network behavior anomaly detection (NBAD). By using these products to locate, monitor, or address endpoint devices' irregular behavior on a network, you can mitigate threats based on signature and policy, as well as network behavior. But, when these systems and appliances can communicate with a NAC solution (and vice versa), NAC can then tie anomalous behavior to specific access and security policies. Therefore, if a NAC solution that interacts with IPS/ IDS, SIEM, or products that offer NBA or NBAD uncovers anomalous endpoint behavior, the NAC solution can propagate policies that address this situation to network enforcement points, and those enforcement points, acting on the policies created by and distributed to them by the NAC solution can shut down the user network session or disable user traffic through that port.

If the NAC solution leverages user name or role, rather than IP address, thus correlating the user name or role to the user's endpoint device and monitoring the user or device's path throughout the network, you can invoke access control and security policies specific to the user or device that's spewing the anomalous behavior through network enforcement points. You have many options open for how to handle a device that's acting anomalously. You can quarantine and remediate it; simply log its actions; or eject the device from the network (even in mid-session), forcing the user to manually remediate their device and reconnect to the network. By interacting and interoperating with additional network and security devices, and by using and referencing user and device identity and role (as opposed to an IP address), a NAC solution can better address insider threats, be more selective in how it handles certain behavior types, and be generally more effective to its organization.

The last word

Although you can find plenty of different types of NAC solutions available that may help define NAC, here's the reality: You may find defining and describing NAC difficult because NAC is a moving target.

How you define and describe NAC can depend on your perspective, the point of view of the user or organization deploying NAC, the issues that you want to address, and the features and functions that you or your organization want to implement. You can also define and describe NAC based on the vendor and the type of solution that the user or organization selects.

No one may ever come up with a single definitive definition or easy description for NAC. Think of NAC as what an organization wants or needs it to be. However, any NAC solution needs to be open and flexible, making it able to evolve so that it can meet ever-changing access control requirements and organizational infrastructure.

Throughout this book, we try to describe and define NAC, but you can draw only one conclusion — whatever your definition of NAC, you need to continue to extend it and allow it to evolve so that it can address the needs of a growing, shifting market and a constant, looming threat landscape.

A Diagram Is Worth a Thousand Descriptions

Although a picture is worth a thousand words, a diagram can help provide a visual definition or description of NAC — especially the different types of NAC solutions and deployment methods. In the following sections, you can find diagrams that illustrate different types of NAC solutions and deployment methods.

The different types of NAC solutions available include

- ✔ Appliance-based, divided by whether the appliance is inline or out-of-band
- ✔ Switch- or network equipment-based
- ✔ Client/host-based
- ✔ Agent-less or clientless

The various types of NAC deployment methods include

- ✔ Integrated with, or as an overlay to, network or security infrastructure
- ✔ Layer 2 or Layer 3 authentication

Appliance-based NAC solutions: Inline or out-of-band

Some NAC solutions are appliance-based, which means that a server, hardened appliance, or a network device of some type needs to reside in the network on which you want to implement the NAC solution. Appliance-based solutions are either inline or out-of-band.

An appliance may act as a policy server for the NAC solution, a receptacle in which an organization can define and manage network access and security policies, and then propagate those policies to NAC enforcement points on the network (out-of-band). Sometimes, instead of or in addition to the policies being propagated to enforcement points, these appliances may also enforce the policies. These network devices, whether inline or out-of-band, may also deliver authentication capabilities, such as serving double duty — working as both policy server and an authentication server; an authentication, authorization, and accounting (AAA) server; a RADIUS server; or even a native authentication data store. These network devices can also include policy management, as well as device management, capabilities. What your NAC solution's policy server can do depends on whether the vendor's solution includes that functionality and capability within their appliance.

Get inline

If you use an inline NAC appliance that addresses policy development and management, and also enforces policies, all network traffic generally flows through the appliance or device, as shown in Figure 1-1. This placement enables you to make the access controls on an inline NAC appliance simple because all network traffic — and all associated individual data packets — flow through the appliance, thereby allowing the inline NAC appliance to apply granular access control.

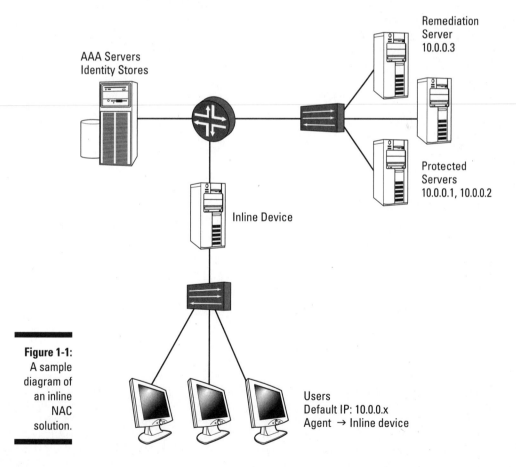

Figure 1-1:
A sample diagram of an inline NAC solution.

Remediation Server
10.0.0.3

AAA Servers
Identity Stores

Protected Servers
10.0.0.1, 10.0.0.2

Inline Device

Users
Default IP: 10.0.0.x
Agent → Inline device

You can easily deploy inline NAC appliances, particularly on a newly deployed or redesigned network. In many cases, these NAC solutions include a single network box that has policy creation and enforcement rolled into the one appliance.

While inline NAC appliances have their benefits (such as simplified deployment in new or renewed networks, a single-box approach, and policy enforcement and control in one place), be aware of a couple of potential challenges when you use an inline NAC appliance:

- ✔ **A single point of failure:** If the inline NAC appliance fails, so could network access control — because it's an inline appliance, it's applied to all network traffic. So, a failed inline NAC appliance could either create a roadblock that restricts access to your network or allow access to all who attempt to sign in to the network, without applying the appropriate policy and access control checks.

- ✔ **Performance:** Particularly in situations involving fast, substantial increases in network traffic, such as during disaster recovery, or mergers and acquisitions, the performance and rate of access control through an inline NAC appliance could suffer. Also, because all network traffic flows through an inline NAC device, that device can become a choke point in a network if too many users attempt network access simultaneously. To prevent your inline NAC appliance from becoming a choke point, you need to effectively load-balance the device and deploy it in a redundant fashion.

- ✔ **Scalability:** An inline, single-box solution can handle only a certain amount of network traffic; while network traffic increases, or the segments of the network on which you've deployed the NAC solution expand, you need to purchase more appliances and deploy them inline. You may not be able to easily maintain this kind of scaling solution or keep it cost effective.

Standing out-of-band

In an out-of-band NAC solution, you position the NAC appliance out of the line of fire of network traffic. Although some network traffic may flow to or through the out-of-band appliance, not all network traffic has to pass directly through it, as shown in Figure 1-2.

You can deploy both inline and out-of-band NAC appliances on an existing network infrastructure, but out-of-band NAC solutions typically are easier to deploy particularly because they are not in the direct line of traffic flow and many times do not require changes in traffic or network design. It can interact with the network components, leveraging them to provide authentication validation (by leveraging authentication data stores or databases), endpoint security policies and updates (by leveraging antivirus or anti-malware policy servers), or policy enforcement (by leveraging switches, access points, firewalls, and so on). You can also deploy an out-of-band NAC solution as a separate appliance, away from an organization's network or security infrastructure, in an overlay deployment.

The NAC vendor can suggest where to place an out-of-band appliance, or your organization's deployment requirements can dictate this placement.

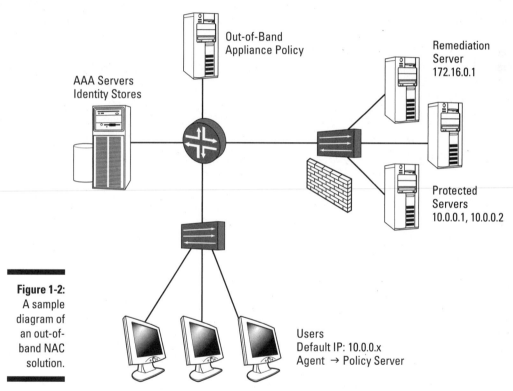

Figure 1-2:
A sample diagram of an out-of-band NAC solution.

Out-of-band NAC appliances sometimes may also incorporate a client or agent, or a clientless or agent-less mode. The NAC appliance can deploy the client/agent to an endpoint device, either as a download or preload, to assess the device's security posture and health, returning the outcome of these checks to the appliance so that the appliance can dynamically incorporate that information into policy or consider it in setting policy. The out-of-band NAC appliance can also use some or all of these capabilities via a clientless or agent-less mode, if the vendor offers such a mode. A clientless or agent-less mode can be Web-based, use a captive-portal design (similar to what a user experiences when he or she attempts to access the Internet from a hotel room or coffee shop), or be deployed by another method. A client/agent can also incorporate some security or access capabilities of its own as an added layer of protection for the user and organization against non-compliant or malware-infested end-point devices. The client/agent may also serve a dual purpose, acting not only as a NAC host or agent, but also as an 802.1X client/supplicant that enables the user's device access to networks compliant with the IEEE 802.1X standard for port-based network access control, which we discuss in detail in Chapter 13.

Deploying an out-of-band NAC solution has several advantages over an inline solution:

- ✔ You can limit disruption on your organization's network and leverage existing network and security components as part of the NAC process.

- ✔ Out-of-band solutions usually scale more easily and quickly than inline NAC solutions.

- ✔ Out-of-band solutions allow for quicker, easier network changes because they aren't in the direct flow of network traffic, unlike inline solutions.

- ✔ In many cases, you can deploy them separate from existing network or security infrastructure.

- ✔ You can pair some out-of-band NAC solutions with inline, infrastructure, or other NAC solution types, as well as other NAC deployment scenarios, combining and emphasizing each other's capabilities while enabling and enforcing NAC from the edge of the network into the network's core.

Switch- or network equipment-based NAC solutions

A switch or network equipment-based NAC solution allows an organization to replace their existing switch or other network equipment deployment with a unit that has integrated NAC capabilities.

This type of solution can operate within an existing network environment, and if your organization is rebuilding an existing or creating a new network, you may find this kind of solution efficient. However, if your organization must rip-and-replace an existing switch environment to obtain NAC capabilities, this process could quickly become cost prohibitive.

Switch-based NAC solutions can deliver NAC capabilities to the network's edge, which enables an organization to implement NAC functionality (such as admission control, access control, and monitoring) from the edge of the network while maintaining performance. The devices can usually integrate within an existing network environment with little disruption; some devices deliver and support multiple ways of enforcing NAC capabilities, such as 802.1X, DHCP, IPSec, or other standards.

Aside from the need to replace existing switches and equipment (which may be costly), this type of NAC solution may also have other hidden issues and costs. Keep these points in mind while exploring switch- or network equipment-based NAC solutions:

- ✔ Some switch-based NAC solutions require that you have an additional device — a controller, for example — on the network to provide policy control and management, which gives you another device that you need to manage.
- ✔ Like many products that combine multiple capabilities, you have to ensure that the device meets all your switching or network security requirements, not just your NAC needs.
- ✔ The device may meet your switching or network security goals but fall short of meeting your NAC requirements.

Client- or host-based NAC solutions

You can quickly and easily deploy client- or host-based NAC solutions. These software-based NAC solutions are usually independent of the network, its infrastructure, and (for the most part) any other equipment, as shown in Figure 1-3. (In many cases, a client- or host-based NAC solution requires a policy server to work with the client- or host-based NAC solution, delivering and managing the needed security and access policies.)

Your organization really needs only software to deploy a client- or host-based NAC solution. To implement NAC, you just have to preload, push, or automatically download the client or host software to an endpoint device. You can typically find this type of NAC solution available from vendors of endpoint security and protection software, and related suites.

Client- or host-based NAC, like all NAC solutions, has its pros and cons. On the pro side of the equation, client- or host-based NAC can

- ✔ Enhance interoperability.
- ✔ Be cost-effective while delivering solid investment protection and scalability.
- ✔ Address security challenges faced by a number of organizations today by combining admission control capabilities, such as endpoint assessment and policy compliance checks, with threat mitigation to protect the endpoint device and ultimately the network from attacks and hacks in economical fashion.

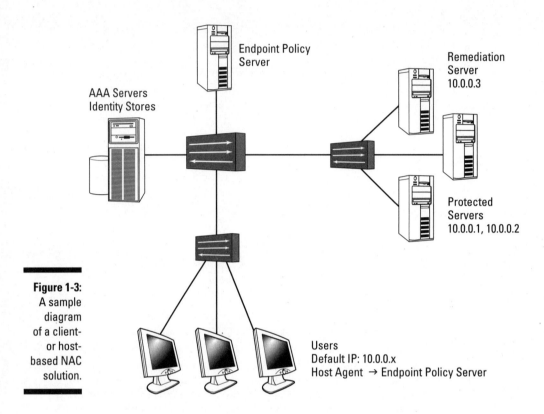

Figure 1-3:
A sample
diagram
of a client-
or host-
based NAC
solution.

On the downside of a client- or host-based NAC solution:

- ✔ **Quick spread of contamination:** If one user device is contaminated, compromised, or a *lying endpoint* (an endpoint device that's infected with malware which presents itself as being policy compliant and up-to-date with all its security inoculations), the organization's network is likely to become compromised, too.

- ✔ **How they handle unmanaged endpoint devices:** If a guest user — a contractor, partner, guest, or other non-employee user — attempts to access the organization's network by using an endpoint device that the organization hasn't provided or doesn't control (an *unmanaged* device), you may not be able to apply a client- or host-based NAC solution against that device. A guest user probably won't willingly agree to have an unknown client (particularly one that he or she may use only temporarily) downloaded to his or her endpoint device. So, how can a client- or host-based NAC solution check the unmanaged device and deem it compliant with the organization's access and security policies? Do you deny unmanaged endpoints network access? Do you funnel all unmanaged endpoints attempting network access to quarantine? Or do you allow unmanaged endpoints to freely access your network? And which scenario is more painful? As you can see, guest users and unmanaged devices can be real issues for client- or host-based NAC solutions.

✔ **Relying only on software on an endpoint device to provide network access control across a network:** A client- or host-based NAC solution can sometimes limit network security. In many cases, by deploying a client- or host-based NAC solution, an organization is attempting to check out and secure the endpoint device at the same time it is also providing the base for the NAC solution.

Clientless NAC solutions

Clientless NAC solutions don't require an endpoint device to have a client loaded in order for the solution to assess the device pre-admission, or for the solution to provide user or device authentication.

Some of these NAC solutions use a Web-based, captive portal-like approach or a dissolvable client that's based on Java, Active X, or some other downloadable applet that can capture user and device credentials for authentication, assess endpoint security state and posture, and measure the device against access and security policies.

Some clientless NAC solutions must deploy a device on the network that monitors network traffic and determines whether a device attempting network access is managed or unmanaged, or whether it's *unmanageable* (a device that's incapable of accepting a client, dissolvable or not, such as a networked printer, cash register, HVAC system, even a vending machine) — essentially, any device connected to the network and that has an IP address. Using predefined policies, the clientless system that uses a network device decides how to handle the network disposition of the unmanageable device.

Types of deployment

There are differing methods of NAC deployment which you may have the option of choosing, or that may be required based on the type of NAC solution you select.

While there are key differences between the various NAC deployment methods, one thing they all have in common is the ability to control access to the network (and in some cases applications) based on a number of variables and settings.

Integrated or overlay

Whether you deploy a NAC solution as an integrated part of a network or as an overlay to network or security infrastructure, for the most part, depends on the NAC solution type that you select.

You usually have to deal with either integrated or overlay NAC deployment when you use any NAC solution type that incorporates or leverages an appliance or network box. If you don't need an appliance or a network component, then you usually don't have to worry about the integrated versus overlay deployment choice.

For example, although you may or may not have an out-of-band NAC appliance integrated within your network environment — it may also be deployed as an overlay to the network environment, ensuring that any changes to the NAC solution or to the network environment don't affect the other — you need to integrate an inline NAC appliance with the network infrastructure, particularly because the inline appliance must be in the network traffic flow to operate.

You first need to determine whether the NAC solution type with which you want to work can support integrated or overlay deployment. If the deployment can be either integrated or overlay (such as when you use an out-of-band NAC appliance solution), then you can decide how intrusive and integrated you want to make your NAC solution.

Sometimes, though, the choice of integrated or overlay comes down to the type of NAC enforcement that an organization selects and uses.

Layer 2 or Layer 3 enforcement deployment

Layer 2 and Layer 3 refer to the data link layer and network layer, respectively, on the Open Systems Interconnection (OSI) Basic Reference Model, which provides a graphic description of computer network communications and protocols.

The data link layer (Layer 2) facilitates the communications and transfer of information between network components. (The IEEE 802.1X industry standard for port-based network access control also operates at Layer 2. Many Ethernet switches and wireless access points deployed in networks around the world today support the 802.1X industry standard.)

Many NAC solutions use Layer 2 as a key enabling technology and the standard for policy enforcement on NAC enforcement points, such as switches, wireless access points, and similar devices. Layer 2 communicates with NAC components during authentication and policy enforcement processes, as shown in Figure 1-4.

Layer 3, the network layer in the OSI Basic Reference Model, provides the means of transferring data from a source to a destination over one or more networks. Also, network routing occurs in Layer 3. Some NAC solutions use a Layer 3 access and security policy enforcement model. This model typically leverages a firewall or a secure router as a NAC enforcement point, enforcing policy-based decisions about how to handle certain users, devices, and even network traffic, as shown in Figure 1-5. A Layer 3 NAC deployment is a strong overlay NAC deployment capability, as well.

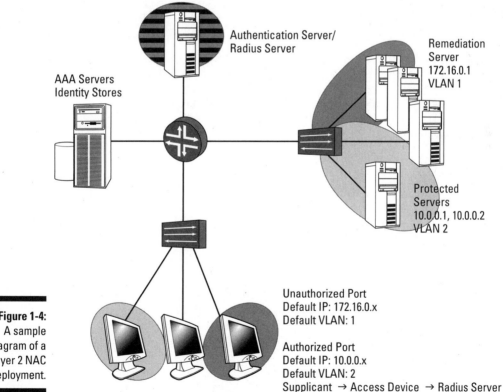

Authentication Server/
Radius Server

Remediation
Server
172.16.0.1
VLAN 1

AAA Servers
Identity Stores

Protected
Servers
10.0.0.1, 10.0.0.2
VLAN 2

Figure 1-4:
A sample
diagram of a
Layer 2 NAC
deployment.

Unauthorized Port
Default IP: 172.16.0.x
Default VLAN: 1

Authorized Port
Default IP: 10.0.0.x
Default VLAN: 2
Supplicant → Access Device → Radius Server

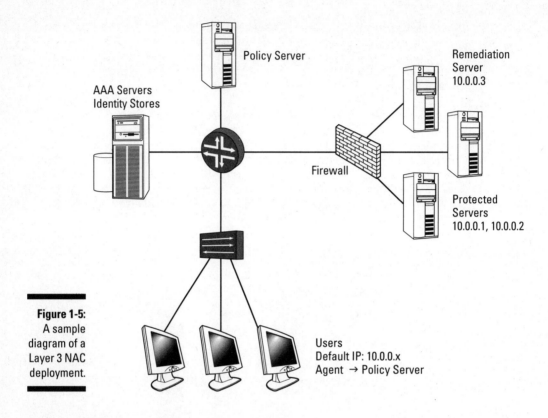

AAA Servers
Identity Stores

Policy Server

Remediation
Server
10.0.0.3

Firewall

Protected
Servers
10.0.0.1, 10.0.0.2

Users
Default IP: 10.0.0.x
Agent → Policy Server

Figure 1-5:
A sample
diagram of a
Layer 3 NAC
deployment.

The Best NAC Approach

So, how do you decide the best NAC solution approach for you, your network, and your organization? How do you select a solution to best meet your access control needs, without forcing yourself to redesign or redefine your network?

No one offers a single, be-all-and-end-all NAC product. First, you and your organization must decide what area or areas of your network you need to secure, as well as what issue is the most dangerous to your organization, network, and resources. A NAC solution can address these kinds of needs:

✔ Giving guest users secure, appropriate access to your network, while protecting your key resources and IP

✔ Differentiating access for different user types, such as employees, contractors, partners, and guests

  ✔ Protecting sensitive data and intellectual property from unauthorized access

  ✔ Minimizing the fear of an insider threat

  ✔ Addressing regulatory compliance and preparing for compliance audits

Your organization first needs to consider whether a particular NAC solution can handle the different device types that will be trying to access the network. Any comprehensive NAC solution should seamlessly address employee or guest user authentication and endpoint compliance *before* it grants a user, and his or her endpoint device, access to a network.

Do your NAC homework

Regardless of the issue or issues that your organization prioritizes — what parts of the network your organization wants to control access to, from whom, and for whatever reason — you need to research and answer all these questions *before* you decide on the NAC solution type, vendor, and product that you want to review or purchase.

Walk through these simple steps:

1. **After you determine that you need NAC, figure out whether budget is, or could become, an issue.**

   Your organization may choose to leverage existing infrastructure, existing endpoint security software, and so on in an effort to maximize efficiencies, maintain costs, and protect existing network investments. If cost is an overriding issue, and scalability and performance aren't as vital, your organization may consider implementing certain NAC solution types, such as an inline NAC appliance that can deliver both a policy server and an enforcement point in a single networked box, a switch-based NAC solution, or client- or host-based NAC.

2. **Decide whether network and resource security is your organization's key concern.**

   If you want the ability to leverage existing network components, but also effectively segment your network so that you can allow only authorized users to access sensitive data and intellectual property, then your organization may need to investigate an out-of-band NAC appliance that has strong Layer 2 and Layer 3 enforcement capabilities.

3. **If your organization is concerned with guest user access, investigate NAC solutions that include a client-less or dissolvable client option.**

We describe these options in the section "Clientless NAC solutions," earlier in this chapter.

4. **Figure out whether your organization is most worried about keeping the wrong people off of the network and away from valuable resources and information.**

   In this situation, consider a NAC solution that supports strong two- or multi-factor authentication.

5. **If ensuring the security of critical networked resources keeps you up at night, then you need a NAC solution that focuses on the segregation of networked resources.**

   This kind of solution ensures that only the correct, authorized users who have the appropriate authority and access rights can access the critical resources.

6. **Determine what use cases are the most important for your organization.**

   If your organization needs to address regulatory compliance, outsourcing or even off-shoring, or business continuity during times of disaster, you can find a NAC solution that can address this for you.

Must-have traits of your NAC solution

Whatever your NAC needs, you can find a NAC solution, deployment type, and environment that can well address your security and access control needs. Just know about any limitations that your NAC solution has and take those limitations into consideration before purchasing the solution.

Absolutely, positively ensure that you find the following attributes and capabilities in any NAC solution that your organization reviews or selects.

Strong user/device authentication and integrity

NAC solutions usually combine two types of checks — user identity and endpoint integrity. A NAC solution, though, should be able to combine user identity, device integrity, and location information with policy to deliver dynamic, comprehensive NAC.

Dynamic identity- and role-based policies

A NAC solution should define policies based on user and/or device identity, as well as the user's role, which a NAC solution should predefine for the user. Also, a NAC solution should be able to create policies on the fly, dynamically, so that if endpoint device integrity, user or device identity, or other factors change, the solution can assign a new policy and take the appropriate actions to ensure network and resource security and integrity. You need the ability to know who's on your network — as well as where they're going and what they're doing — particularly if you have to worry about regulatory compliance and audits. Tracking users and devices by IP address just isn't enough any longer.

Complete network protection

The NAC solution that you choose should be able to deliver a rich set of predefined endpoint integrity checks, as well as the ability to create custom endpoint checks right out of the box. It should also be capable of making dynamic network status changes if the endpoint device's security state, network information, or user information changes — even if the changes occur in the middle of a network session. Your NAC solution must enforce dynamic policy in real time across a distributed network. And any NAC solution that you select needs to effectively address the quarantine and remediation of an offending user, and his or her device, prior to granting network access. You also want a NAC solution that includes automatic or automated remediation, in addition to self-remediation capabilities.

Network and application-level control, visibility, and monitoring

If your organization must comply with industry or government regulations, then you really need to ask whether, and how, the NAC solution can accomplish this compliance. The best NAC solution simplifies adherence to regulatory compliance requirements, as well as providing the required security for and necessary data to prove compliance with industry and/or governmental regulatory requirements. A NAC solution also needs to address application access control, which enables an organization to apply user and/or device level policies for access to sensitive or protected applications, limiting access to critical data to only authorized users and devices. A NAC solution that addresses application access control can also provide a quick, effective way to virtually segment your network. Finally, any NAC solution today must have the ability to provide visibility into and monitoring of users and devices attempting to access a network and its applications. The ability to match user identity and role information with network and application usage enables the NAC solution to better track and audit network and application access. Plus, a NAC solution can leverage and use a user's role when determining access control policy.

Robust extended security

Consider whether the NAC solution leverages your investments in existing access and security devices. Your NAC solution needs to work with your existing firewalls, Ethernet switches and access points, and AAA infrastructure. Your network access control solution shouldn't require costly, time-consuming upgrades or a rip-and-replace scenario. Any NAC solution should integrate quickly and seamlessly with your existing AAA infrastructure to validate user identity. Your NAC solution should also deliver interoperability with existing network and security infrastructure components, effectively extending NAC capabilities to include intrusion prevention systems (IPSs), security information and event management (SIEM) solutions, and other vital network infrastructure components to deliver investment protection and comprehensive NAC.

Flexible, phased deployment and ease of operation

When you look at NAC solutions, consider what you need to deploy the solution. Most organizations are best suited to a phased deployment approach to NAC. Flexibility in your NAC solution is vital because a network is fluid, not static; your NAC solution should be able to change with and adapt to your network while that network grows and changes. The NAC solution should be able to add an additional enforcement method without requiring you to rip and replace the network that you've already deployed. One of the best ways to ensure this level of interoperability is to seek solutions that are based on open specifications and standards.

Simple administration and management

Consider the ease of administration and management of a NAC solution when you select a solution for your organization. You can determine a NAC solution's ease of administration by considering whether you can use existing network management capabilities to manage that NAC solution. Can solutions or access control devices share or reuse security and access control policies? Does the NAC solution have a centralized management console that can aid in administering and provisioning various solution and/or infrastructure components? Also take into account how easily the NAC solution can create or edit policies, or deploy endpoint integrity checks, and whether the solution can predefine host checks or policies.

Value

The value that you can get from a NAC solution combines factors of deployment flexibility, ease of use, the time that you have to spend administering and managing the solution, the actual acquisition cost, and the time that you need to spend redesigning your network (if required). What security or access control components or policies can you leverage, reuse, or repurpose on your network to help enforce NAC? If a solution requires that you upgrade your switching infrastructure, you must also factor in the time you have to spend inventorying the devices on your network, determining what types of switches you already have deployed, and what version of code they're running; getting hardware and/or software upgrades, as required; and testing the network. You may find a phased approach to deployment easier to justify to your organization or management because it can save valuable time and expense. Be aware that you can easily deploy some NAC solutions in a phased manner, but you can't so easily deploy others in this way.

Leveraging What You Have Today

If you can leverage pieces and components of your existing network to deliver NAC, you can save time and expense when deploying a NAC solution.

Ensure that the NAC solution you review or select can leverage your existing network, policy, and reporting capabilities and resources as much as possible; work across standards and different platforms; and save yourself some headaches and a lot of wasted time and cost. The rest of this book shows you how.

You can use your existing network infrastructure, endpoint security software, security products, and other network hardware or software for NAC by considering any of the points in the following sections.

Standards

If you want to use the network that you have today to address NAC, you first need to determine whether the NAC solution that you're considering incorporates or uses industry standards; for example, the IEEE 802.1X standard for port-based network access control, which we cover in greater detail in Chapter 13. If the NAC solution that you're considering or reviewing utilizes the 802.1X standard and can work with an existing 802.lX network by leveraging 802.1X-compliant switches and wireless access points already in the network as NAC enforcement points, you've just leveraged a very vital — and expensive — portion of your existing network infrastructure. The more components that you can leverage on your existing network to deliver NAC, the more easily you can deploy NAC — and for less money. And, NAC doesn't just reuse or leverage existing network hardware, either.

Reuse policies

If you already have access control policies in place, repurposing or even copying those policies so that you can use them on your NAC solution can save you valuable time in policy definition, as well as in NAC deployment time and expense. For example, if you already have remote access or endpoint security policies defined and deployed, you can leverage them again in your NAC solution, which could save you a significant amount of time. Your staff, who might have needed to redefine, rewrite, or create new security policies if they couldn't be reused or repurposed, can instead address more pressing or strategic needs.

Interface with existing systems

The ability of a NAC solution to simply interface with your existing authentication systems or AAA infrastructure can save you a great deal of time and cost. Imagine that you have to duplicate your user database, which you've already spent time creating, redefining, and updating for your existing network access methods, for your NAC solution. You can save all that time, effort, and resources — and use those administrators to address other, vital projects — simply by ensuring that your existing authentication data stores can be leveraged as-is with your NAC solution.

Reporting

A hidden area of reusability — and one that some organizations seldom think about — is reporting. If you already have a series of reports defined and use an external reporting solution or an SIEM device, you can find your NAC solution's inability to interface or interoperate with those devices or to export information into existing report templates maddening — especially if you didn't even think about this sometime neglected, but very important, consideration before purchasing or deploying a NAC solution.

Chapter 2

Knowing Why You Want NAC

. . . .

. . . .

*Y*ou know that NAC is the acronym for network access control, but you may be wondering why someone's network access needs to be controlled. Like with any business operation, technological and market drivers influence the need for network access control or limitations. Also, the number of network users, the information they use, and the type of work they do affect the frequency and level of access they need.

In this chapter, we explain some of the key reasons why companies need to control access to their networks. We also briefly discuss ways for companies to ease into a NAC solution, as well as why some companies may choose not to control access to their network and the possible ramifications of that decision.

What Are the Reasons for NAC?

Companies need to deploy a NAC solution for many reasons:

✔ Some of these reasons are positive, such as

   • Leaps in business

   • Productivity

   • Technology

✔ Some reasons are negative, such as

   • Hackers

   • Information poachers

   • Identity thieves

   • Data-nappers

Both reasons for NAC dictate greater control over networks, access to those networks, and who requires network access.

Other grounds for deploying NAC might be completely business- or market-driven, such as to address

✔ Guest access

✔ Outsourcing

✔ Business continuity

Still other purposes are driven by industry or government, such as regulatory compliance and audits.

Ask yourself (and your business) a few questions:

✔ Who needs controlled access to your network?

✔ What driving forces dictate the need to control access?

Regardless of industry, size, or demand, NAC is fast becoming a requirement. But you need to understand the reasons and forces behind the motivation to deploy NAC so that you can best match a NAC solution to your need.

That's Why They're Called Trojan Horses

Today, users are accessing networks from anywhere in the world, at any time of day, through an array of access technologies and devices that may run any number of operating systems and applications. Although mobility has helped raise productivity and profits for companies around the world, it has also meant sleepless nights and headaches for administrators and trouble for their networks. Administrators now have no idea where a user's device — whether it's managed by the company or not — has been before it attempts to access the enterprise network. The user could have been surfing the Internet and accessed Web sites that carried hidden dangers (such as worms, keystroke loggers, rootkits, botnets, backdoors, or other nefarious forms of malware). Or, even though company policy may forbid it, the user may have allowed his or her child, significant other, or another individual to use his or her device; that person may have launched a chat site or sent an instant message to friends, or even disabled antivirus or other anti-malware checks because they made the PC run too slow, providing an open invitation to malware or other culprits.

These and other traps could be lying in wait for the user whom the company trusts and who uses a trusted, managed device. When that user reconnects to the company's network, the malware or hack lying in wait uncoils its wrath upon an unknowing company network, that network's users, and its connected devices. They didn't name that nasty malware Trojan Horse for nothing!

Of course, sophisticated, well-funded hackers can spawn and launch virulent forms of malware. Many times, these hackers aren't in it for the glory or bragging rights; they're in it for the cash, holding ransom the vital data that they retrieve from corporate networks through insidious means. Data-nappers ransom the data back to the corporation that they breached; or, if the company doesn't meet their ransom demands, they sell the stolen data to the highest bidder.

These malware attacks typically use the managed, trusted device of an unknowing trusted user as a transfer agent for the spread of viruses, spyware, adware, Trojan horses, worms, bots, rootkits, keystroke loggers, backdoors, dialers, or other malicious applications onto the enterprise network or directly to other unsuspecting user devices. These attacks put intellectual property, personal data, and sensitive information at risk, and they can have a serious impact on productivity, safety, cost, and even reputation.

Not knowing where a user's device has been before it connects to the network can be dangerous. Not having a way to protect against malware and breaches can be disastrous.

Where Have You Been?

When deployed, a NAC solution makes sure that a user device can meet a preset level of security standard. NAC can also assure that a device is free and clear of malware before allowing that device to access the company network; and some NAC solutions can even check whether the user's device maintains the corporate security standard, even after network connection. Your company can decide how you want to enforce access control. For example, if a NAC solution determines that a device has been infected with malware or doesn't meet the organization's security standard prior to connecting to the company network, the NAC solution can either

✔ Deny the device network access.

✔ Accept the device onto the network with a warning (or without a warning).

✔ Place the device on a quarantine network.

A *quarantine network* is like purgatory for unclean devices. Just like its medical counterpart, a quarantine network segregates an infected, non-compliant, or potentially dangerous device with potential for contaminating others from the remainder of the healthy, normal network by putting it in an ancillary network — perhaps a virtual network — apart from the company's core network and resources.

While a device is in the quarantine network, a NAC solution can begin the procedure of cleaning or repairing the device itself or in conjunction with a third-party server, a process called *remediation*. A NAC solution can use several forms of remediation:

- ✔ **Automated:** Little to no human interaction necessary; remediation of the infected device happens automatically.

- ✔ **Hands-on:** A person from support (or another corporate department) may need to clean or repair the infected device.

- ✔ **User-driven:** Various forms of remediation that may include instructions on how a user or other individual should clean or repair a quarantined device on his or her own, or directions to a specific Web site that can walk the user through the process to clean or repair his or her system.

After the infected or non-compliant device has been cleaned and repaired, the user can be instructed to manually re-authenticate the device so that it can access the network or the NAC solution can automatically reauthenticate it and place the device on the appropriate network with the appropriate authorization rights, depending on the NAC solution.

NAC can make sure that all devices requesting network access are free of malware that might infect the network and its users' devices, as well as assuring devices that access the network have and maintain a certain, specific level of predefined malware and data protection.

Wireless Networks and NAC

Mobility is attractive. It promises hassle-free, anytime, anywhere access that enables employees to connect to the network, around the clock and around the world. Companies also deploy wireless local area networks (WLANs) because these networks are simple to install and expand the work environment, providing a localized type of mobility, and lead to increased productivity.

A wireless LAN doesn't need much wiring, which can make deploying it more cost-effective than traditional wired networks. A WLAN is also more flexible for implementing physical office changes, which can also save cost and time. However, although mobility and WLAN access are both desirable and increase productivity, maintaining network security for mobile or WLAN users and devices is a concern. The more wireless LANs your company deploys, the greater the risk that someone can hack, breach, or attack your network and its resources. The open nature of WLAN access brings additional security concerns. Without the proper credentials, security, and controls in place, a hacker can snoop or steal sensitive user information and corporate data while a user establishes a wireless connection and even after a user is connected to the WLAN.

NAC can address WLAN access — without impeding the openness of the WLAN network or its accessibility — by applying strong authentication controls to check the authenticity of the user, and his or her device, before granting that user and device access to a network by WLAN. After authenticating the user and device credentials, the NAC solution can apply the appropriate security and access policies against the user device, making sure the device meets a baseline of security and access capabilities *before* it's allowed onto the company's network. With a NAC solution protecting their WLAN, the company can ensure that

- ✔ The user, and his or her device, are authorized to access the LAN (although no solution is perfect or a panacea)
- ✔ The device's antivirus and anti-malware software is active and up to date, and meets a minimum baseline of security and access policy
- ✔ The user and device gain access only to the areas of the company's LAN and to sensitive resources that the user is authorized to access.

NAC can also allow companies to limit network access to specific areas of the LAN based on access type; in other words, if a user, and his or her device, access the LAN through a WLAN, he or she may be granted access to a limited set of corporate network resources and applications. But if that user accesses the network directly over wired Ethernet, the user and device may be allowed greater access.

Some companies deploy a NAC solution supplying limited access to the network and resources when accessed by a device over a WLAN because they fear WLANs are easier to hack than wired LANs. But this concern is unfounded, particularly if the organization has deployed the IEEE standard for port-based access control, 802.1X. The 802.1X standard requires and implements powerful, government-grade, standards-based encryption methods between the device and the network resources, ensuring the security of data in transit. Many NAC solutions implement the 802.1X standard because of its strong authentication and data security features.

Whether or not a NAC solution uses the 802.1X standard, you can both maintain the openness of the WLAN and ensure protection and privacy for vital corporate assets by using NAC to effectively segment a network, allowing authorized WLAN users appropriate access rights while keeping unauthorized WLAN users from peering into sensitive corporate data.

NAC and Compliance

A litany of compliance regulations (which industry and government entities launch and enforce) scrutinize many companies, as well as their networks, applications, and data. Various compliance regulations may

- ✓ Prescribe how the company must assure data and network integrity.
- ✓ Demand that users comply with company security policies.
- ✓ Mandate companies implement policies that adhere to the regulations and dictate penalties if the company or their users don't meet policy.

The difficult news

Many industry and government regulations have been created, and most of them focus on specific industries or markets. These regulations include Payment Card Industry Data Security Standards (PCI DSS), Health Insurance Portability and Accountability Act (HIPAA), and Sarbanes-Oxley (SOX), just to name a few. If you Google any of these regulations, you can spend a fun-filled afternoon reading about them.

In many cases, compliance regulations reach around the world, such as PCI DSS; but many countries or world regions also have their own compliance regulations, in addition to worldwide compliance regulations. Many of these national or regional regulations have additional paragraphs and sections that dictate protection for the company, users, and data from unauthorized access, as well as for non-compliance and non-adherence. Particularly if a breach or attack occurs, or if an audit or check is failed, your organization may face severe ramifications — including fines and, in extreme cases, imprisonment of the violating company's senior officials.

For example, many compliance regulations require companies to ensure that an organization authenticate users who and devices that request network connection before bestowing network access. Many times, these same regulations require *two-factor authentication,* which means that the company needs to require more than just a user name and password to enable network access. The company would require users to use an additional authentication method, such as a password key, identity card, biometrics, or other means before they could be granted network access.

Here are some examples of other compliance issues that you might encounter:

- **Device adherence:** Some regulations require all devices that request network connectivity to have the latest, most up-to-date antivirus software and signatures up and running. These same regulations mandate that devices have installed the most current patches and hotfixes for operating systems and applications before they can gain access to a company's network. And organizations must provide proof to a compliance authority — an industry body, government agency, or another similar authorizing organization — that they're following and meeting these requirements.

- **Data protection in transit:** Most compliance requirements have a stipulation about protecting data in transit to and from the user's device and the network. They require that the data — which can include sensitive patient data, credit cardholder information, or financial records, to name a few examples — be encrypted in some manner — via software or hardware encryption, by a client or other means — while that data is communicated between the user's device and the network so that no one can hack, steal, or render useless the sensitive data.

- **Segmentation:** Regulatory bodies can also require that companies segment their most secretive, sensitive data from the rest of their network and user community when companies store that data on their network. They can also stipulate that accessing the stored data requires additional authorizations.

- **Proof of compliance:** Industry and governmental regulatory agencies require proof of adherence to their rules and regulations. In many cases, the regulatory bodies perform their own audits of participating companies. Or they may require that a certified third party audit the security records of companies annually or on a defined periodic basis to ensure their compliance with the entity's rules and regulations. A company that doesn't comply with the industry or government regulations may face severe penalties, including fines.

Although all these rules and regulations might seem like overkill, you can face large penalties for not complying with industry or government regulations: Stolen user data or hacked systems can lead to fines, imprisonment of company officials (in the most egregious cases), and significant loss of reputation and revenue.

Your company can find losing reputation many times worse, and much more costly and time-consuming to gain back, than a simple fine. Loss of revenue just makes matters worse.

The good news

NAC addresses most, if not all, of the requirements placed on corporations by industry and government regulatory bodies, which we talk about in the following sections.

So, if your network and company needs to comply with any kind of industry or governmental regulation, no matter how complex, NAC can protect against data breaches; data and identity theft; and other forms of data snooping, hacking, and unauthorized access. A NAC solution allows you to address regulatory compliance and keep your company's reputation intact.

Network security

A NAC solution can check a user's device to ensure that it has the latest, most up-to-date antivirus signatures, that its operating systems and applications include the most current patches and hotfixes, and that they're all operating. A NAC solution usually can perform these tasks for a number of other anti-malware and security applications, as well.

Encryption

Most NAC solutions provide a level of encryption for data being transmitted from the user device to the network. Some NAC solutions also offer data encryption from the network to the device, as well. The level and standard of encryption can vary.

Insider threats

As discussed in the section "Wireless Networks and NAC," earlier in this chapter, some forms of NAC implement the IEEE's 802.1X standard as part of their deployment. The 802.1X standard, which requires the user or organization to deploy and load a client (or, in 802.1X parlance, a *supplicant*) to the user's device, can help to ensure data security and integrity while that data is in transit. The 802.1X standard uses powerful, standards-based encryption on data communicated from the user's device to the network, effectively discouraging data snooping and theft. Some NAC solutions also provide encryption for data communicated over a wired network. Many NAC solutions can provide encryption via the implementation of the 802.1X standard, by Internet Protocol Security (IPSec), or other means. This level of NAC can protect against insider threats, such as information theft or hacking by trusted employs who use managed devices. We talk more about this scenario in the section "Insider Access and Threats," later in this chapter.

Authorization

NAC can effectively segment sensitive data from unauthorized users. Whether through re-authentication before data access or by checking the user's role — if access is identity- or role-based — a NAC solution can make sure that only authorized users, whether external or internal to the network, may access servers storing sensitive data.

Logging and reports

Most NAC solutions provide comprehensive logs and, in many instances, detailed reports on user actions. In the case of logs, you can often import the logs into existing reporting tools or report structures, providing regulatory compliance audits and auditors with the reports and data that they need. You can also export NAC reports to existing reporting tools and report structures, in most cases, which aids in viewing the collected data and regulatory compliance audits. Depending on the particular NAC solution, the logs or reports may correlate IP addresses to user identity, making it easier to follow and understand which user accessed sensitive data at what time.

Be Our Guest

Because of the exponential growth of user mobility and mobile devices, the number and types of users requesting and requiring network access is also growing exponentially. In fact, you can categorize almost anyone — aside from trusted employees who use managed devices — as a guest user.

Guest users come in many shapes and sizes. All guest users require their own level of distinct network and application access:

- **Contractors:** You may treat contractors like employees, giving them access to the corporate offices, access rights to the corporate network, and sometimes even a managed device. And, like employees, they often require access to sensitive network resources to get their day-to-day jobs done. However, in many cases, contractors use *unmanaged devices* (devices that your company hasn't provided, therefore you must consider those devices potential threats). Although you treat these users like employees in many ways, for the most part, with network access, you often have to give them a different level of access — for instance, access only to specific servers or applications, and not to others — than you give to an employee.

✔ **Partners:** Partners often provide specific services to companies. They may be part of the corporate supply chain — for example, your company may consider its shipping agency or import/export agent a partner. A partner may provide a piece of your company's end product, such as an OEM manufacturer. Or they may be a sales partner, an organization that helps market and sell your company's end product or service to your end users. You can come up with countless other examples of partners, but all partners need to have access to core portions of your company's network — either locally or remotely — to ensure that they can perform their duties, whatever they may be, in the manufacturing, processing, sales, support, or delivery of your company's products or services. If a once-trusted partner attempts to launch an attack on your network, they become an insider threat, and can be addressed by the NAC solution. This scenario is covered in "Insider Access and Threats" later in this chapter.

Hackers have begun to recruit partners to assist in stealing sensitive corporate or consumer data, using a disgruntled partner's approved credentials to access sensitive areas of the corporate network. Those disgruntled partners won't have the ability to access those sensitive areas if the company has the proper access controls in place. To secure your company's network and data, make sure that partners have access only to the portions of the corporate network that they need to perform their services and do their job effectively.

✔ **Customers:** Customers may require network access; for example, a customer visiting your company site may request access to his or her own network via a virtual private network (VPN) or to the Internet. In order to gain this access, he or she first needs access to your company's network. Even though your company's network is simply the conduit for the customer to access another network or the Internet, your company needs to ensure that the customer can gain only Internet access and not be able to access any other portions of your company's network, accidentally or intentionally.

✔ **Guests:** Some guest users are *truly* guests. For example, on Take Your Child to Work Day, your company really wants to protect your child from unintentionally surfing to dangerous or inappropriate Web sites or chat rooms, and their core data from inadvertent access. For instance, they don't want your child to be able to access the company's financials or its order-processing application while he or she is IMing friends or surfing the Internet. They also don't want your child's messaging or surfing to accidentally infect and launch a virus or other malware on their network.

NAC can regulate which guest users can access which networked resources. It can check the user's and device's credentials and, based on that data, provide the access for which the user is authorized.

For example, a contractor may have different network access rights and be authorized to access different applications, servers, data — any network asset — than an average guest user. Each form of guest user may have different network and resource access rights — all defined, implemented, and managed by a NAC solution. If a user attempts to access data or a portion of the network for which he or she isn't authorized, the NAC solution can deny that user access.

Now, add to this scenario managed and unmanaged devices.

A *managed device* is a device that your company has provided to the user, so your company can, to some extent, control that device. An *unmanaged device* is any device that your company didn't supply or doesn't manage.

NAC can ensure that an unmanaged device — just like a managed device — meets a minimum requirement for security before the NAC solution and enforcement points grant that device network access. If the unmanaged device doesn't meet the baseline of security policy, as dictated by the company — for example, the device isn't running the latest antivirus signatures — the NAC solution may place the unmanaged device onto a quarantine network, depending on the enforcement of the company's policy. Or the NAC solution, in conjunction with enforcement points, if needed, may limit the unmanaged device to Internet access only. The NAC solution may allow the device to go through remediation, in the same way that the NAC solution enables managed devices. Or the company may choose to limit network access to only managed devices, not allowing unmanaged devices to have any network access, or only Internet access.

When deploying NAC and defining access control policies, the company usually decides how leniently or stringently they want to enforce their access control policies for compliant or non-compliant unmanaged devices.

Off-Shoring and Outsourcing

The ability to find the best product or service at the best price helps keep companies profitable. Outsourcing aspects of business helps companies grow and retain their margins. A form of outsourcing, called *off-shoring* (outsourcing production of a good or service, or outsourcing a business process such as manufacturing, to a company that's based outside of your company's country) has helped to grow the world economy while keeping spiraling prices in check, allowing companies to keep their margins up by controlling the cost of goods or services. These savings also help keep consumer prices in check.

Although outsourcing and off-shoring provide clear benefits to business, these services include very real gotchas for networking and security. Outsourcers and off-shore partners, like contractors and local partners, may require access to sensitive corporate resources and assets stored on the company's network to be productive and perform their duties. And, like contractors and partners, they may be conducting their business either locally or remotely.

Whether the outsourcer or offshore partner accesses the corporate network via Ethernet at the corporate offices or via VPN, your company should provide them with differentiated network access that has unique authentication credentials:

✔ Your company's NAC solution needs to check the devices that the outsourcer or off-shore partners use to connect to the corporate network to make sure that those devices meet the access policies put in place by your company.

✔ Outsourcers and off-shore partners should receive access rights only to the servers where the information is stored on the corporate network for which they need access to perform their jobs effectively.

✔ Your company — through its NAC solution — probably should segment the information to which outsourcers or off-shore partners require access from the rest of their corporate network data by using firewalls or a virtual local area network (VLAN), by segmenting the information on physically different servers, or by other means.

NAC can deliver secure, necessary network, application, and data access by outsourcers and off-shore partners for your company. It can ensure that the outsourcer and off-shore entity, no matter how they access the corporate network, can't access the network until the NAC solution authenticates them; that their devices meet (and, in many NAC cases, maintain) compliance with corporate access and security policies; and that the NAC solution — either standalone or working through network enforcement points, such as switches, wireless access points, and firewalls — grants them access only to the network areas and applications to which they have appropriate access rights. If an outsourcer or off-shore entity doesn't meet any one of these requirements, or if they attempt to circumvent appropriate access rights, the company — through its NAC solution, and network enforcement points — can terminate outsourcer or off-shore partner's network session and revoke their access rights.

Off-shoring and outsourcing addresses a vital need for business, and you can ensure that it doesn't become an issue or problem for your company or their network. Securing your network, applications, and data for outsourcing and off-shoring depends on how your company wants to deploy NAC, and how sternly and strongly you want to enforce your policies.

Insider Access and Threats

After you have a NAC solution in place, you can begin to address a growing problem that sometimes seems rampant — insider access and threats.

An *insider* is a trusted network user who has a managed device. The user is authenticated, his or her device meets policy, he or she is authorized to be on the corporate network, and all necessary and required processes have checked him or her — all of which ensure and validate trust in the user and his or her device.

Then, it happens: The user or their device begins to snoop internal data, accessing servers, files, and folders that he or she isn't authorized to access; and the user can begin removing sensitive data or transferring it from the network. Or the user's device launches an attack on the network.

How can a company stop such an insider threat scenario from playing out, even though the user is trusted, and his or her device clears policy?

If your company effectively *segments* your network using your NAC solution — alone or in concert with network enforcement points, you can ensure that even trusted users can gain access to only the servers and data to which they have approved access. If a trusted user attempts to access a server or data to which he or she doesn't have approved access, the NAC solution — alone or via enforcement points — can deny him or her access.

For example, say that the NAC solution has granted access to a user who has access rights to the engineering servers, but she attempts to access the finance server. If you have a NAC solution, the solution (alone or in concert with network enforcement points) will invoke the appropriate access control policy, and denies her access to the finance server, logs her attempted access of the finance server, and (depending on the NAC solution), flags the unapproved access attempt, or alerts an administrator of this access attempt.

Most NAC solutions include a flagging and/or alerting mechanism, or they may interface with existing alert systems or security information and event management (SIEM) systems that have threat detection or network behavior anomaly detection (NBAD). NAC solutions may even be able to leverage the threat detection and NBAD data to identify and mitigate threats.

A NAC solution can also interoperate with existing network infrastructure and security components, such as intrusion detection system (IDS) and intrusion protection system (IPS) appliances. If the NAC solution interfaces with an IDS/IPS appliance, it may (depending on the interaction) enable the IDS/IPS to notify the NAC solution of anomalous network behavior. If identity-enabled, it may even be able to isolate the anomalous behavior down to a specific user or device, thus empowering the NAC solution to apply decisive, actionable policy against the offending user or device, depending on the corporate policies in place. This level of NAC interaction with existing network components can stop an insider threat before it can even get started.

Unapproved resource or asset access by trusted users and devices can lead to loss of revenue, fines, lawsuits, ransom demands, and even prison for perpetrators or company officials, not to mention loss of reputation and profits. A NAC solution that can interact with existing network and security infrastructure while effectively segmenting network assets can stop these transgressions from happening.

Keeping Business Running

You may want to deploy NAC in your network for one (or more) of several rational business reasons.

Continuity

Business continuity — particularly during natural or manmade disasters, or pandemics — can keep a business running and afloat.

For example, say that a city is in the midst of a natural disaster. The city or state government has declared a state of emergency and instructed everyone to stay off the roads. A company's headquarters is located in that city, and they need to keep the company running — otherwise, they risk losing millions of dollars in revenue and productivity.

To enable their employees to remain productive, they may employ a VPN that their employees can use to access the networked corporate resources that they require to do their daily jobs. Or the company may have employees who aren't affected by the natural disaster work remotely from a nearby branch office. But the company still needs to maintain their network security and data protection, ensuring that their users can access only the network resources that they need to effectively do their jobs; the company's NAC solution needs to authenticate the users accessing the network and assure that their devices meet corporate policies. A local emergency or disaster doesn't mean that one has to occur within your corporate network, too.

Telecommuting and remote access

While most NAC solutions and VPNs can ensure that users are authenticated and that their devices adhere to and maintain corporate security and access policies, only NAC solutions and VPNs working together ensure remote users can access only the network resources to which they're authorized, whether they're accessing the corporate network remotely from home via VPN or from a remote office.

Merger or acquisition readiness

Merger or acquisition readiness involves the integration of an existing network and policy set with another existing network and set of policies. For example, say that one company acquires another company. Both companies have operational network security and access policies. But both may be running different antivirus and anti-malware applications. How can the acquiring company enact these policies simultaneously, while ensuring that each company — the acquiring and the acquired company — maintains the same or a higher level of access control, and application and data security? A NAC solution can help bridge the gap between the two company's policy sets. The NAC solution may be able to readily employ both sets of policy via an either/or mechanism, which can ensure that, regardless of which set of policies the acquiring company selects and ultimately invokes, the user (and his or her device) adheres to a combined policy set, is authenticated, and can gain access only to the areas that he or she is approved to access.

Chapter 3

The NAC Lifecycle

*T*o determine the level of access that a user receives when he or she authenticates into a NAC-enabled network, the NAC policy server evaluates several elements. Each of these steps is as important as the next in ensuring that NAC can meet the goals of your corporate security policy and its associated network access control policy. This chapter discusses the entire NAC lifecycle so that you can get an overview of the process associated with getting a user and a machine on the corporate network.

Policy and the NAC Lifecycle

Any NAC solution will go through five steps in determining the level of access provided to a user or machine:

1. Assess

2. Evaluate

3. Remediate

4. Enforce

5. Monitor

You must incorporate continual updates to policy into every step, ensuring that while the security and access control needs of your organization change, so too do the policies and actions that your NAC deployment takes. These necessary changes will help you to refine your NAC lifecycle as business needs change.

Figure 3-1 shows these steps in the NAC lifecycle. In the shaded area, you define the security policy that ultimately determines how your organization implements every step in the NAC process.

Your NAC implementation has very little hope of being successful unless your organization has plans and goals in place.

When rolling out NAC across your organization, you need to understand the implications of your corporate security policy and its impact on NAC, shown in the shaded area of Figure 3-1. NAC is the key component of your corporate security policy when it comes to how you handle access control on your corporate networks.

Chapter 6 covers how you actually write a corporate security policy.

For the first step in the lifecycle, the NAC implementation team reviews the corporate security policy and, from that document, develops a more detailed policy and implementation plan for your NAC deployment.

This plan includes the specific policies that your organization implements:

✔ The corporate security policy might stipulate that end users must use strong authentication in order for employees to access the corporate network.

✔ Your corresponding NAC policy might detail that stipulation, indicating that the organization will implement strong authentication in the form of a token-based one-time password system from Vendor X.

✔ The NAC policy might also specify the level of access that an employee in the Finance department gets from his or her smartphone, or the consequences for having an improperly patched machine that an NAC system can't remediate.

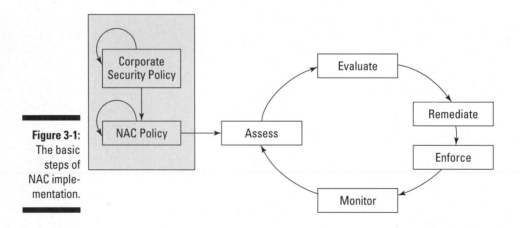

Figure 3-1:
The basic
steps of
NAC imple-
mentation.

Like with any rules and regulations, both the corporate security policy and your NAC policy must evolve over time to accommodate changing business and security requirements.

Ensure that while these changes occur, you feed these changing business requirements back into the NAC lifecycle as part of a continual change process.

Schedule periodic reminders or meetings to re-evaluate your NAC policies or build continual update reviews into your normal work processes.

After you have a mechanism to ensure that your policies are up to date and you deploy NAC in your network, you need to move to the five continual phases of the NAC lifecycle.

Taking Inventory

Your users and machines go through the first phase of the NAC lifecycle — assessment — when they attempt to join your network and access network resources, as shown in Figure 3-2.

Typically, this step involves two primary sets of policies:

- User or machine identity
- Machine security posture

In some instances, you might also want to include other environmental factors related to your policy.

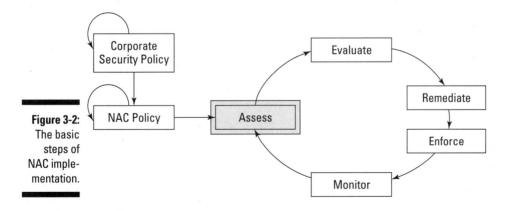

Figure 3-2:
The basic steps of NAC implementation.

User and machine identity

Knowing who's on your network is a key advantage of deploying NAC.

In today's environment, mobile users, authorized third parties, and users on non-standard corporate devices make it more and more difficult to figure out exactly who's accessing your corporate resources. NAC allows you to

- ✔ Determine who's using which machine
- ✔ Tie that information to specific policies for that user's access

When a user first comes onto the corporate network, the NAC system authenticates him or her.

Authentication can take many forms — ranging from a statically defined user name and password, to more complex forms such as biometric identification and X.509 digital certificates. Regardless of the credentials used, the goal of authentication is to prove beyond reasonable doubt that people coming onto your network are who they say they are.

The same authentication holds true for machines, too:

- ✔ In some cases, organizations simply want to determine whether a particular machine is a trusted asset, and then make the access control decision based solely on that information.
- ✔ In other cases, that machine might be an unmanned machine on the network. For example, an employee might have logged off of his or her machine and gone home for the evening, leaving the machine running. IT can take this opportunity to patch that particular machine without having to interact with the end user. In these cases, NAC authenticates, assesses, and patches the machine, making it ready to go — fully compliant — when the user returns to work in the morning.

A NAC-enabled system can prompt a user for authentication in many ways:

- ✔ If the user is an employee using a company-owned asset, that asset may have a NAC software agent installed as part of your standard corporate image.
- ✔ If the user is a guest or partner, coming to your network for a short duration with no need for a permanently installed agent, his or her machine's Web browser may act as the agent, redirecting the user to a captive portal for authentication.

When the user comes onto the network (through some method or another), NAC determines who that user is and feeds the info into the next step of the lifecycle — evaluation (which we talk about in the section "Putting the Pieces Together," later in this chapter).

Chapter 8 covers identity in much more detail.

Clean machines

In the assessment phase, NAC takes note of the security posture of the machines attempting to join the network to ensure that you don't inadvertently allow insecure, improperly patched machines onto the network. The risks of allowing just anything onto the network are staggering — with the potential for spyware, malware, viruses, remote exploits, and more breaking out on your network, NAC needs to gauge the risks associated with allowing unmanaged devices on the network and then take appropriate action.

Chapter 9 covers endpoint assessment at a much more detailed level.

How's the weather?

The assessment process also involves determining other environmental factors such as location or access time.

Environmental factors can include any number of additional pieces of information, other than identity and machine integrity, that you might use as part of your policy decision:

✔ Location might be one factor that plays a part in your decision about whether to allow a user on the network.

For example, you might restrict guest access solely to certain areas of the corporate network — such as conference rooms and public areas. If a guest machine suddenly shows up in a restricted area, NAC provides you with the ability to deny access.

✔ You might employ time of day or day of week restrictions for certain users. For example, you might want to ensure that certain employees or other users are accessing corporate data only during business hours. When that employee tries to access sensitive corporate data from home and on the weekend, you can have a policy in place that automatically denies access.

Putting the Pieces Together

During the assessment phase (discussed in the preceding sections), you collect a lot of information about the user, his or her machine, and the environmental factors associated with the access request. The next step in the NAC lifecycle, indicated by the shaded area in Figure 3-3, is evaluation. In this phase, your NAC system puts together all the pieces of information collected during the assessment phase.

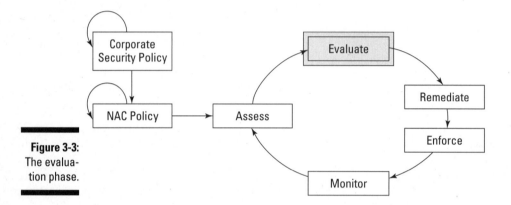

Figure 3-3:
The evaluation phase.

Most NAC deployments have different sets of policies related to different groups of users. In the evaluation phase, the NAC system examines the tens, hundreds, or thousands of new session requests coming onto the network and determines exactly which policy should apply to which request.

For example, your NAC system performs user authentication, but at the same time, it pulls from your corporate directory any additional required information related to that user. Your corporate directory might include group membership information, which indicates what groups the user is a member of in the organization, allowing NAC to automatically differentiate employees from contractors or members of the Finance department from members of the Engineering department.

NAC uses this information to determine which, of potentially many, policies apply to a particular authentication request. It then evaluates the next steps required to provide the appropriate level of access. For example, an employee on a managed laptop might have his or her machine automatically remediated if it doesn't have an up-to-date antivirus program, whereas a contractor who uses his or her own machine might end up in quarantine because your organization's IT department can't patch that machine.

Not So Fast . . .

Remediation, shown in Figure 3-4, is an optional step in the NAC process.

Some users might never go through remediation if their machines stay in compliance with policies at all times. For example, your desktop deployment group might have a very firm handle on software distributions and can manage to keep all the employee machines on the network patched and up to date. When a user comes onto the network with such a machine, NAC can bypass the entire remediation step, moving right on to enforcement, which you can read about in the following section.

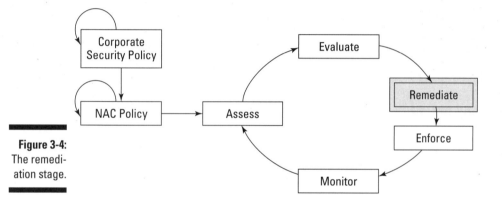

Figure 3-4:
The remediation stage.

Remediation is an incredibly important part of the NAC lifecycle. In this step, your NAC system gets any machine compliance issues corrected so that the user gets full access to any resources for which he or she is authorized. Properly chosen and deployed remediation can make the difference between a safe and secure network, and a horrible situation where machines are out of compliance and your helpdesk is flooded with calls from frantic users.

You ultimately want to get all your users onto the corporate network with full access to everything that their roles imply they should be able to access. Nobody wants to be the person keeping the CEO from her e-mail simply because her antivirus program is out of date. If users can't get their work done, they either try to circumvent access control restrictions (though hopefully your NAC system can prohibit this action) or call the helpdesk. You don't want either of these scenarios to happen in your organization, but you likely don't have to worry about them if you have a well-designed NAC implementation.

Wherever possible, use automatic remediation mechanisms as a first line of defense for machines that are out of compliance. By using this function, your NAC system automatically corrects issues that it finds in the endpoint device. For example, if your NAC system finds that an antivirus program is out of date, it can automatically initiate the update mechanism with no end-user interaction. Or the NAC system might push a machine to retrieve the appropriate patches if it doesn't find them all on the end user's system.

Avoid end-user interaction. Use manual remediation, available on all NAC systems, as a backup. Although most systems provide a mechanism that can give users custom instructions on how to update their antivirus programs, for example, this unnecessary step can cause delays and potential helpdesk calls. The authors have seen many deployments in which end users can't even identify which piece of software is their corporate antivirus program, let alone open it, update it, and enable real-time protection! A good guideline in any security policy, NAC or otherwise, is that the less the end user needs to do, the better.

Let Me In!

After collecting all the information related to a new session request, correcting any deficiencies, evaluating all your policies alongside this collected information, and figuring out exactly which resources your end user can access, the NAC system now needs to enforce those policies.

We give you a detailed look at policy enforcement in Chapter 10, and Chapter 12 covers the advantages and disadvantages of the various NAC policy approaches that we mention in this section.

After the NAC system determines the level of access that an end user can have, enforcement becomes the next hurdle, as shown in Figure 3-5. If you think about varying complexity and size of many organizations' networks, you can get an appreciation for how difficult organizations may find enforcing NAC policies across their entire network.

Ultimately, the main policy server in your NAC implementation has to provide to the various network and endpoint elements specific instructions about what a particular end user is allowed to access on the network.

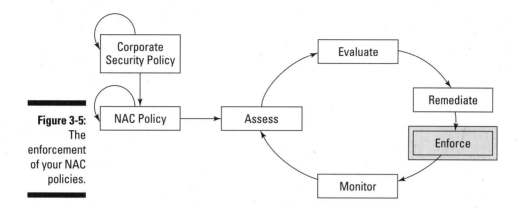

Figure 3-5:
The
enforcement
of your NAC
policies.

Most vendors' NAC solutions utilize one of three primary enforcement points:

- ✔ **Endpoint:** Uses the pre-installed NAC agent software as a means of polic-ing traffic and enforcing access control policies.

- ✔ **Corporate switching infrastructure:** Either wired, wireless, or both. These solutions typically leverage the 802.1X standards for access con-trol, and prohibit or allow traffic right where the user connects to the network.

- ✔ **Inline appliances:** In these architectures, instead of pushing policy enforcement out to separate enforcement points, the appliances them-selves become the enforcement points, and all traffic transits through the devices.

Each of these approaches has its pros and cons. But when your NAC system determines a user's level of access, it will inform all the various enforcement elements that the user should be able to access so that those elements can perform the appropriate policing.

We're Watching You

After you allow users and machines onto the network, you need to ensure that they remain in compliance with the policies that they passed in order to get on the network.

Implementing a security solution such as network access control has no point if you check for policy compliance only at the very beginning of the session. That's like the highway patrol checking for speeders at the beginning of the freeway, and then assuming that everyone stays under the speed limit for the rest of the freeway.

The final phase — monitoring — comes into play when you want to make sure that everyone stays compliant.

When NAC monitors your network, it continually watches users and endpoints for updates or changes in their compliance status, as shown in Figure 3-6.

- ✔ If a user switches off his or her personal firewall or antivirus application, your NAC system should be able to detect that change and react accordingly.

- ✔ Perhaps your operating-system vendor just rolled out a very high severity patch that corrects a gaping security hole. Your NAC system should allow you to roll out a policy that scans for that patch after IT pushes it to all the managed systems so that you can ensure everyone has accepted and installed the patch.

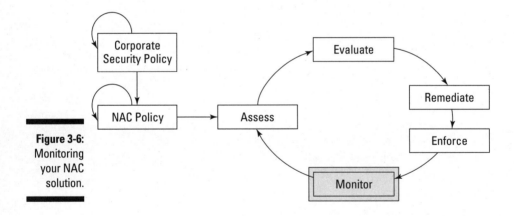

Figure 3-6:
Monitoring
your NAC
solution.

You can choose from two primary types of monitoring:

- ✔ **Time-based:** Scans the system at an administrator-defined interval and makes adjustments when it finds changes

- ✔ **Event-driven:** Actively watches the system and reacts immediately to any changes

In general, you want to implement monitoring functionality that reacts to new events as quickly as possible, which event-driven monitoring can do. But you may not always be able to implement these solutions for various reasons, including performance of the endpoint device. In some cases, event-driven monitoring will consume more resources on the endpoint device, which can be of concern, especially for older or less powerful systems. This determination will need to be made on a case-by-case basis.

Through one mechanism or another, watch the important policies that you roll out so that you can ensure that your end users and machines stay in compliance throughout their sessions.

When or if the part of your NAC system that does the monitoring detects a change in status, this information should feed directly back into a change in access control or possibly remediation for the endpoint device. At this point, the NAC lifecycle essentially starts over and runs through the first four steps of the lifecycle, ensuring that this process happens not only at the beginning of the session, but also on a continual basis throughout every user's and machine's session on the network.

Chapter 4

NAC Components

*A*fter you cover the business cases and know that you have a reason to deploy network access control (NAC), what exactly do you deploy? You can find many different flavors of endpoints, enforcement devices, and policy engines, but all NAC solutions are made up of three parts:

- ✔ Policy engine (also called policy decision point)
- ✔ Endpoint agent (sometimes the endpoint agent is agentless)
- ✔ Policy enforcement point

Although all NAC solutions use at least these three parts, sometimes those parts can be combined. For example, a policy engine can sit inline on the network and enforce policy. You might also have a solution that's agentless via a Web browser; in this situation, the Web browser is your agent.

Picking the right mix depends on the network the NAC solution is going to protect. This chapter helps you define your network access policy and then it shows how you can enforce it.

Creating Policy

One of the most important pieces of any network access control infrastructure is the policy engine. The policy engine is central to a NAC deployment because it controls your entire NAC deployment by creating user access rules and controlling enforcement point in the network infrastructure.

NAC central policy engines are called many different names:

- ✔ Policy engine
- ✔ Policy decision point
- ✔ Policy server
- ✔ NAC manager
- ✔ NAC controller

The policy engine is responsible for determining whether a device or a particular usage should have access to the network. The policy engine also controls all the enforcement points on the network, whether the policy engine is a network appliance or a software agent running on a desktop machine or network server.

One of the primary roles of a policy engine is to make network access decisions based on access control policies determined by the NAC administrator. The core of the NAC policy typically includes three pieces of information:

- ✔ **Network information:** Source, destination, port, and protocol

  Traditionally, a firewall policy examined the network information. The policy engine incorporates that function.

- ✔ **Endpoint integrity:** Identifying hardware, applications, and the security posture of the endpoint.

- ✔ **User identity:** Identifying the user and the user's groups.

Controls

With NAC, this policy includes network, user, and device information, using the policy engine and its primary job functions.

802.1X control

The policy engine provides a RADIUS service with which the switch can communicate.

In an 802.1X deployment, the policy engine provides the RADIUS server to provide an authentication source for the switch or access point. The policy engine makes the final decision about whether the client should be allowed on the network and what restrictions the client should have. These restrictions can include access controls such as Virtual LANs (VLANs) or Access Control Lists (ACLs).

Layer 3 control (inline enforcement)

For a Layer 3 deployment, the enforcement points are controlled by the policy engine, meaning that the enforcement points enforce the policy that the policy engine creates.

Here's an example corporate policy: If you're a corporate user on a compliant corporate machine, you can have access to the datacenter or some other protected resource controlled by the Layer 3 enforcement point.

User authentication

The policy engine verifies user or device identity for any device that connects to the network. For instance, when a corporate user connects to the network, the policy engine verifies the user's credentials against the authentication server (we talk about authentication servers in the section "Authentication server," later in this chapter). If the user has valid credentials, the policy engine performs a group lookup to see what kind of a user is connecting — for example, the user might be an employee in human resources. The controller then knows that the user is a valid employee and should have access to the human resources network or servers. If user authentication is the only part of the policy being enforced, the policy engine can now signal an enforcement point and push a policy that gives the user access.

Endpoint posture

The policy engine verifies endpoint posture for any device connecting to the network.

One of the greatest benefits of a network access control deployment is the ability to be able to verify the state of an endpoint before it connects to the network. This ability gives you a lot more control over your network. You can now create a policy that says, "If you're an employee (who has valid user credentials that have been verified via user authentication) and you're connecting to the network with a corporate asset that's compliant, you can have access to the network."

If a device goes out of compliance (for example, if it doesn't run the correct antivirus software that has the latest virus definition files), you can

- ✔ Remove the user from the network.
- ✔ Quarantine the user to another network.
- ✔ Block the user's access to certain parts of the network.

Pop quiz: Your network needs

Can you create and maintain policies in your own NAC deployment?

✔ Is my policy engine flexible enough so that I can create all the policies that I need?

✔ Can I maintain the policies when my organization or deployment grows?

✔ Can I delegate administration to my operation group?

✔ Can I give delegated access to the helpdesk so that the helpdesk support technician can help users that can't get on the network?

✔ Can I scale my policy engine to fit my network?

Continuous monitoring

The policy engine creates dynamic network policies that are pushed out to devices on the network and therefore must keep track of them.

For instance, a user receives access to the network because his or her device is compliant and meets all the NAC policies that you've defined, but after gaining access, the user changes his or her device so that it goes out of compliance. You want to make sure that endpoint agent recognizes the changes, communicates the changes with the policy engine, and then takes action on them. You could configure remediation messages so that the user receives a simple message or the network changes to give the user limited access.

Don't leave open holes in your network. Holes defeat your whole NAC deployment and increase your risk whenever a user unplugs from the network. Remove the policy that you have set (typically static network policy on firewalls) so that the next user can't just piggyback on the access created for the prior user.

Although all these functions are relatively simple to manage on their own, the usability and flexibility of the policy engine becomes critical to the success of your deployment when you combine these functions to create complex access policies. There is a potential for management to become very difficult when many functions are used together.

Location

The policy engine's location in your network is a critical deployment consideration.

If your network access control deployment is going to control access for all your users who get on and off the network by controlling devices deployed in the network, you need to place the deployment in a location where all the devices that it's controlling can reach it.

For most networks, it makes sense to put the policy engine in the datacenter. But you need to consider these high availability concerns:

- **Datacenter survivability:** Make sure that you have a redundant datacenter or backup policy engine store that Layer 3 devices (such as switches and access points) can contact if your primary datacenter falls off the face of the Earth.

    If your network access control deployment is controlling access for all users getting onto the network and you lose a datacenter, you lose the policy engine that allows people to get onto the network.

- **Branch survivability:** If an off-site central policy engine controls access to your branch locations, you need a backup plan. Otherwise, if you lose your WAN link to the central datacenter, you can't get users on the network.

Oh, one more thing . . .

You're adding a layer on top of your network called NAC that can potentially block all users from getting access to the network. Hmm. Users aren't going to be too thrilled if something happens to the policy engine and they can't work. If your NAC goes down, access goes down. Your NAC implementation is a service that controls your network which must *always* work and be available.

Do your homework

When you evaluate a network access control solution, make sure that the vendor can demonstrate high availability and survivability of the policy engine. You want to make sure that when the primary policy engine goes down, your users can continue to work and connect to the network like nothing has happened.

Check the reputation of your network access control vendor:

- Do they have a history of reliability?

- Have they solved your problem for other customers?

Doing a little homework can save you many headaches down the road.

Because you want your NAC to always be on, you need to identify a solution that has high-availability options (such as an active/passive pair of policy engines) that protect you from a large network access outage if one of the policy engines were to explode. *High availability* means redundancy and backup, and it requires a combination of network design, hardware, and software configurations.

Dealing with Clients

An *endpoint client* is a component typically responsible for collecting information from the endpoint and forwarding it to the policy engine for verification and validation.

Client functions

An endpoint client needs to be able to collect user and endpoint information from the connecting user and endpoint.

Collect posture

If endpoint identity is one of the most valuable bits of information that you need to collect, an endpoint client can do that collection efficiently and correctly. Every endpoint is different, so you need to have the flexibility to collect the information that you need to make decisions. You should also look for open standard support for endpoint integrity collection so that if something isn't in your current NAC solution, you can find another company that supports the standards and leverage the integration, or in very rare situations, write or develop something yourself.

When collecting posture, don't limit it to a single check. Configure the endpoint agent to continually monitor the endpoint for changes.

Collect user credentials

Identity is a critical aspect of network access control, and the endpoint agent typically collects this information. An endpoint agent can collect several kinds of authentication, such as

- User names and passwords
- User names and passcodes (two-factor authentication)
- Certificates

The endpoint client must have the flexibility to collect any form of authentication that you plan to use in your network.

The endpoint client should also have support for some form of Single Sign On (SSO) authentication. If you plan to add an agent to the endpoint that's going to request credentials, try to get rid of the password prompt to make logging into the network more usable. Think of the situation this way: How would you feel if you had to log into Windows and then log into an agent right afterward? You'd probably find it quite annoying. SSO gets rid of the second login request by using the credentials that it gets from the Windows login. If you use Group Policy Objects (GPOs) in a Windows network, you may need the Graphical Identification and Authentication (GINA) library integration to get the endpoint on the network so that you can start login scripts, map drives, and so on.

Network enforcement support

If you're rolling out a Layer 3 NAC deployment, you may need support for Layer 3 enforcement in the agent you're deploying, such as IPSec enforcement for data privacy. The agent would have to support IPSec to be able to connect the user to the network.

Network supplicant functionality

If you plan to leverage 802.1X as an enforcement mechanism, then the supplicant functionality of the endpoint agent becomes very important. You need to make sure that it supports all the Extensible Authentication Protocol (EAP) methods that you need for your deployment, as illustrated in Figure 4-1.

EAP is a framework for universal authentication, as described by RFC 3748. Although you can find many different EAP methods, the most common are EAP-TTLS, EAP-PEAP, EAP-TLS, and EAP-MD5.

Deploying, supporting, and troubleshooting

If you're planning to roll out an agent to 25,000 or more users in your network, you need an endpoint agent that you can easily pre-configure before deploying it to the users. Also, you need to figure out whether you can lock down the configuration and how easily you can upgrade it. Look for these features in your endpoint agent, as well as other features, such as an option to deploy the endpoint agent by using tools such as SMS or Active directory. You need to be able to troubleshoot endpoint agents easily if something isn't working.

Not-so-secret agents

Although many different types of endpoint clients can fit a multitude of network needs in the world, you can divide endpoint clients into three general groups.

The client depends on type of device or endpoint that you are going to be running it on.

Smartphones, PDAs
iPhone, Win Mobile
Android, Symbian, etc.

Desktop OS
Windows, Linux, Mac

Figure 4-1:
An EAP
authen-
tication
diagram.

Laptops
Windows, Linux, Mac
Personal, Corporate Machines

Full agent

The full agent is typically a large agent that you need to pre-install on the endpoint before it can get on the network. The agent usually includes

- ✓ A supplicant
- ✓ Layer 3 enforcement functionality
- ✓ Endpoint integrity collection
- ✓ Remediation support

✔ Troubleshooting tools

✔ Some sort of tray icon

The full agent is usually targeted at corporate employees.

The challenge with full agents is that you usually need administrator rights on the local machine to install the agent. So, a network administrator typically uses a software deployment service that exists on the network already, usually SMS or Active Directory.

You can dynamically install some full agents via an ActiveX or Java installer, but these full agents are larger in size than lightweight agents, so a network administrator can pre-configure them before a user gets the agent deployed to their machine.

Lightweight agent

The lightweight agent is a client, which you typically run via ActiveX or Java, that includes

✔ Layer 3 enforcement functionality

✔ Endpoint integrity collection

✔ Remediation support

✔ Not much else, usually

You use the lightweight agent mainly for guests or contractors who come into the network.

The biggest benefit of the lightweight agent is that you typically don't need administrator privileges on the local machine to do the endpoint integrity query and perform Layer 3 enforcement in the network.

You usually use the lightweight agent in conjunction with a *captive portal feature,* which is best described as the hotel-room experience. At a hotel, you plug into the network and try to browse somewhere, but instead of getting what you want, you see a web page that asks you for your room number and last name. In the case of network access control, you're redirected to a page that runs the lightweight agent via ActiveX or Java. After that has happened, it will ask the user for their username and password.

Clientless

Clientless access typically takes the form of a Web page to which a user submits his or her password to get access to the network. Clientless access usually uses a captive portal feature to provide a redirect of the user's web browser to the location for the clientless access page.

Clientless access is typically limited to user authentication and Layer 3 enforcement only. Clientless access is often targeted at guest users or devices for which no agent exists. The only requirement on the device is a Web browser.

Left behind

Each of the types of agents behave slightly differently when you sign out or close the agent.

Persistent

The persistent state is typically what you get if you have a full agent. After you install a full agent, it starts every time that the operating system does.

The persistent state is really targeted at managed corporate users, who want you to install the full agent once and then have it persist so that it can continue working for the users.

Dissolvable

A dissolvable agent is usually an ActiveX control or Java applet that runs when the user tries to get on the network. It uses captive portal functionality to redirect a user's Web browser to a page that can run the dissolvable agent. This agent persists only while the user has the Web browser open. When the user closes the Web browser, the dissolvable agent closes. To get back on, the user needs to launch the dissolvable agent via the captive portal Web page.

The dissolvable agent is best suited for contractors and guests, or anyone on whose machine you don't want to leave a client.

None

No client is targeted at devices that aren't capable of running ActiveX or Java applet, including guest machines. For any machine that you don't want to run ActiveX or Java, the no client option provides network access only when the Web browser is open.

Enforcement Time

After you define the policy, you decide how and where to enforce your policies. Enforcement gives your network access control policies teeth, so to speak, allowing them to have meaning and purpose on the network.

Most network access control deployments use several enforcement methods. When selecting the best method to enforce policies, take a look at each method and see what makes sense in your network. You may even choose to do no enforcement at all and just run the entire deployment in monitor mode. Whatever you decide to do, do your homework and test each option thoroughly.

Endpoint

Endpoint enforcement, the most basic form of enforcement, involves the endpoint client enforcing policy that the policy engine pushes. The enforcement can be network-access-based or software-based. For network-access-based enforcement on the endpoint, the endpoint client restricts or changes access for a network user based on a policy that the policy engine sends. Endpoint enforcement can use a couple of different methods, but the most common method uses a software firewall-based approach. The other method of enforcement is software based, which is limited only by your imagination. For example, the software based approach can block certain applications from running or start a virtual desktop.

Try to avoid using endpoint enforcement on its own. Malicious users can get around endpoint enforcement alone more easily than a deployment that includes another form of enforcement.

802.1X

802.1X enforcement, which is becoming one of the most popular methods of enforcement, is an authentication standard that's supported on most modern switches and wireless access points. 802.1X uses the Extensible Authentication Protocol (EAP) that's defined in RFC 2284.

802.1X enforcement has some really big advantages for most networks. Because 802.1X is a Layer 2 based authentication mechanism, you can authenticate users or machines before they have an IP address and are a part of your network. 802.1X allows you to be pro-active and decide who you want on your network before they actually get on your network.

Enforcement stages

For 802.1X to work, you need three stages of hardware and software.

Authentication server

The authentication server is a RADIUS server. In the case of network access control, the RADIUS server is typically a part of the policy engine. The authentication server takes all the authentication requests, validates them, and then says yay or nay to the access request.

Authenticator

The *authenticator* is your switch or access point and is the simple device in the middle:

1. The authenticator takes authentication requests that it receives from a supplicant and forwards those requests to the authentication server.

2. After an authentication server determines that the endpoint should have access, the authentication server sends an access accept to the authenticator.

3. When the authenticator receives the access accept, it allows the endpoint to have access to the network.

Supplicant

The *supplicant* is a piece of software that enables an endpoint to communicate over Layer 2 for 802.1X authentication. In network access control, the supplicant is typically a part of the endpoint client. The supplicant needs to support the form of EAP that your network uses. The supplicant collects all the user credentials and any other information that the authenticator needs for authentication, and then sends that information to the authenticator (the switch or access point) for authentication.

Usage

802.1X enforcement is typically used in conjunction with VLANs. VLANs are a way of separating traffic at Layer 2 into virtual networks that don't have access to one another. In the case of NAC, think of having all your valid compliant endpoints in a corporate VLAN and all your non-compliant machines in a quarantine VLAN. The endpoints in the quarantine VLAN don't have access to any of the resources in the corporate VLAN, so the quarantine VLAN has restricted access, as illustrated in Figure 4-2.

Typically, the only access available in the quarantine VLAN is the access needed to update virus signatures or any other remediation that the machine needs to become compliant. After the machine is compliant, the 802.1X authentication transaction happens again, and the endpoint is put in the corporate VLAN.

Component	Policy	Result
Antivirus	Installed	Passed
	Up-to-date	Passed
	Real-time protection enabled	Passed
Personal Firewall	Installed	Passed
	Real-time protection enabled	Passed
Disk Encryption	Installed	Passed
	Active	Passed
OS Patches	Installed	Passed

Figure 4-2:
VLAN
endpoint
enforcement.

Inline

Inline enforcement is a method of enforcement that enables you to differentiate between different Layer 3 IP addresses and provide the appropriate
access to protected resources on the network.

With inline enforcement, you put a device in between the user and the
resources that he or she is accessing so that you can control the access of
the user's access as it flows through the device.

For example, when you have two endpoints, those endpoints are both connected to the corporate network and have IP addresses in the same subnet,
but the users are two different people with two different job functions —
one is an engineer, and the other works in human resources. The engineer
shouldn't see the HR database, and the HR person shouldn't see the engineer's source code server.

The most popular form of inline enforcement is the firewall. Firewalls allow
administrators to define a policy based on IP addresses, specifying which IPs
can reach which resources. Network administrators defined this policy statically in the past. Network access control now extends firewall policy and creates dynamic policy based on any number of attributes that the policy engine
checks.

Think of inline enforcement as a firewall in front of a datacenter. In the past,
a firewall had static policy based on source IP, destination IP, ports, and protocols. But if your users have Dynamic Host Configuration Protocol (DHCP),
the users' IP addresses are always changing, so you can never fix a policy that
applies to the users directly. If you switch to an inline enforcement point
(a firewall controlled by the policy engine), you can have dynamic policies

created on the enforcement point when a user is authenticated and joined to the network. So, the HR guy can see only the HR server, and the engineer can see only her source code.

IPSec

IPSec enforcement, an extension of inline enforcement, is used to create an IPSec connection from the endpoint to a virtual private network (VPN) concentrator in the network. The VPN concentrator can also be a firewall or other appliance, but its main purpose is to provide data privacy across the internal network.

You can use IPSec VPN where encryption of traffic is important, such as your company's financial information. If you don't want anyone else to see the traffic, then IPSec is for you.

Remediation

When you define and enforce the policy, the policy engine triggers the enforcement point to move users that don't meet your NAC policies to a quarantine network. When users are in the quarantine network, unable to work, you have to fix them.

The method of fixing users and allowing them to get back on the network is called *remediation*.

You can use two types of remediation:

- ✔ **Auto remediation:** Remediation happens automatically.
- ✔ **User self-remediation:** The endpoint client provides instructions that the user must follow to fix his or her machine.

The outcome of your remediation can change any number of enforcement methods discussed in this chapter. You can easily block all your users from getting on the network at all! Review and test your access policies before you deploy them into the network.

Chapter 5

SSL VPNs

Many SSL VPN (Secure Sockets Layer virtual private network) vendors have repositioned the marketing of their products to claim that they're NAC products. Is there any truth to these claims? Absolutely. However, the devil is in the details. Although SSL VPN products provide many of the same functions that a NAC offering does, most SSL VPN products have been architected with the remote user in mind, whereas most NAC offerings have been architected for the local user — possibly a minor distinction until you account for the differences in experience and throughput expected by end users when they're on the local area network (LAN) as opposed to when they are remote.

Can you use SSL VPNs for a NAC deployment? It depends. In this chapter, we introduce you to SSL VPNs, compare them to traditional NAC products, and then provide an introduction to when and where you can and should use each product.

In the Beginning, There Were SSL VPNs

SSL VPNs have been around long enough to have their own overall product category. In many ways, SSL VPNs were the very first NAC products available.

We have dozens of customers that originally used SSL VPNs to do the job that NAC provides today.

Historically, organizations used SSL VPN to protect their Wi-Fi (wireless fidelity) deployments and their remote access deployments. When users wanted to access the wireless network, they needed a valid SSL VPN session, in addition to possessing wireless credentials (such as a WEP key). Because SSL VPNs provided this functionality, organizations could layer role-based access control onto their wireless networks and up the ante for wireless security.

SSL VPNs are primarily a remote-access–oriented technology that acts as a gatekeeper between the end user and network resources and applications. Access control decisions are based on user identity/role and endpoint integrity, among other things.

Sounds a lot like NAC, doesn't it?

User identity with SSL VPN

User identity validation (authentication and authorization of users) with SSL VPN is very similar to an NAC solution. For the most part, these products are architected to integrate seamlessly with the organization's existing authentication infrastructure.

The similarities between user identity with NAC and user identity with SSL VPNs is a bonus for many organizations. They can leverage a single authentication and authorization infrastructure for both local and remote users.

User authentication

From an authentication perspective, most leading SSL VPN offerings provide integration with a mix of standards-based and proprietary authentication servers, such as the options discussed in the following sections.

Local authentication

Local authentication is an on-board database for authentication of users. The entire user account management and record storage is done on the SSL VPN appliance.

Most SSL VPN vendors offer this type of authentication, though it's used primarily for administrator authentication or for smaller organizations. Most large organizations invest in (or plan to invest in) an external user authentication solution.

Lightweight Directory Access Protocol (LDAP)

LDAP is a standard protocol for querying a directory database and for making updates to database records. As one of the more commonly used interfaces in SSL VPN deployments, LDAP acts as the protocol of choice for querying many types of databases, including Active Directory.

Active Directory (AD)

Active Directory is one of the leading directory servers, and most organizations deploy it, to some extent. Many SSL VPN servers offer a native Active Directory authentication server interface, but AD deployments can also leverage LDAP/LDAPS (LDAP over SSL) for queries and updates.

RADIUS authentication and one-time password systems

Multiple-factor authentication, such as one-time passwords (OTPs) and digital certificates (see the following section), have become very popular for remote access use, replacing static user names and passwords in many organizations. Like with digital certificates, a number of technologies have evolved that make it far easier and less expensive to deploy and manage one-time password solutions, and organizations have adopted these technologies as a result of those developments.

Most SSL VPN systems provide a standard way to interface with these OTP systems through the RADIUS protocol. Remote Authentication Dial-In User Service (RADIUS) provides authentication, authorization, and accounting services, and most OTP systems available on the market today support RADIUS. Some SSL VPNs also provide native support for proprietary OTP systems, but you don't need this special native integration for most deployments because the RADIUS interface can provide the same functionality.

X.509 certificate authentication

In recent years, X.509 digital certificates have gotten more popular as an authentication method. X.509 certificates are issued by several trusted certificate authorities to organizations and to end users. These trusted certificate authorities (CAs) hold the power to revoke these certificates at any time. Because they are based on secure digital certificates, this form of user or machine credential is impossible to spoof or steal without acquiring the private key, which is kept protected and never exchanged. The U.S. Federal Government has been a huge driver for adoption of X.509 certificates, due to mandates requiring their use not only by government agencies, but also by government contractors and other private sector organizations. As a result, both software and hardware support has improved significantly over recent years, making deployment and ongoing administration much simpler.

When an SSL VPN appliance supports X.509 digital certificates, that appliance must perform validation of a certificate to ensure that the certificate hasn't been revoked. The SSL VPN validates the certificate with either

- **CRLs (certificate revocation lists):** CRLs are essentially lists of revoked certificates that are distributed by the certificate issuer.
- **OCSP (Online Certificate Status Protocol):** OCSP was introduced as a way to bypass some of the limitations of CRL checking (such as the size of the lists), and it specifies a way to verify certificate status in real-time.

In addition to certificate status validation, the SSL VPN might also retrieve user attributes from the certificate so that the SSL VPN access control system can compare those attributes to attributes in a directory, for example, or map users to specific roles in the SSL VPN implementation. Most SSL VPNs also allow the administrator to specify which certificate authorities (CAs) result in a successful authentication.

Security Assertion Markup Language

Security Assertion Markup Language (SAML) is a standard for authenticating and authorizing users across different systems. Essentially, it's a Single Sign-On (SSO) technology. Some SSL VPN appliances provide support for SAML, allowing users that are already logged in to other systems the ability to be seamlessly logged in to the SSL VPN system, as needed.

You can find a variety of identity and access management platforms available that support SAML. In most SSL VPN deployments that use SAML, the primary use case is SSO to SSL VPN–protected resources and applications, not signing in to the SSL VPN itself, so not many enterprises have used this authentication method, according to the authors' experiences.

User authorization

User authentication (discussed in the preceding sections) is only one piece of the puzzle in identifying and providing appropriate access to users. Another piece is authorization.

Authorization maps information about a user to the credentials provided at login.

In some cases, the relevant information is stored in the authentication request itself. For example, an X.509 digital certificate or an SAML assertion might contain information that allows the SSL VPN to do the appropriate role mapping. In other cases, however, the SSL VPN appliance needs to query the directory.

Many organizations have stored information, such as group membership or other attributes related to each user, in Active Directory or some other LDAP database. Upon login, the SSL VPN queries the database to get these details and uses that information to assign the user to a specific role. For example, an LDAP query for John Doe might return information indicating that John is an employee in the Engineering group. As a result, John gains access to the intranet, corporate e-mail, and various engineering-specific resources.

Endpoint security with SSL VPN

When you compare SSL VPNs and purpose-built NAC systems, endpoint security (or endpoint integrity verification) for each is almost identical.

For the most part, organizations want to ensure an appropriate machine posture prior to allowing a user access to the network. In addition, most organizations see more variance in the types of machines from which end users want to gain access to corporate resources when those users access the resources remotely, versus when they access them locally. For example, end users might need to access their e-mail from their home PCs, or they might want to download a PowerPoint presentation from a kiosk in a hotel lobby.

For these kinds of reasons, it becomes crucial to validate the endpoint machine prior to allowing the user to come on the network in a remote-access setting.

Some SSL VPN vendors have created protected sandbox technologies and cache cleaners that can remove sensitive information from these types of machines at the end of an SSL VPN session, limiting the risk of data theft. Chapter 8 covers many of these capabilities with a NAC perspective, rather than an SSL VPN perspective.

Figure 5-1 shows users accessing the SSL VPN from three different locations. In this case, the SSL VPN policy dictates that a different level of access is granted to the end user based on whether the user's machine is in compliance with the policy. Figure 5-1 is similar to typical policies used in active SSL VPN deployments:

- **Home PC:** This machine doesn't have an antivirus application installed, so the user is prompted to remediate the device. The user downloads and installs the appropriate antivirus software, and then is allowed access.

- **Kiosk:** The user is accessing the SSL VPN from a public machine. Obviously, the user doesn't have privileges on the machine, so the user can't install additional software. Because the user can't remediate the machine, the SSL VPN fails the policies, but the administrator has set up a policy to grant the user minimal access in this type of situation.

- **Managed PC:** The user is accessing the network from an appropriately patched and compliant managed laptop, so the user is granted full access to the SSL VPN.

Although Figure 5-1 may be too simple for you and your network needs, it shows a small piece of the flexibility available with SSL VPN systems. Other types of policies are available with SSL VPNs for endpoint integrity verification, too.

Endpoint security applications

One of the most commonly used and easiest to configure types of endpoint security policies are those that verify the presence, operation, and up-to-date nature of third-party endpoint security applications. These types of policies ensure that endpoints connected to your network have the appropriate self-protection mechanisms in place.

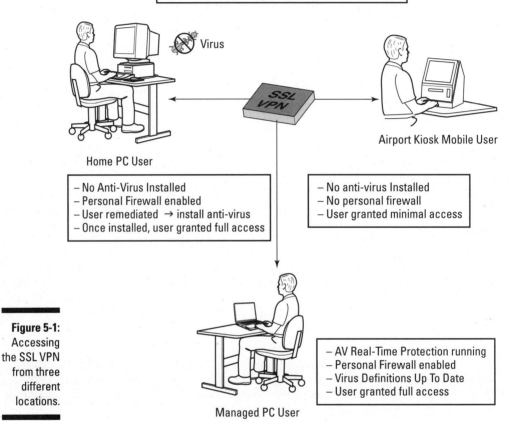

Host Checker
- Check devices before & during session
- Ensure device compliance with corporate policy
- Remediate devices when needed
- Cross platform support

Virus

SSL VPN

Airport Kiosk Mobile User

Home PC User

- No Anti-Virus Installed
- Personal Firewall enabled
- User remediated → install anti-virus
- Once installed, user granted full access

- No anti-virus Installed
- No personal firewall
- User granted minimal access

Figure 5-1:
Accessing
the SSL VPN
from three
different
locations.

- AV Real-Time Protection running
- Personal Firewall enabled
- Virus Definitions Up To Date
- User granted full access

Managed PC User

Most SSL VPN products available have a list of predefined policies, though the level of comprehensiveness varies from one implementation to the next.

Look for these common policy types provided by NAC vendors:

✓ **Operating system:** These scans allow you to verify the operating system, and potentially the service pack, of the incoming endpoint device, which is especially important in an SSL VPN deployment in which you have no advance idea the type of device from which the user is trying to gain access.

Operating system policies can help you to verify which type(s) of additional endpoint security mechanisms to put into place. You might have a different endpoint security policy for a Windows XP SP2 device than for a Windows CE or Macintosh OS device. Even within something like the Windows OS, you might have some differentiation — for example, your corporate standard personal firewall might be different on Windows XP machines versus Windows Vista machines. This information also helps the SSL VPN system itself to appropriately display login pages, home pages, and application interfaces to end users. For example, the login page on a Macintosh might look quite a bit different on a Windows Mobile Smartphone.

✔ **Antivirus:** Scanning for antivirus applications is one of the most common types of endpoint integrity policies implemented with SSL VPNs. Organizations want to ensure that machines connecting to their networks have an appropriate level of protection, and an antivirus application is pretty much a standard requirement for verifying endpoint integrity.

You can't simply scan the machine to ensure that it has an antivirus application installed — scanning for particular files or registry settings, for example, doesn't necessarily guarantee that the antivirus application is actively protecting the machine itself. Also, you may find looking at processes running in memory troublesome, even if you're verifying an MD5 checksum of the process, because modern antivirus applications may have several processes running at any given time. Without an in-depth knowledge of what each process does, endpoint integrity agents can have difficulty determining the processes that must be running to verify normal operation of the antivirus application. Throughout normal operation, some processes might start at different times, making this a very difficult task.

Most NAC vendors offer a solution that checks not only whether the machine has an antivirus application installed, but whether it's also running and up to date. Some of the available policies on the market include

- Verifying installation of a particular version or vendor of antivirus solution(s).

- Verifying that real-time protection is actively enabled on the system.

- Verifying that virus signatures are fully up to date or that they've been updated at some point in the recent past, depending on your policy.

- Ensuring that a successful full system scan has been completed in the last few days. (The number of days depends on your antivirus vendor's update schedule, and your organization's willingness to allow machines with slightly outdated antivirus policies to join the network.)

Depending on your organization's security policy, you might want to verify one or more of those attributes related to antivirus.

Your verification might vary, based on the user and machine in question. For instance, you might want to be very specific in your scan when an employee comes onto the network by using a company-owned and -managed machine, but when that same employee tries to access the network from his or her home machine, you might allow some level of restricted access only if his or her machine is running an up-to-date antivirus application from any vendor supported by your SSL VPN appliance.

✔ **Personal firewall:** Checking to ensure that a machine has a personal firewall installed and enabled is a common endpoint security measure. This scan ensures that the endpoint device has active protection enabled. Like with antivirus scans, make sure that you're verifying the personal firewall is actually running, not just installed.

✔ **Disk encryption:** With the number of data loss incidents in the news — not to mention the thousands of laptops lost or stolen in airports and other public areas every year — disk encryption is becoming more popular by the day. These scans allow you to ensure that the sensitive data on a mobile device or laptop hard disk is secured and encrypted.

✔ **Antispyware:** You want to ensure that the antispyware application is running and actively protecting the system, not only installed on the machine.

✔ **Peer-to-peer applications:** Many organizations fear peer-to-peer applications because a user can inadvertently download viruses or malware, and the application could potentially allow an intruder to gain access to a machine. SSL VPN products are increasingly beginning to scan for these types of applications so that you can verify their presence and, if necessary, shut them down before allowing the user to have full access onto the network. If you have users accessing the SSL VPN from their home machines, you probably want to shut down their teenagers' BitTorrent or other file sharing applications before allowing those users to view sensitive corporate data.

The Windows operating systems has a much more comprehensive list of policies than any non-Windows OS — Macintosh, Linux distributions, and mobile platforms. Windows is the most heavily targeted operating system with the most known vulnerabilities, so you find the largest selection of endpoint protection suites for Windows. While other platforms gain or lose market share, you'll see an expansion or contraction in terms of the number of offerings for these devices. For example, the number of antivirus and personal firewall applications for Windows Mobile and Macintosh machines has increased significantly, mostly as a result of increased popularity of these systems, which leads to an increased likelihood that hackers will target these machines.

Operating system and application patches

New application and operating system vulnerabilities are discovered on a daily — even hourly — basis. Hackers are increasingly motivated by profit, rather than by fun and glory, so exploitation of these vulnerabilities happens alarmingly fast. As a result, you absolutely must appropriately patch operating systems, middleware, and applications as often as possible.

In the datacenter, where servers and applications are tightly controlled, applying such patches is a relatively easy task. Virtualization and datacenter management technologies allow the administrator to easily take machines offline, patch them, and then bring them back online with minimal user disruption.

Outside the datacenter, especially with mobile users, the myriad devices connecting to the average corporate network changes frequently due to the frequency with which device vendors release handset and new operating system versions. Because most SSL VPN users are mobile users, their devices frequently connect to a dizzying array of 3G networks, Wi-Fi networks, and wired connections — and many of these networks are very insecure. These devices might be holding intellectual property, customer information, or sensitive financial data, so you need to both scan these machines when they come onto the network (to protect the network and network assets) and ensure, at least on a periodic basis, that the device can be patched to protect against known exploits, thereby protecting that data on the machine.

To help solve this problem, many SSL VPN solutions offer a mechanism to check the endpoint machine for required patches *prior* to allowing that machine onto the network. This mechanism helps to not only validate endpoint security, but also ensure that even fully remote machines can stay patched and up to date. Because patches change all the time, SSL VPN appliances implementing this type of scan typically include some sort of update mechanism that allows them to stay up to date and dynamically enforce policies that scan for new patches.

For example, Microsoft sticks to a monthly release schedule for their new patches on what is known as Patch Tuesday. After Microsoft releases these new patches, most vendors publish new patch scans as soon as possible. The SSL VPN appliances are updated dynamically, usually by the SSL VPN vendor, and after that update, the SSL VPN, through its endpoint integrity agent, enforces those new policies for new sessions or for policy reevaluations.

But what to scan for? A fully loaded system might have dozens, or even hundreds, of applications. Certainly, you don't need to ensure that every single application is fully patched and up to date.

Most patches are classified by severity, so you probably don't have to scan every single one. And when these patches are released, you might determine that the potential impact of some vulnerabilities is higher than others, so you want to make sure that you install the patches corresponding to the impactful vulnerabilities on all devices. For example, in the retail marketplace, your customer relationship management (CRM) software might have had a critical vulnerability that was recently patched. You'd find it more important and prudent to ensure that this patch is installed on the endpoint systems, as compared to ensuring that iTunes was patched on your endpoint machines.

If you go overboard with patch scanning, you might end up causing a bad end-user experience. Scanning for hundreds of patches on dozens of applications might take a long time to complete on an endpoint machine — which becomes even worse if the user is on a low bandwidth connection, such as dial-up, or just has a slow connection. During that time, the end user is waiting to get onto the network and do his or her job. Use caution or, at the very least, assess performance implications when you implement scans for a large number of patches.

Machine identity: Who's on first?

Most organizations trust the machines that they own and manage to access networks more than they do foreign devices. They can control the patch levels, software distribution, and (to some extent) who uses the device. As a result, they feel more comfortable providing access to sensitive corporate data from these machines.

If you find yourself in this boat, you might want a programmatic way to identify your own machines versus outsiders. You can make this identification easily enough when you can look at the PC and see your corporate asset tracking barcode or other physical identification, but identification isn't so easy when you must differentiate between two seemingly identical Windows XP SP2 machines that have nearly the same installed software, one of which is a corporate-managed laptop, with the other being some employee's untrusted personal use machine.

Over the years, we've seen customers use many different methods to trick this identification step, some of which are more secure than others.

Given the native, custom endpoint security scans that many SSL VPN appliances provide, some of the less secure and easily bypassed tricks have included

 ✓ **Registry setting identification:** Some administrators have hidden information in Windows registries that identify corporate assets. This is a method of security by obscurity — although someone can easily spoof this "secret" registry setting, the administrators know that a person isn't likely to come across this secret and identify it for what it is.

✔ **Secret files:** Similar to the registry setting, this scheme relies on security by obscurity, but instead of hiding something in the registry, it hides a file somewhere in the file system where no one is likely to find and delete it. The endpoint integrity agent uses a custom scan to find this file and identify the machine.

✔ **MAC address:** This technique involves storing the MAC address(es) of a user's machine in the corporate directory or somewhere accessible by the NAC solution. When the user logs in, the MAC address of the endpoint machine is extracted and compared to the addresses stored in the directory. If the endpoint machine's MAC address matches one on the list, the SSL VPN policy results in the machine being classified as a managed device.

Identifying a machine by MAC address has two primary problems:

• Someone can easily copy or spoof MAC addresses.

• Most modern machines have multiple adapters, so they have multiple MAC addresses.

  Make sure that you have all network adapters categorized and available to support this portion of your SSL VPN deployment, if necessary.

A machine coming onto the network via a wired switch port is going to have a different MAC address than that same machine connecting via your 802.11 wireless network.

Get your certificate

Many companies have begun using a method of device identification more secure than MAC addresses or secret files to identify corporate assets. Many have turned to machine (or computer) certificates. These certificates can be somewhat expensive and difficult to deploy, but luckily, many SSL VPN appliances and many NAC solutions offer such capabilities, so you don't make the investment for only one piece of the network access control deployment. If you're looking for a secure way to identify corporate assets, machine certificates might be your best bet.

Machine certificates are standard X.509 digital certificates, similar to what you might find on a Web server or in user identification such as a smart card or USB drive. The key distinction between machine certificates and user certificates, however, is that machine certificates are stored in the computer or machine on the endpoint device, so they're used to identify the machine, not the user. As a result, the user can't present these machine certificates to the browser as identification — another mechanism must exist to extract and validate the certificate.

Machine certificates have one advantage: They use private key infrastructure (PKI), which is designed to protect against spoofing, man-in-the-middle type attacks, and other security concerns associated with authenticating a previously unknown third party.

Many IT administrators don't feel comfortable with some of the PKI concepts, and many think that rolling out certificates will be difficult or costly. Luckily, many resources available online describe PKI, and certificate management tools have made huge advances in the past few years, making the process of creating, distributing, and managing certificates much easier than in the past.

Custom policies

You might find yourself wanting to scan endpoint devices for certain applications, patches, or other types of information that don't fall into the predefined list of applications provided by your vendor. Instead of scanning for a known personal firewall, for example, your organization might have implemented its own endpoint security application. Or you may want to scan for some endpoint security application that's available from an outside vendor, but for which your vendor hasn't yet provided a predefined policy. You don't have to stick with predefined parameters.

Almost every SSL VPN offers the ability to create your own custom endpoint integrity policies, which allow you to scan for such system attributes as

- ✔ Presence or absence of certain files on the file system
- ✔ Whether a particular process is running on the endpoint
- ✔ The MD5 checksum of that process
- ✔ Particular registry settings

These scans can provide you with a picture of whether a particular application is running on the system or other customized information that might be applicable to network access control for your organization, as set forth in the corporate security policy.

Cache cleaning, as opposed to money laundering

If your organization needs to enable access to corporate resources from unmanaged machines (whether those machines are partner-owned laptops, shared machines in kiosks or Internet cafes, or home PCs), you want to make sure that any evidence of an SSL VPN session, including the details of that session, be deleted from the machine before others begin using the device.

To respond to this requirement, many SSL VPN vendors have implemented *cache cleaning,* which clears temporary Internet directories, the browser history, cookies, and other remnants of the user session from the machine when that user logs off. You can also use cache cleaning to clear temp files from certain directories on the endpoint device.

Most cache cleaning implementations execute on an explicit timeout, if they encounter an abnormal termination, if the user session expires, or if a loss of connectivity with the server occurs — which means that, regardless of how an SSL VPN session ends, this temporary session data is securely removed from the machine. Most solutions also utilize a secure delete functionality to ensure that data cleanup is complete and comprehensive, protecting the device from malicious attempts to recover erased data from disks.

Stay out of my sandbox

Protected sandboxes (marketed under different names from various vendors) provide complete control over corporate information that's downloaded to a local machine during an SSL VPN session. These client applications create a secure, quarantined environment within which a secure SSL VPN session is completely contained on an end user's PC, limiting the use of downloaded data to only the current SSL VPN session.

The SSL VPN agent creates the sandbox within the user's real desktop after the endpoint integrity agent validates the host integrity of the end user's machine. The sandbox provides a secure environment within which only administrator-specified programs can run and where extremely strict control is enforced over user interactions with the data. In many implementations, the sandbox entirely controls the registry and I/O access of these programs, their network communications, and the interactions with the resources and programs running on the real desktop. Additionally, information stored on the disk or in the registries is encrypted during the session.

At the end of the SSL VPN session, the sandbox is destroyed, and all the information pertaining to the virtual environment is permanently deleted from the endpoint so that any user accessing data from a remote kiosk can be assured that no other user on the shared PC can access the data. The net result is that no data is saved locally, printing and clipboard operations are tightly controlled, and session specific information is securely deleted from the endpoint.

Organizations that have strict information security policies use protected workspaces in kiosk and shared-PC environments. Protected workspaces are typically dynamically downloaded from the SSL VPN gateway and installed on the endpoint when a user initiates a new session.

Protected workspaces might seem, on the surface, to be an effective data-leakage prevention mechanism. Make sure that you check with your SSL VPN vendor about the scope of the sandbox protection — different implementations vary in design and how you should use them. Some implementations are more effective at preventing data leakage from the machine than others. Many are designed to simply clean corporate data off the machine, but they don't prevent data from leaving the machine through explicit end-user actions.

Remote access policy enforcement

The biggest difference when comparing SSL VPNs to NAC products is policy enforcement. SSL VPN devices require all traffic to transit through the appliance itself, instead of distributing enforcement throughout the network and security infrastructure. Before directly comparing SSL VPN and NAC pros and cons, we discuss the policy enforcement tactics that you can apply with SSL VPNs in the following sections.

Clientless SSL VPNs

SSL VPNs were first introduced to the market as a way to consolidate extranet deployment. The value proposition stated that as more and more applications were externalized for outside access, it became more expensive to build up the secure, Internet-facing infrastructure for each Web application. Separate, Internet-facing deployments for each application would require hardening of servers, authentication and authorization on each server, appropriate security infrastructure, and more. SSL VPNs offered the first way to consolidate access to all these types of applications without providing people (such as partners and customers) a full Layer 3 IPSec VPN connection onto the network. Since that time, SSL VPNs have evolved to meet the needs of many more use cases, but the clientless mode of operation remains a primary deployment option, largely because of two key benefits:

- ✔ **You don't have to install any client software on the endpoint device.** So, an end user can access the SSL VPN from anywhere — home, kiosk, Internet cafe, and so on — and still be able to access relevant corporate information, provided that the machine has a Web browser that supports SSL. Platform and device independence is a huge gain over client-based technologies that require a special client installation on every machine.

- ✔ **Organizations can have a very granular level of control over what the end user can access on the network.** In many cases, the administrator can control, down to the individual file or URL level, what the end user can access. So, if a partner needs access to only a single Excel spreadsheet on a file server, SSL VPNs can provide that level of granular access control.

Although clientless SSL VPNs can't handle client-server applications, they generally provide access to a large range of Web-enabled content. Clientless access methods provide Web access to HTML, Javascript, Java applets, Flash, Terminal Services/Citrix, file shares, Outlook Web Access, SharePoint, Lotus iNotes, and much more. Most of today's Web-enabled enterprise applications (whether they're internally developed or commercially available) can work with clientless SSL VPN access methods.

How does the clientless mode of operation work? It depends on the implementation, and most vendors have developed this key intellectual property over time. For the most part, clientless SSL VPNs use something called a rewriter. A *rewriter* actually intermediates every request and response that goes through the SSL VPN, and it modifies embedded links so that, to the outside world, the content appears to be served directly from the SSL VPN. This rewriting capability provides granular access control and, at the same time, allows organizations to mask the details of their internal application deployments from would-be hackers. If a hacker can easily get the IP address or URL of an application server that's housed inside the network, he or she can begin to formulate a plan for attacking that server — a less than desirable outcome for your network.

Client-based SSL VPN access

Despite SSL VPN's beginnings (and reputation) as a clientless VPN technology, vendors and customers quickly realized the need that exists, and will exist for the foreseeable future, to support full client/server versions of applications. For example, few users rely only on Outlook Web Access and never use the full version of Outlook.

As a result of customer requests for support of full client-server applications, vendors developed client-based technologies that frequently combine some of the advantages of clientless SSL VPNs with some of the functionality provided by traditional IPSec VPNs. Vendors created two main types of SSL VPN clients:

- Layer 3 network-extension clients
- Port forwarding client applications

Layer 3 network extension clients

Layer 3 clients, offered by every SSL VPN on the market, are very similar to traditional IPSec VPNs in terms of the connectivity that they offer. When a user is granted access through one of these clients, he or she is assigned an IP address and has full network connectivity, short of any access control lists (ACLs) that the administrator puts in place to control that user's connectivity.

Connecting through a full Layer 3 SSL VPN client gives the user the same type of experience that he or she has when connecting through an IPSec VPN or attaching directly to the LAN itself.

The SSL VPN version of a Layer 3 client offers some significant advantages over traditional IPSec VPNs, however. Among the key advantages is the much easier deployment of an SSL VPN client. Installing and configuring IPSec VPNs can be difficult, typically requiring manual intervention to set some of the configuration options. With SSL VPN, however, most offerings provide dynamic delivery of the client itself:

1. When the user first needs to log in to the SSL VPN appliance, he or she browses to the appropriate URL.

2. After the authentication and authorization process has been completed by the SSL VPN, if the policy states that the user should have a full Layer 3 access, the client is dynamically delivered and installed on the user's machine with no intervention required on the administrator's part.

The SSL VPN appliance handles upgrades in a similar fashion — seamless to both the administrator and the end user.

Although most SSL VPNs do offer dynamic delivery and installation, the user typically needs administrator or root privileges on his or her machine to install the appropriate drivers. Many IT shops have locked-down managed endpoints so that end users don't have these types of privileges. Some SSL VPN vendors have responded by creating installer services, which temporarily elevate privileges on the client machine for the purpose of installing or upgrading SSL VPN agents. Administrators can install the installer service as part of the corporate image, allowing the users to upgrade freely without the need for elevated privileges on their accounts.

Many SSL VPNs offer the ability to package their clients into an install package that administrators can push out to endpoint devices via software distribution mechanisms. Make sure that you determine how you plan to resolve any potential challenges, such as lack of administrator privileges, when rolling out an SSL VPN deployment — regardless of whether you use it for

- ✔ Internal NAC access
- ✔ Its traditional purpose as a remote access control technology

When evaluating SSL VPN solutions (or any NAC offering), make sure to pay attention to cross-platform support. In recent years, many organizations have begun offering more choices to end users in terms of the types of devices that those end users can use to access corporate resources. You certainly don't want to make a large investment in an access control solution only to find out that it doesn't support the Macintosh that the CEO of your company recently purchased.

Port forwarding client apps

Not all SSL VPNs provide port forwarding technology, but you may see it. Like with the Layer 3 network extension, the *port forwarder* is a dynamically installed and delivered client application that provides access to full versions of client/server applications.

The primary difference between port forwarding applications and Layer 3 network extenders is that the port forwarder controls access at a more granular level, specifying exactly which resources can access the VPN. With these technologies

1. The application itself believes that the client application is the destination application server.

2. The client then intercepts this traffic and forwards it to the SSL VPN appliance over the secure connection

3. It's then forwarded to the final destination, the application server.

 In some cases, the port forwarding application can also specify which processes on the client side are allowed to access the tunnel, not only the destination. In other words, you might have a policy that states that only `outlook.exe` can use the connection, and it can only pass traffic to certain ports on the exchange server. You get a much more granular level of control than a Layer 3 network extender can provide, and depending on your organizational needs, you might use port forwarding for some users and network extension for others. This is a policy choice, not a hard and fast rule:

✔ Some organizations will want to simplify their policies by providing only one option.

✔ Other organizations might have specific requirements for each user group, and would want to provide port forwarding for one group, and network extension for others.

For example, the authors have frequently seen organizations provide full network extension for employees, but port forwarding for only a defined set of applications for partners, specifically because their security policies prohibit partners from having full network access.

Dynamic access control

One of the advantages of SSL VPNs versus IPSec VPNs is their ability to provide access from any device — any time, anywhere. SSL VPNs simply vary the
level of access that the user gets based on administrator-defined policies.

Figure 5-2 shows the ideal user's perspective — logging in from any device,
in any location, to perform the same behavior: opening a Web browser and
browsing to the URL of the corporate SSL VPN gateway.

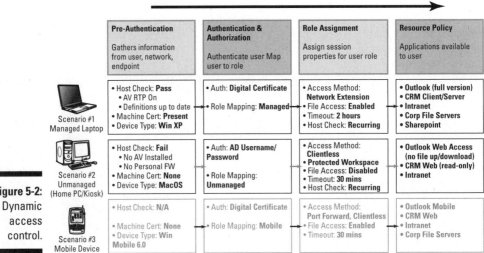

Figure 5-2:
Dynamic
access
control.

	Pre-Authentication	Authentication & Authorization	Role Assignment	Resource Policy
	Gathers information from user, network, endpoint	Authenticate user Map user to role	Assign session properties for user role	Applications available to user
Scenario #1 Managed Laptop	• Host Check: **Pass** • AV RTP On • Definitions up to date • Machine Cert: **Present** • Device Type: **Win XP**	• Auth: **Digital Certificate** • Role Mapping: **Managed**	• Access Method: **Network Extension** • File Access: **Enabled** • Timeout: **2 hours** • Host Check: **Recurring**	• **Outlook (full version)** • **CRM Client/Server** • **Intranet** • **Corp File Servers** • **Sharepoint**
Scenario #2 Unmanaged (Home PC/Kiosk)	• Host Check: **Fail** • No AV Installed • No Personal FW • Machine Cert: **None** • Device Type: **MacOS**	• Auth: **AD Username/ Password** • Role Mapping: **Unmanaged**	• Access Method: **Clientless** • **Protected Workspace** • File Access: **Disabled** • Timeout: **30 mins** • Host Check: **Recurring**	• **Outlook Web Access (no file up/download)** • **CRM Web (read-only)** • **Intranet**
Scenario #3 Mobile Device	• Host Check: **N/A** • Machine Cert: **None** • Device Type: **Win Mobile 6.0**	• Auth: **Digital Certificate** • Role Mapping: **Mobile**	• Access Method: **Port Forward, Clientless** • File Access: **Enabled** • Timeout: **30 mins**	• **Outlook Mobile** • **CRM Web** • **Intranet** • **Corp File Servers**

✓ **Managed laptop:** The user is logging on from her corporate laptop,
which is fully patched and up-to-date, and also includes a machine certificate that verifies the machine as a corporate-owned and -managed
asset. The user then proceeds to authenticate with her digital certificate and is mapped to a role that the administrator has defined called
Managed:

 • Because the user has passed all the pre-authentication endpoint
 integrity scans and used strong authentication, she's allowed full
 Layer 3 access via the network extension functionality.

 • Additionally, she has a relatively long timeout and access to corporate file shares.

As a result, she can use all the client-server applications available on her
machine, while also accessing Web applications.

✓ **Home PC:** No endpoint security applications are installed on the machine, remediation has failed, and the PC has no machine certificate. Because this machine doesn't have a smart-card reader, the user can't use certificate authentication and must authenticate with his static Active Directory username and password.

As a result, even though he has performed nearly the same behavior as when using his managed laptop in an effort to log on to the system, the SSL VPN has assigned him to a much more restricted role:

- He's quarantined inside a protected sandbox and has access to only Web-enabled applications, such as Outlook Web Access.

- The policy has also determined that he might be coming from a shared machine, so the timeout on his session is very short (30 minutes).

✓ **Mobile device:** In this case, the SSL VPN doesn't conduct a host check, and the mobile has no available machine certificate. That said, the IT department has pre-installed a digital certificate on the user's mobile device, so she can authenticate herself by using strong authentication.

Based on the credentials provided and the type of machine, she's allowed access through the SSL VPN port forwarding application, she can access files, and she can use a variety of client/server and Web-enabled applications.

Figure 5-2 and its access scenarios are indicative of the types of policies that many organizations have put into place for their remote access users by using SSL VPN, and very similar to a typical NAC policy:

✓ Verifying the user, role, and endpoint integrity status

✓ Varying the level of access that the user is allowed based on these verifications

So . . . NAC to Get In

You find few differences between what a particular SSL VPN can do and what a particular NAC solution does. So, why does the industry make a distinction between the two types of products? Can you use an SSL VPN interchangeably with a NAC solution?

To muddy up the topic a little more, some NAC implementations include a remote access VPN component, or they might tie in closely with a similar technology from that same vendor. In these cases, you can achieve some level of coordination between SSL VPN and NAC by using the solutions together. (You might also save on costs by consolidating remote access control with local access control.)

When using both SSL VPN and NAC together, use consistent sets of policies for both remote access and local access. For example, don't force a user to use strong authentication and pass endpoint integrity scans on the local LAN if he or she can log in remotely via SSL VPN by using a static user name and password without endpoint integrity scans.

When evaluating an SSL VPN device for local access control (NAC), the biggest issue is scalability:

✔ In the remote access world, an inline appliance, such as an SSL VPN, is ideal for terminating the user traffic:

  • All the remote users come into the network from the same location (the corporate Internet connection).

  • The total amount of bandwidth is limited by the size of that connection.

✔ In the LAN environment, you can have problems finding a location in the network that allows the traffic from all the end users to traverse a single appliance or group of appliances. End users are

  • Spread throughout the corporate campus and potentially across many branch locations

  • Constantly mobile

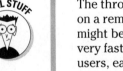

The throughput expectations on the LAN are much different than those on a remote access connection. Users on a remote access connection might be used to low bandwidth availability, but on the LAN, users expect very fast application performance and high throughput. If you have 1,000 users, each expecting maximum throughput of 100 Mbps, you might need quite a large number of inline appliances to pass this amount of traffic. Then comes the question of where to place these appliances to protect all resources while users are dispersed across the network. Due to these challenges, most larger enterprises use a distributed enforcement architecture, such as one based on 802.1x, because that architecture is much more scalable.

In small deployments that have simple network topologies, an appliance-based model might be appropriate and simpler to deploy than an infrastructure-based solution. In these cases, you simply need to figure out whether the SSL VPN appliance in question can scale to meet the performance needs of your user group.

An SSL VPN appliance might also fit the bill in today's current wireless deployment. But, in the coming years, when faster wireless LAN (WLAN) technologies become common in the marketplace, WLAN performance will be expected to be as fast as wired LAN performance (or close to it). Keep not only your current needs, but also your future business needs, in mind when choosing an access control technology such as SSL VPN or NAC.

You can best use a product for the use case that it was *designed* to meet. A product that's touted as a remote access product that "can also do NAC" has likely been designed with remote access in mind, rather than local access. That product likely has functionality missing or implementations of features that don't make sense when force-fitting a product into a different type of scenario. Because of this uncertainty, focus on a dedicated NAC solution for local access control, rather than another type of solution that has similar features, such as SSL VPN.

SSL VPN Use Cases

Because of their flexibility, a wide variety of remote access use cases include SSL VPNs. Enterprises use many of these appliances for all their remote access needs — not only employee remote access, but also partners, contractors, and even customers. Refer to Figure 5-3 to see the SSL VPN use cases discussed in the following sections.

Business Continuity

Because you can deploy SSL VPNs dynamically to just about any machine available (as long as it has a Web browser that supports SSL), many organizations have deployed SSL VPNs as part of their business continuity plans.

Many organizations have planned for disaster situations that result in loss of a datacenter or some other disruption to primary locations, but plenty of other potential scenarios can result in a different type of problem — geographical isolation of employees.

In recent years, concerns about situations such as a potential avian flu or SARS outbreak, and worries about more mundane events such as public transit strikes and snow days, have resulted in employees, even those that don't normally work remotely, working from home or from some other location for a period of time. When these last-minute events happen, you can use SSL VPNs to easily allow users to connect to the corporate network from home, even without a preinstalled client. You get an extension of your local NAC deployment: Because you can enforce many of the same access control rules with SSL VPNs, you have to deal with a much smaller impact on the productivity of the end user during these types of events because he or she can still perform required functions remotely, even if he or she hadn't planned for such an event.

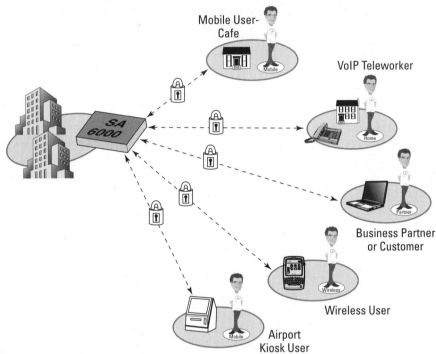

Figure 5-3:
SSL VPN
use cases.

Mobile users

One of the primary uses of SSL VPN is for the mobile user — someone who's potentially in the network/NAC deployment one day, and then traveling from one remote connection to the next the following day.

Managed laptop

In addition to ensuring user authentication and granular access control, SSL VPN offers the ability to ensure that the laptop user's machine stays up to date, even if it remains remote for long periods of time.

This automatic updating helps to avoid the configuration drift that frequently results from permanently mobile employees.

Mobile device

Historically dominated by RIM BlackBerry, the enterprise mobile device space has seen a large range of new devices enter the network — from Windows Mobile and Symbian devices to newer platforms such as the Apple iPhone and Google Android. End users are demanding choice in mobile platforms without any loss in their ability to access mobile data.

SSL VPN is the ideal platform for mobile device users because all these platforms offer a Web browser, and many SSL VPN vendors have also developed client access technologies for these platforms.

Fixed telecommuters

Fixed telecommuters (employees who work remotely from one location and are not mobile) have become more popular in recent years because organizations are focusing on downsizing real estate and containing costs. SSL VPNs fit well for this type of deployment.

Many fixed telecommuters are provided with a hardware device, such as a wireless access point, deployed by the organization at the user's home office. In these cases, consider whether SSL VPN is a better fit, or whether you can extend your NAC deployment to also incorporate access controls on this home office equipment. The primary decision point here is whether your NAC solution offers the ability to enforce NAC access controls remotely, such as on the wireless access point.

Mobile users on a kiosk or home machine

You can use SSL VPN for essentially any machine other than the user's own managed machine, such as his/her mobile device, home machine, or on an Internet kiosk.

Because of SSL VPN's granular access control and endpoint integrity capabilities, an organization can determine a risk factor and associated access policy before a single machine hits the SSL VPN. Then, when users attempt to log in, SSL VPN can evaluate the attributes and dynamically grant an appropriate level of access.

Business partners or customers on their own machines

Because most organizations don't want to allow business partners or customers full Layer 3 access onto the corporate network, SSL VPN allows organizations to establish extremely granular access controls.

These controls allow the organization to provide exactly what the user needs and nothing more.

Part II
NAC in Your Network

The 5th Wave   By Rich Tennant

©RICHTENNANT

"My spam filter checks the recipient address, http links, and any writing that panders to postmodern English romanticism with conceits to 20th-century graphic narrative."

In this part . . .

This part gets personal and brings in all the variations that can enable a NAC solution to fit your network needs. A NAC solution can really do a lot for you, after you realize the scope of its capabilities.

Chapter 6

Writing a Corporate Security Policy

*I*n this chapter, we look at the many elements that you might want to include in your corporate security policies. You must cover a variety of areas, many of which have a direct impact on the goals of your NAC implementation. This chapter also shows you some example security policies and covers some best practices that can ensure everyone in the organization — from IT administrators to end users — adopts and follows your security policies. Following these best practices up front makes planning your NAC implementation easier and ensures that the implementation follows the broader goals of your organization as closely as possible.

A good security policy charts the course of security across your entire company. NAC might be a crucial element of that policy, but the broader corporate security policy has many different pieces, and many of them affect your NAC rollout. Before you start down the path of deployment, you need to know what your goals are for NAC — and the security policy that your team has in place drives those goals.

What Policies Do You Need?

The Internet resources mentioned in the section "Getting Started: Standards and Web Resources," later in this chapter, illustrate that you can find a lot of different policy types available. The ones that you end up implementing depend on the type of business you're in and the specific security concerns for your organization. Just about every organization requires some types of policies, but some policies may be critical in one company but completely insignificant in another.

Depending on the specific needs of your company, you might have some, all, or none of these policies. Every organization is different, so make sure that before sitting down to address your policy needs, you first figure out the risks and goals of your company.

Acceptable use policy

One of the more commonly implemented policies in corporations today, this policy explains to end users the activities in which they can participate while using corporate assets and services. These assets and services might include a laptop or desktop computer, the company's e-mail and Internet access, specific software, and more. Many companies use the acceptable use policy as the primary communication vehicle for informing end users of what they can and can't do electronically while on company time or while using company assets or network resources.

Antivirus policy

An antivirus (AV) policy generally specifies that every machine should have an installed, running, and up-to-date antivirus application. It might go beyond that, however, to also specify how users should handle spam, strange attachments, or other files that might look like viruses. The AV policy might also specify whether guests, contractors, and other users on non-corporate machines need to have an antivirus application running on their machines prior to connecting to the corporate network.

Your AV policy might end up being a key policy for your NAC implementation. If your organization has an antivirus policy, NAC can be the piece of technology that helps you to enforce this policy, as well as getting machines remediated and up to date. Make sure to take this linkage between your NAC solution and your antivirus policy into account when designing your NAC solution.

Data backup policy

A backup policy specifies what your organization, and specifically, your users need to do to keep corporate data and information stored safely. A data backup policy is particularly important if you have a lot of laptops or other types of mobile devices that can be lost or stolen. Having this data properly backed up becomes critical, and this policy specifies what types of data users need to back up and how often. The policy might also specify how the user must back up the data and who needs to make sure that the backups happen as scheduled.

E-mail use policy

Depending on how your organization chooses to shape policy structure, you might make the e-mail policy part of the acceptable use policy, or you might create an e-mail use policy on its own. An e-mail use policy dictates appropriate use of e-mail — whether users can send and receive personal e-mails, the types of content that your organization restricts and wants users to avoid, and so on. The e-mail use policy might also specify that the company reserves the right to monitor and intercept any employee communications, stipulating that users have no right to privacy when they use corporate assets to conduct either business or personal communications.

Extranet policy

An extranet policy describes the process by which third parties can gain access to corporate resources via an extranet. Many companies require that a contractor, guest, or partner go through an approval process before he or she can remotely access the network. An extranet policy might also specify acceptable use and other rules that the third party must follow. The extranet policy also includes recourse if the third party breaks these rules.

Mobile device usage policy

Because many organizations are beginning to allow employees to use mobile devices (such as PDAs and smartphones) to access their networks, mobile device usage policies have become common. Mobile device usage policies specify that employees who want to use mobile devices to access corporate resources must first gain approval from appropriate personnel before they can receive access. The policy might specify whether the device must protect itself by using disk encryption, remote disk-wipe functionality, and other theft or loss mitigation technologies. The policy also includes acceptable use for the mobile device and whether such a machine can reach all resources. A mobile device usage policy discusses appropriate use of portable media that can attach to these devices and store data (if your organization doesn't have a corresponding storage media policy).

The mobile device usage policy might also discuss who's allowed to use these types of devices to access the network because your organization may forbid certain roles or job titles from using these devices to access the network.

Your NAC or SSL VPN rollout (depending on whether the policy is for remote or local access) plays a part in your ability to control access from these devices. Both of these technologies can determine the user's device type and, in most cases, whether that machine has the appropriate theft and loss mitigation technologies that your policy requires. As a result of these checks, it can provide the user with the appropriate level of access. (See Chapter 5 for more on VPNs.)

Network access control policy

The NAC policy might specify any number of items related to the level of access a user gets when he or she comes onto the network, including the type of authentication that employees, guests, contractors, partners, and so on receive. This policy also specifies the types of endpoint security applications that the endpoint device must have, the high-level patching policy, authentication types, authorization and group membership, resource access policies, remediation, quarantine, reporting, and auditing.

Password policy

A password policy specifies everything related to the management and maintenance of passwords. The policy might outline different types of passwords, each with its own security requirements; for example, users who have access to highly sensitive systems might have more strict password requirements than users who don't have such access.

The password policy usually specifies the duration of time between password changes — quarterly, for example. Also, the policy usually includes the complexity and minimum length requirements of the password itself. Many organizations specify a mix of characters, numbers, and symbols to make passwords more difficult to guess. The policy might also specify whether you can reuse old passwords, password recovery policies, and so forth.

Like with any policy, the password policy is only as strong as the weakest link, which unfortunately is often the end user. The password policy should also stipulate when and to whom the end user can provide his or her password. For example, you might state that your IT department will never ask for a user's password, so users should never provide it over the phone, via e-mail, and so on.

You might also require that users not write their passwords down on sticky notes and place them on their desks somewhere — a frowned-upon practice that's no doubt still in existence today. (Many of the most successful hackers in history were more skilled at user manipulation and social engineering than at brute-force hacking into secured systems.)

End users can never have enough training on password management and handling.

Physical security policy

The physical security policy concerns access to your company's physical locations. You might question such security as part of your overall plan, but like with password policies, physical security is of utmost importance if you're trying to secure and protect sensitive corporate assets.

The physical security policy might describe mechanisms such as badge readers and surveillance. It might also describe how to avoid security lapses such as *tailgating* — a common practice in which an unauthorized user follows a legitimate employee through the doors of the building, bypassing the badge reader. These possible security breaches deal with end users as potential sources of security holes, so you absolutely must make them aware of the reasons behind, and the importance of, these policies.

Remote access policy

The remote access policy specifies acceptable usage and behavior for those users who access computing resources from outside the corporate network. Depending on the way that the company provides remote access, this policy might dictate personal use of Internet access and company equipment. It might also specify how employees can use the corporate-managed laptops outside of the office, requirements about when the user must maintain the connection back to corporate, and so on.

Security configuration change policy

A security configuration change policy might describe the rules and procedures for configuring and maintaining network and security devices on the network. It can outline roles and responsibilities, specify audit and documentation requirements, and detail approval processes. Such a policy applies directly to IT personnel, not necessarily to end users, who typically don't manage and maintain network and security equipment, such as routers and firewalls.

You Want Me to Do What?

You can write all the policies that you want — but if you can't enforce them and your users don't follow them, they're useless. With security policies, you need to ensure that you have the appropriate support from across the organization in order to be successful. End users are an important part of this equation, but a host of other groups need to buy off on your policies, so you must account for all of them.

Chapter 7 talks about some of the numerous groups and teams you have to interface with when forming and deploying your security policies. You have to write and review the key components of your policies with these groups.

Being reasonable

Unreasonable policies can easily alienate everyone involved in the security policy process — from upper management to the end user. Never lose sight of the fact that all these people are your customers, and your (not so simple) task is to ensure that they're productive and happy, without risking security.

By keeping policies reasonable, you can actually increase the odds that employees follow the policies (ensuring your ultimate success in the task). The following sections discuss some sample policies, outlining what's reasonable and what's not.

Backup

Backup policies are very common these days — corporate data is extremely valuable, yet so much of it is stored on laptops and other PCs that can be lost or stolen, or simply fail. For these reasons, it makes a lot of sense to have a backup software policy. Here are two ways that you might address this requirement:

✔ *Unreasonable: At the end of each work day, every employee must save all newly created or edited files to both their hard disks and a network file share.*

This policy is obviously unreasonable. Backing up their files to a shared drive themselves requires the users to go through an unnecessarily manual process. At the same time, employees may forget or simply won't want to do this manual save. If users don't back up their files, you have no recourse — how can you even tell whether employees are bypassing the policy?

✔ *Reasonable: The company installs backup software on every corporate managed system. The user must not uninstall, bypass, or alter this software in any way.*

This policy is more reasonable than the preceding one, so look to implement this kind of policy. In this example, you simply ask employees not to tamper with their backup software so that automatic backups can continue. Because you're rolling out NAC, you can use NAC to check whether the software is still installed and running, ensuring that you can enforce the backup policy.

Passwords

End users have dozens of passwords related to various systems, and users must update and change most of these passwords periodically. People like you, trying to figure out the best possible policies for password management, have put these policies into place.

Today's systems make it simple to set timers and limits on passwords, forcing the end user to change his or her password within the defined limits. But you need to balance end user convenience with security to keep your password policy reasonable:

✔ *Unreasonable: Employees must change their passwords every week. All passwords must have a minimum of 15 characters, including at least one letter, one number, and one symbol.*

This policy is simply unreasonable, and end users won't be able to remember the extraordinarily long and frequently changing passwords.

Password policies such as this example frequently lead to one of the top causes of password theft — your users start to write their passwords down (putting sticky notes containing their passwords somewhere near their desks, for example) or rely on similar insecure behavior to remind themselves of their passwords. Or they might end up forgetting their passwords altogether, resulting in a lot of calls to the helpdesk, which costs the organization unnecessary dollars.

✔ *Reasonable: Employees must change their passwords once per quarter. All passwords must have a minimum of eight characters, including at least one number and one letter.*

This policy is much more reasonable than the preceding policy. Some employees might complain about changing their passwords every quarter, but they should be able to deal with this type of policy. At the same time, the eight-character minimum meets current, industry accepted best practices of a reasonable password length — and should cut down on the number of people either forgetting their passwords or writing them down so that someone else might find and use them.

Book 'em, Danno!

Enforceability is a key aspect of any security policy. Regardless of the amount of training, reminding, and retraining you do, if you can't enforce your policies, end users can bypass those policies, leaving your organization with security holes.

Enforceability has two aspects:

- ✔ Making it very difficult for users to bypass the policies
- ✔ Implementing recourse if users do bypass the policies

When possible, you want to ensure that you have policies that are very difficult for users to bypass. For example, you can enforce a password policy fairly straightforwardly. You simply set your systems so that after the user's password expires, that user must change the password before he or she can access the network. In the case of antivirus software policy, ensuring that every machine has antivirus installed and up to date can get a bit more complex, but quarantine is perfect for one of your NAC policies — allowing you to restrict or even forbid non-compliant machines access to the network.

In some cases, you might not be able to enforce specific policies all of the time through technology. In these cases, you need to have management buy-in.

Before going to management and asking for new people to help deploy and enforce policies, make sure that you have a good idea of the projected cost, the likely tradeoffs, and what might happen if you don't implement these policies. Just don't exclude the cost of enforcement.

Impressing the big wigs

You really need management support for your security policy. Not only do executives hold the purse strings, but they also act as a key ally when you roll out your new policies, and need a big-gun sponsorship or maybe a little extra management motivation to get the masses to readily adopt the new plan.

From a financial perspective, every new policy that you try to roll out has some cost and (hopefully) some benefit. When making the case to management, you need to devote PowerPoint slides to these key metrics.

In some cases, the key benefit of a particular new policy is cost savings. Maybe the policy makes employees more productive or cuts down on the number of helpdesk calls that your support team receives. In other cases, new security technologies bring reduced risk to the organization, justifying spending a large amount of money for those technologies. For example, new policies that protect data on laptops might prevent your CSO/CIO from appearing on the front page of the world's newspapers after a massive data theft or loss incident. You can't easily put a number on the value of such threat prevention, but you need to hint about the value that your data protection policies offers to the organization as a whole.

Management can present your policies to the end users when you're ready to deploy those policies. If you're a network or security administrator, you probably don't have the clout to convince end users about the importance of new security policies. If, however, you have an upper-level sponsor, he or she can be the big gun you need.

Coercing your colleagues

In most companies and organizations, a number of groups are responsible for the design, implementation, and maintenance of the IT infrastructure — including application developers, desktop support groups, network and security infrastructure engineers, and so on. The security policies that you implement impact each of these job functions.

We've seen many NAC implementations go awry because different groups within the organization don't work well together, so we devote Chapter 7 to the topic. You can easily make a statement such as, "All PCs must have backup software installed and running." But you need to communicate this policy to your desktop team to ensure that you can logistically implement it (ideally *before* you deploy the policy solution).

In fact, depending on your organization and its size, you can often pull the corporate security policy together most effectively and efficiently via committee. Involving several groups not only ensures that everyone signs off on the policy, but you also benefit from the diverse backgrounds and knowledge that these other groups have to offer.

Don't create policies in a vacuum. A well-designed NAC policy always takes into account everyone's feedback, so it's just good practice to involve as many people as possible from the start.

Training the masses

After you put together the appropriate policies and decide how to implement each policy, you need to educate the end users on the policies — how the policies may impact the users and the consequences if the users don't follow the policies.

End user training can be a daunting experience. But with a little bit of creativity, the rollout can go smoothly, with little negative impact.

Most importantly, you need to consider your audience. Are your end users technical or non-technical? If you happen to work in a company in which everyone is up to speed on the latest security and networking technologies, you might be able to train your end users very easily. We're willing to guess, however, that you don't work in such a company. As a result, take a step back and try to think through how a typical end user might think about security policies.

If you're having difficulty figuring out whether your users are techie enough, ask yourself, "Do they think IP is an acronym for intellectual property or International Paper?" Similarly, "Do they think NAC stands for North Atlantic Conference or the National Aerobics Championships?"

Anything about security often seems a foreign topic to users because, to be perfectly honest, most of them don't think about this stuff on a day-to-day basis. Therefore, you need to phrase concepts in common language wherever possible — and make it as fun as possible, too. End users often simply ignore or bury an e-mail that you send about new security policies, so you don't get your message across. Try something more unique, such as posters in break rooms or notices on elevators. Post notices in the restrooms if you think that can help get the point across. Raffles, contests, lunchroom placards, free prizes — it can all prevent future problems and bruised feelings.

Make the message as fun as possible, too. Don't use acronyms and NAC-speak security idioms. Just use conversational language. We don't expect you to become an ace marketer overnight, but a little bit of effort towards making security enjoyable for your end users can pay hefty dividends over the course of the policies.

Like with any policy — from NAC to your rules for your kids — end users are likely to forget over time. You need to have periodic reminders of the policies. At the same time, you need to bring new hires that come into the organization up to speed on the existing policies. Many organizations have new-hire training and/or manuals, as well as periodic retraining or reminder requirements. Many organizations distribute a copy of the security policy (written in plain English) to every new worker. The worker must read the policy and then sign an affidavit indicating that he or she has read and agrees to abide by the policy. Periodically (perhaps annually, for example), the employees must view the updated policy document (if you've changed it) and again confirm that they understand the policies and agree to abide by them.

Figures 6-1 and 6-2 show example posters that you might hang in various areas around the workplace. Figure 6-1 reminds people of acceptable e-mail use, and Figure 6-2 shows the example company's mobile device use policy.

When you roll out your policies to your user group, keep it simple. Unnecessary technical jargon only confuses (and possibly scares) your user group. If you can't spell out the policy in terminology that a non-technical user can understand, then probably no one will follow it.

Figure 6-1:
This poster tells employees to stop and think about proper e-mailing.

Only YOU Can Prevent the Spread of Viruses!

Follow these steps to help us all maintain a safer and more productive workplace. Virus outbreaks cost the corporate world millions of dollars each year – let's make sure we are not the next victims!

– Do not open any unexpected email attachments or unrecognized files
– Do not click on ANY links in any suspicious emails. This includes unsubscribe links and even normal looking web links.
– Make sure that your antivirus application is always running and up-to-date
– Immediately report and suspected virus infections to the helpdesk.

Figure 6-2:
Remind
employees
that their
mobile
devices
need
watching.

Help Keep Your PDA or Smartphone Out of the Wrong Hands!

Your PDA/Smartphone contains extremely valuable data – follow these steps to ensure that sensitive corporate data doesn't end up in the wrong hands.

- *Make sure that you've installed the corporate security application, which includes full disk encryption and remote disk wipe capabilities*
- *Lock the unit with a strong password, preferably 8 characters or more.*
- *Keep only corporate information that you absolutely must have on the device.*
- *In airports and other public areas, be more diligent than usual in keeping your device protected. Try not to leave it in the airport security line!*

A Living Document: The Security Policy Lifecycle

Like with many of the policies that you deal with on a day-to-day basis as part of your job, the security needs of your organization continue to adapt and evolve over time. In some cases, new business initiatives drive security concerns. In other cases, new threats determine how you adapt security. Regardless of the reason, your security policies need to adapt, if only to add new policies when the security landscape changes or to remove old ones that no longer apply to your business needs.

You might think that you should change policies every time that a new threat comes to your attention. Nix that idea because end users and the people who must implement those policies will be hesitant to change frequently, and will likely be slow to adopt new changes.

Instead, we recommend that you

- ✔ Make major policy changes only when absolutely necessary.
- ✔ Roll out new policies only when you're sure that the organization needs them, and they'll stay current and applicable for the foreseeable future (in other words, you don't think that you will be changing them again next week).

Up to date

Keep tabs on the IT, and more specifically, the security industry. Monitoring new types of products, staying up to date by reading trade journals, and speaking regularly with peers in other organizations can help you stay on top of new developments in the security field.

While hackers exploit new classes of vulnerability and develop new types of attacks, you may need to implement new policies (and potentially even use new technologies) in order to deal with evolving attack types. If you constantly keep yourself educated about the security market, you can better equip yourself to act quickly and decisively when necessary.

In sync

Keep yourself apprised of changes in your company's business.

For example, if your company is entering into a new line of business, new security requirements might come along with that new product or service offering. Say that your company has a new product that's intended for the federal government market. In some cases, companies have product requirements, such as Common Criteria, that involve product development practices. Vendors adapt their products to make sure that they pass the rigorous tests and audits associated with Common Criteria. If the product doesn't comply, it doesn't receive Common Criteria certification.

Security policies can have an impact on the product that your organization sells or provides — a fact that you might point out to your management when you present your vendor recommendations.

Also, keep abreast of new rules and regulations, or compliance mandates, that apply to companies in your market.

In recent years, credit card processors imposed the Payment Card Industry Data Security Standards (PCI DSS) for retail, Health Insurance Portability and Accountability Act (HIPAA) in healthcare, and Sarbanes-Oxley (SOX) for public companies. Each of these regulations has greatly affected the security policies of the companies in these markets. You have to ensure that your company doesn't run afoul of these kinds of requirements because not complying can result in hefty fines or other penalties.

Getting Started: Standards and Web Resources

If you're not yet ready (or don't have the time) to create your own security policy from scratch, fear not — you can find a lot of excellent information available on the Web that can help you to develop your own policy:

- **ISO/IEC 27002 (www.iso.com):** The International Standards Organization (ISO) and the International Electromechanical Commission (IEC) wrote this standards-based security policy, formerly known as ISO 17799. The goal of this standard is to describe the current worldwide best practices in a variety of areas related to security. Simply put, it helps take the guesswork out of developing a corporate security policy. ISO/IEC 27002 consists of 12 primary sections, each describing best practices for a different area of security. Topics range from physical security to access control. Even if you don't use all (or any) of the content in this standard, it can show you best practices as collected by internationally recognized standards bodies.

- **SANS Institute (www.sans.org):** The SANS Institute's Web site includes templates for a large number of security policies, as well as a great deal of additional information that can help you develop your own security policies, regardless of whether you use their templates. The Institute has been kind enough to include some easy-to-consume materials, similar to the ones that we discuss in the section "Training the masses," earlier in this chapter. For example, the site offers some easy-to-understand and humorous posters that explain a variety of security policy concepts, which you can download free of charge.

Writing Your Own Security Policy

To help you get a jumpstart on writing your security policies, we include two sample policies in the sidebars "A sample corporate antivirus policy" and "A sample mobile device usage policy," in this chapter. Feel free to use these policies, or policy templates that you find on the Web, and fill in the needs of your organization.

Your security guidelines specify how to

- ✔ Put a policy into action.
- ✔ Define who has responsibility for deployment of the technologies required to support the policy.
- ✔ Decide what the systems or users do if there is a breach in the security policy.
- ✔ Take recourse when policies have been violated.
- ✔ Assign responsibility for correcting the issue.
- ✔ Establish a timeline for an action such as "all viruses outbreaks will be investigated and a plan put in place within 24 hours of the first reported infection."

A sample corporate antivirus policy

Overview: This policy describes the Company XYZ policy on antivirus applications. Included in this policy are guidelines specifying antivirus updates, scan intervals, and recommended antivirus applications. It also specifies e-mail antivirus policies — blocked attachments, network antivirus scanning, and anti-spam techniques.

Purpose: This policy has been designed to protect Company XYZ from the ongoing threat of viruses, worms, and other forms of malware.

Policy:

- ✔ All corporate managed laptops must have the corporate standard antivirus application installed and running at all times. This software is installed as part of the standard corporate operating system and must at no point be tampered with, uninstalled, or disabled.

- ✔ Antivirus definition files must be updated on a regular basis. The desktop application group will define an update mechanism and schedule for antivirus software updates. At no point should any employee interfere with the regular update of the antivirus software.

- ✔ System real-time protection must be running at all times. Full-disk system scans must be run on a regular schedule of not less than one time per week.

- ✔ Any user who suspects that his or her machine has been compromised with a virus or any other form of malware must immediately inform the helpdesk for corrective action to be taken.

- ✔ Users must take care not to download suspicious or unknown files from any source, including e-mails, file servers, and Web sites.

- ✔ All incoming e-mail will be scanned for viruses by the corporate network antivirus server prior to being processed. If a virus is found, the policy is to immediately delete the attachment and notify the intended recipient of the action taken. A separate list of permanently blocked attachments is updated and maintained by the IT security group.

Depending on the size of your organization, you might have more or less thorough and detailed policies. If your company is large, you might need formal procedures. For a smaller company, you might simply be able to establish a common understanding among employees, although we recommend documentation as a best practice for recording procedures, regardless of the size of your organization.

A sample mobile device usage policy

Overview: This policy describes the Company XYZ policy on mobile device usage. A mobile device is any PDA, smartphone, or other portable device that has the ability to access the corporate network and is able to store sensitive corporate data.

Purpose: This policy has been designed to ensure that Company XYZ employees protect mobile devices and corporate data from theft and loss.

Policy:

- All devices used by Company XYZ employees to access *any* corporate data must be approved by IT security and the employee's manager prior to being used.

- All devices must be from the available list of approved mobile devices. Under no circumstances will non-approved devices be allowed.

- All devices must have the corporate-approved full-disk encryption and remote device disk-wipe protection package installed and running at all times.

- Employees must employ all reasonable means to ensure that mobile devices are not lost or stolen, which requires extra diligence on the part of every employee to mitigate carelessness.

- Sensitive corporate data must not be downloaded to mobile devices. Data access is restricted to corporate e-mail, the corporate CRM application, and the company intranet. Sensitive attachments received via e-mail must not be stored permanently to the device disk drive or to any removable media.

- Employees must immediately report any lost or stolen devices to the helpdesk.

- Any requests for exception to this policy must be approved by Company XYZ's IT security.

Chapter 7

Herding the Cattle

A NAC solution must cover a great deal of technological territory within an organization if it's going to effectively keep unknown users and unwarranted, non-compliant devices from accessing the network. This chapter discusses how best to cover all that territory in your network organization.

Analyzing the Terrain

Deploying a NAC solution — in most cases — involves more than simply plugging the solution in and letting 'er rip. Deploying a NAC solution can mean dealing with managed user endpoint devices, such as laptops that the organization owns and operates, and that employees use; and unmanaged devices, such as devices that guest users (including contractors and partners) own and operate.

In some instances, organizations don't provide employees with endpoint devices, instead giving employees a budget and allowing them to pick their own devices. So, how do you control and manage devices in that sort of situation?

In some organizations, you will have to deal with endpoint devices that really don't belong to any particular owner. These devices have an IP address on the network, and users may share the devices. Many industries operate in this manner, with devices passing between employees from shift to shift. Although your organization *manages* (meaning it owns and maintains) the devices, different users can run into different issues, require different policies that they need to adhere to, and so on.

The unmanagables

Some devices that have no clear owners — and may be used and shared by many users — may not be able to accept downloads or identify themselves to a NAC solution in the way that a desktop PC, laptop, handheld, or other user-driven device can. You can categorize these devices as unmanageable because no particular, individual user manages, meaning owns and operates, each unmanageable device. Some examples of unmanageable devices include printers, fax machines, copiers, cash registers, bar code scanners, and even HVAC systems and vending machines.

If a network-connected device that has an IP address doesn't allow a NAC solution to analyze or question it, you may consider that device unmanageable. But even an unmanageable device can serve as an entry point for a malicious person bent on wreaking mayhem on or pilfering vital information from your network. The malevolent user only has to unplug the unmanageable device from its network jack and plug in their system to hack or infect a network, or steal vital data; or hijack the device's wireless signal to breach the network, and potentially can launch additional breaches and malware exploits. The inability to control network access by unmanageable devices makes a network vulnerable.

Your NAC solution needs to make sure that any unmanageable device attached to your network acts as expected, day in and day out.

Authentication

Authentication is a crucial part of most NAC solutions. So, after a user, and his or her device, attempt to access the organization's network, your NAC solution needs to *authenticate* both the user and device; that is, determine that they're who they say they are.

In Chapter 1, we give an airport metaphor for NAC — when you go to an airport, you need to present a valid, government-provided ID to the personnel at the airline customer-service counter, who check to be sure you're who you say you are. That is authentication. These same airline customer service personnel also check to see that you're authorized to fly to your destination; that you have a reservation for that flight to Cucamonga. Well, that process is authorization, and a NAC solution does basically the same thing to you and your endpoint device when you attempt to access a network.

A NAC solution checks to see that you and your device are authorized to access the network, and what level of authorization you and your device have on that network — where you can go on the network, what servers and data you can access, and so on — based on several different criteria, often including from where you're attempting to access the network.

Endpoint checking

Throughout this book, we discuss NAC solutions that include the ability to check and analyze endpoint devices that attempt network access so that you can ensure that those devices meet your organization's access policy baseline — for both pre- and post-admittance. Most NAC solutions can check whether the endpoint device features items such as antivirus and other malware protection capabilities; the level of malware protection invoked; and (depending on the NAC solution) even the existence of specific files, applications, registry settings, or security hardware and devices. Many NAC solutions can then leverage this information when deciding whether to grant or deny you and your device network access. A number of NAC solutions can integrate with an organization's existing antivirus or other malware policy servers, leveraging those existing policies for a baseline of access policy. This integration helps organizations because it saves time and energy by allowing your NAC solution to use existing policies, meaning that your organization doesn't have to re-invent the policy wheel. Integration can even help ensure that the NAC solution enforces uniform policies across the organization.

Clients and agents

Some NAC solutions include a client or agent that the solution needs to push or preload automatically (or the organization need to preload manually), or even download dynamically, onto a user's device before or during an attempt to access the network. Some NAC solutions provide a Web-based interface for network access, without needing an agent or client of any kind, but others deploy a *dissolvable* agent or client — an agent or client that lives on a user's device for a limited period of time and ceases to exist after the user leaves the network or shuts down his or her system.

Throughout this book, we write about client-based NAC solutions, solutions that add an appliance to an existing network, and still other solutions that utilize both clients and appliances. You can even find client-less NAC solutions. Some NAC solutions that use a network device can allow their device to deploy inline, serving double duty as a policy server and an enforcement point for access control policies. NAC solutions that include a network device can deploy their appliance out-of-band in an existing network environment.

Scanning the NAC terrain

You can use and deploy NAC solutions to handle a number of pressing security and networking issues, as well as to address your organization's need to comply with industry or government regulations. You can use a NAC solution to address control over wired or wireless access. The NAC solution may be able to interoperate with a number of already-deployed security, compliance, or network infrastructure components in an existing network environment. Some NAC solutions can leverage data from the existing network infrastructure and devices to use in formulating or updating access control policies, and as well as in their access control decision-making process.

Most NAC solutions can also cordon off endpoint devices (whether those devices are managed, unmanaged, or unmanageable) that don't meet or maintain access or network policies. A NAC solution can then repair those devices — manually, semi-automatically, or automatically; on demand, or without human or user intervention; or without the user even knowing — until the devices comply with policy.

So, do you know how many different groups within an organization a NAC solution can affect? Get your best herding horse ready and figure out where you stand.

A Team Security Blanket

An organization's network security team typically secures anything that's on, that connects to, or that even attempts connection to their enterprise network. The long and impressive list of items that connects or attempts connection to a network encompasses network devices, network monitoring (such as SNMP), file servers, print servers, applications servers, computing devices (particularly for their connections to the network), networked fax machines and printers, and so on. Basically, any device that connects to the network usually falls under the network security team's purview; in today's typical organization structure, those entities can include just about every device used in the organization.

In some organizations, the scope of the network security team even crosses over into covering network authentication or security devices, such as RADIUS servers or appliances, or network access databases or data stores. In other organizations, even Voice over Internet Protocol (VoIP) or networked e-mail devices, such as e-mail servers, fall under the auspices of the security team. Whether authentication or security devices are the bailiwick of the network security team really depends on your organization and their corporate make-up.

From organization to organization, independent of their corporate make-up, the charter of the network security team typically doesn't change. The charter of the network security team focuses on network security and the policies that can assure and enforce network security. The network security team usually defines, deploys, and sets the enforcement of network security policy for an organization, which helps provide a roadmap for the breadth, depth, and reach of the network security team within most organizations.

It's our policy

Security policies for any organization require a level of uniformity and conformity. Keep what the security policies control and how you enforce them consistent, regardless of the type, scope, or purpose of the device attempting to connect to the network. Consistency is a key — but only one of the keys — to defining security policies and making those policies enforceable.

The network security group in most organizations is the team in charge of ensuring that consistency exists between security policies.

The network security group needs to make sure that their organization has security policies in place, as well as ensuring that those policies are up to date. A network security team must understand the art of designing and defining a security policy that's robust and stringent, but also malleable and resilient. Any security policy that the network security team defines and deploys must be extensible and flexible because while the network — and its users, the devices and tools that they use to access the network, and their access methods — evolves, the network's security needs to evolve, as well. If you — through your organization's network security team, in most instances — don't define strong yet adaptive security policies, the threat of a hack or breach, such as unauthorized individuals or devices accessing the network, or unapproved hardware and software connecting to the network, can occur and spread quickly and exponentially throughout your network, threatening the security of the network, its applications and services, users and their devices.

In most organizations, the network security team determines who may be eligible for or requires administrative privileges and rights. An organization can grant administrative rights to specific users for their own devices or for the network. In this instance, the network security team typically focuses on granting network administrative rights. Device administrative rights usually fall under the control of an organization's desktop or device management team, which we discuss in the section "A Clean Desk(top)," later in this chapter.

The billing of rights

Administrative (admin) privileges and rights are the network security team's collateral — their cash, so to speak.

Admin privileges and rights are akin to the keys to the kingdom because these rights can gain a user access to many highly-confidential, secure areas on (and tools for) a network. Access to the nooks and crevices of the network may also be part of the admin rights grant, too. A person who has admin rights gains a level of unchecked, unfettered freedom and openness to the network — and its security. In the wrong hands, admin privileges and rights can be lethal to a network and organization.

Review, review, review

To keep up with the ever-changing threat landscape, the number and type of devices connecting to the network or that require an IP address, and the amount of users and devices (not to mention types of devices) attempting to access the network, the network security team has to keep tabs on the security of the network. The network security team can accomplish this through consistent and regular — or, in many cases, constant — review of the network's security and the threat risk that it faces.

Like emergency first responders (such as firefighters and police), this team of network first responders runs tests and security audits, and even stages their own network security events, to test their network alert and response times — as well as the team's own response times. The security team uses many tools and means to assess the risk to their network, how they respond to those risks, and how long those responses take, from a variety of threats and breaches.

Armed with this data and insight, the network security team can verify (to some predetermined and predefined level of assuredness) that their network, networked devices, applications, data, and services have current security measures in place. They can also assure that their network has (and maintains) low vulnerability and exposure to malware explosions, exploits, breaches, attacks, and other negative network events. But this predefined level of verification isn't perfect. Like any fortress, no network is impregnable. A network security team needs to be forever vigilant, current, and focused on the task at hand — the safety and security of their organization's network, protecting sensitive data and intellectual property.

With these privileges and rights, a malevolent user can breach confidential information, as well as access rights to applications, data, and devices. Such a user can even modify the network itself, leaving it in jeopardy from hack, breach, or other threat. The user can drill holes into the network's security and make the network easily accessible to hackers, whether those hackers are external or internal. Because of these issues — and more, the network security team considers admin privileges and rights collateral, and they guard those rights and privileges as securely as the keys to a safe, cash or jewels, or any other precious possession. The network security team doesn't grant these privileges or rights lightly. They make admin rights and privileges available only when required, ordered, or under great duress. The safety and security of their network kingdom — and its coveted crown jewels, such as information and accessibility — are at stake.

The team job description

The network security team, in all likelihood, is very actively involved in any investigation into or decision regarding a NAC solution. They

- Quickly stand behind your organization's adoption of NAC (if they don't make it happen themselves).

- Driving the NAC selection and adoption process from the start, determining the organization's and network's NAC need, defining the NAC solution criteria, and helping in the selection of vendors and products.

- Work with other organizational teams and groups to determine and define their access control needs.

- Lead the testing of a NAC solution, in conjunction with other organizational teams, all the way up to the selection and deployment of a NAC solution.

The network security team needs to do all these NAC implementation processes and tasks because that team usually defines and implements the security policies that drive the selected NAC solution, not to mention enforcing those policies and taking remediation actions against non-compliant devices or unauthorized individuals attempting to access the network.

This team needs to ensure the following:

- Any selected NAC solution has strong, powerful means to control who and how users and their devices can access the network and corporate resources.

- Robust, inclusive user and device authentication and authorization procedures secure network and application access as stringently as possible, without forcing users to contact the helpdesk because they can't access the network and its resources. After all, the network security team doesn't want to face the ire of angry helpdesk personnel!

- Any policy engine associated with the NAC solution needs a simple, easy-to-use user interface, particularly because the network security team most likely has to define, create, and implement the security policies.

- The selected NAC solution enables the network security team to reuse or repurpose existing security policies — either policies that they already have in place with existing policy servers, such as those for organizational antivirus or other anti-malware capabilities; or policies that they've already defined for other access methods, such as security and access policies for virtual private networks (VPNs); network infrastructure security devices (such as intrusion detection systems [IDS] or intrusion prevention systems [IPS]), or existing security appliances (such as firewalls, routers, or integrated security devices).

The network security team must adamantly demand that all network users and their devices — including all layers of organization management, as well as guest users, including contractors and partners — adhere to the security policies and access control procedures because the more unauthorized, unauthenticated users and devices denied network or application access, the lesser the chance of those same users or devices breaching network security and causing the network security team more work, aggravation, and heartburn.

Networking Social

You may have the networking team (as opposed to the networking security team, discussed in the section "A Team Security Blanket," earlier in this chapter) involved in the search for a NAC solution. They can help set criteria for network access control, as well as help select and purchase the right NAC solution for your organization. The networking team may even, in some cases, drive the NAC decision-making process — particularly if the NAC solution or solutions that you're considering include any sort of network appliance or device.

Here are the differences between a network security team and a networking team:

- The networking team at most organizations is responsible for the selection, deployment, management, and administration of the network infrastructure. *Network infrastructure* can refer to the backbone of the network, as well as the access points for, types of appliances and devices on, and the appliances and devices that connect to the network. It also refers to the appliances and equipment — the physical devices themselves — that the organization uses to communicate data and information throughout the network and beyond. So, devices such as routers, hubs, gateways, bridges, and even Ethernet switches and wireless access points can fall under the control of *the networking team*.

  The networking team is in charge of

  - **Wired network infrastructure:** The miles and miles of cables that connect network infrastructure devices, the operating systems and management software for those devices, and any software that operates on the network infrastructure fall under the watchful eye of the networking team.

  - **Wireless network infrastructure:** This team also has responsibility for the repeaters, gateways, hubs, and access points for wireless networking.

  - **Network infrastructure equipment:** This category can include virtually anything that's connected to a network, including wired or wireless network infrastructure components. And, if something is part of the network infrastructure, it likely falls under the scope of the networking team.

- **Managed services:** *Managed services* are networking services and applications that a third-party provider supplies. These providers are often referred to as managed service providers (MSPs). MSPs can provide services such as user authentication, security, storage, remote access, and so on. You can find a managed service for virtually any service available locally to a network. (Although the networking team can select and manage managed services, a security-related managed service, such as authentication, may fall under the responsibilities of the security or network security team.)

In some organizations, the security or network security team may reside under the umbrella of the networking team. Rarely does the networking team reside under the security team; but never say never.

The networking team, in most organizations, is responsible for managing the network infrastructure and its components, which normally includes

- ✔ Determining the organization's need for various networking solutions (including NAC solutions)
- ✔ Creating the selection criteria for network infrastructure products
- ✔ Selecting the network infrastructure device or solution vendors and products
- ✔ Evaluating the vendors and products by piloting or lab testing chosen network infrastructure devices and solutions
- ✔ Selecting products
- ✔ Negotiating with the vendors for their products
- ✔ Installing the products — or contracting with a third party to install the products
- ✔ Troubleshooting and testing the products — which can be done in a lab environment with a network mock-up, or live on the network environment
- ✔ Determining the lifecycle of the products that constitute your organization's network

You gotta have heart

If your network is the brain of your organization, the network infrastructure is your organization's heart — pumping vital information and coordinating the mix of collaboration, communication, and information that allows the network to live and thrive. The infrastructure acts much in the same way that the human heart mixes blood and oxygen that it sends to the human brain.

If malware, a breach, or even an attack that brings down a server or switch affects a network, any interruption in the network or its sensitive mix can make an organization cease to operate efficiently. In some cases, an organization can stop operating at all, like the human brain does without its supply of fresh blood and oxygen mix. In some extreme cases, in which the network is extremely vital to the organization's life or the attack against the network lasts a long time, the organization might cease to exist. So, the networking team is sort of like the cardiologist for the network, ensuring that the life-giving pump — the network infrastructure — continues to feed the brain of the organization (the network), and all the information and communications on it.

Because of the importance of the network infrastructure to the life of the network and even the organization, in most cases, you need to have the networking team actively involved in any NAC solution investigation, decision, and deployment. If the NAC solution can affect the organization's heart and damage its brain, this team wants to know all about the NAC selection process and have a say in it!

Don't tread on me

If you involve the networking group in defining or selecting a NAC solution, they will likely want to be reassured that the NAC solution doesn't disrupt the way that they deploy their internal network architecture or how that architecture works.

The networking team can be very particular about their network footprint and topology. The networking team will greatly scrutinize anything that now affects or could ultimately affect the network infrastructure and the network's operation — not to mention its security. The networking team will also want assurances that the implementation and deployment of any security device, especially a solution as intrusive and all-encompassing as a NAC solution, won't impact the current performance or interfere with the ongoing, day-to-day operations of their network.

You can approach the networking team with a NAC solution by showing them how quickly and simply they — or the organizational or third-party team chosen to deploy the NAC solution — can deploy the solution within their existing network environment. Illustrate and discuss how the networking team won't have to go through any kind of painful infrastructure upgrades. Any upgrades expose the networking team to a lot of work, and more importantly, upgrades expose the organization's network, leaving it potentially vulnerable to attacks or breaches.

Anytime you add anything new to the network infrastructure — no matter what that thing is or how you deploy it — you introduce a risk to the network and, ultimately, to the organization. This sort of action can send shivers up and down the spine of even the most hardened networker. The mere mention of upgrades can make the little hairs on the back of a networker's neck stand on end because of the potential for breaches, hacks, and other bad things happening.

Showing how easily the networking team — or the organizational or third-party team chosen to deploy the NAC solution — can deploy your selected NAC solution — particularly if it involves a network component, appliance, or even network software — can make all the difference between getting the networking team onboard or having them act as a roadblock to your NAC solution's implementation. Build consensus for deploying NAC on your network and solidify your NAC decision with the networking team.

Use your phasers

Deploying your NAC solution in phases (for example, component by component, group by group, department by department, floor by floor, or wired then wireless) can help assuage the fears of your networking team.

Like my lab rats?

We highly recommend that, if possible, you conduct a small pilot or other method of pre-testing — such as a lab environment — for your NAC solution of choice. Prior to *any* deployment, whether full or phased, a pilot or lab test eases the networking team into the whole NAC idea. You may find this approach helpful or useful when trying to convince other's to deploy NAC organization-wide, or to deploy a NAC solution at all, particularly if you run into a networking-team roadblock right off the bat when it comes to a NAC solution. Most times, depending on the NAC solution, even the most hard-boiled, anti-NAC networking team member can begin to see the benefits of implementing a NAC solution in the network infrastructure, particularly if the NAC solution plays well in the test sandbox.

By starting off small (such as with a pilot or lab test environment), and then growing outward in small increments (such as a phased deployment scenario), the networking team can get their collective feet wet with NAC. They can set up and access the solution in a small, controlled environment until they become comfortable with it or fully configure it with organizational security and access policies. Then, you can deploy the solution to a small group or "tiger team" in a phased approach. You can also phase the NAC solution setup to only audit the network and user traffic, without policy enforcement, so that the networking team can see whether (or, more likely, how) the NAC solution and their network can play well together. One way or another, try to help your networking team ease into NAC.

By deploying in phases, you likely need less labor, so the networking team doesn't have to expend as many resources, saving the team time and cost, as well as decreasing the opportunity costs faced by the networking team. You also cut the costs of other organizational teams that don't have to focus all their resources on your large-scale, multi-tentacle NAC rollout.

A phased deployment scenario also enables the networking team and other teams involved with a NAC deployment to work out any issues during the NAC solution's shakedown cruise. The team or agency deploying the NAC solution can then apply these lessons during the next rollout phase, again limiting labor used and exposure. A phased deployment also limits the organization's and the network's exposure if something goes awry with the deployment, eliminating a lot of helpdesk calls. The fewer users adversely impacted, the fewer calls to the helpdesk and the lower the overall cost.

Don't approach the networking team like you've just happened upon the network security Holy Grail, a cure for all the network's ills, delivering pervasive access with locked-down network security — otherwise, they may banish you and lock you out of their labs!

A Clean Desk (top)

If your organization is large, you might also have a desktop team, known as desktop management, desktop security, or other monikers. This team manages any and all computing (and input) devices that your organization owns and operates, or manages. So, any device that the organization owns or manages, or that an employee or a contractor operates, falls under the purview of such a desktop management team.

If you don't have a desktop management team, you might consider creating one or at least focusing someone's duties to cover all the devices.

A desktop management team is ultimately responsible for

- ✔ The actions of any computing device that the organization owns, operates, or manages, including what happens when a device attempts to access the organization's network.

- ✔ Anything and everything that's initially loaded or subsequently downloaded onto the device, including any software applications.

- ✔ Any sort of hardware, storage, or other device type that's ultimately attached to a computing device.

✔ Policing desktop and other computing devices to ensure that users are maintaining the devices properly, which includes checking the devices for applications that the organization bans or hasn't approved. These applications can include instant messaging, peer-to-peer, file sharing, and other applications that can act as a Typhoid Mary of malware or open the network, applications, data, and the whole organization to hack or attack.

✔ Ensuring users don't use devices that the organization's security policies forbid, such as USB drives. Or the team may restrict a user from using specific devices and programs, such as USB drives, Bluetooth devices, or IM, when accessing certain servers.

✔ Creating and enforcing the desktop and endpoint security policies of an organization, and helping police the endpoints to ensure that users comply with these policies.

✔ Making sure that any endpoint device which the organization manages has required antivirus, anti-spyware, or any other anti-malware software loaded onto it. If the device requires patch-management capabilities, the desktop team needs to make sure that the device receives those capabilities.

Desktop rights

A desktop team provides administrative rights and privileges for endpoint devices. Like the network security team, the desktop team holds administrative rights and privileges for endpoint devices very close to their vests. They don't hand those rights and privileges out to every user, and for good reason.

If a user receives administrative rights and privileges to his or her endpoint device, he or she can enable the endpoint's access privileges, or delete or alter the endpoint's security capabilities. For example, if a user deactivates malware scans or turns off other forms of endpoint protection, he or she leaves the endpoint vulnerable to attack. That endpoint can even become a Trojan horse for a hacker, who can gain entry into the inner sanctum of the organization's network by piggybacking on the unsuspecting user, who (along with his or her endpoint device) is an authentic, authorized employee or other user in good standing. Then, after the user and the device access the network, the hacker springs his or her attack onto the network, capturing once-private, sensitive customer or corporate data and intellectual property, selling it to the highest bidder or holding it for a king's ransom to be paid by the bilked organization; or, threatens to unleash a malware attack to take down the organization's network, unless they are paid handsomely.

So, the desktop team, like the security team, holds the endpoint's keys to the kingdom — the administrative rights and privileges — and doles them out only to certain users, as needed.

Not-so-secret agents

If your organization has a desktop management team, get that team actively involved in the definition, selection, and deployment of a NAC solution — particularly if the NAC solution includes any type of software that needs to be loaded or downloaded onto the endpoint device or if the NAC solution requires a piece of hardware (or even firmware) to secure the endpoint device.

Many NAC solutions include a client or an agent. The client or agent may be a full preloaded client, an 802.1X supplicant, a persistent agent, or even a dissolvable agent. If an organization-managed endpoint device needs to upload or connect to any software or device as part of the NAC solution, the desktop management team should and likely will be involved in the NAC solution selection and test process.

If the organization's desktop management team needs to become involved in the NAC process, particularly if the NAC solution has a client or agent involved, that team will likely want to discuss the configuration and download process; the speed and size of the client or agent; and whether the NAC solution preloads or downloads the client package, or whether the NAC solution downloads a persistent or dissolvable NAC agent. The desktop management team wants to be involved in the NAC process so that they can ensure

- ✔ No impediments prevent users from accessing the network with their devices in the shortest time possible.

- ✔ The client or agent, as well as the complete NAC solution package, doesn't interfere with the already-created and -defined policies of their existing malware protection (that the organization has approved and the desktop team has loaded or downloaded to each endpoint device that they manage).

- ✔ If the NAC solution requires a client download, the client operates seamlessly with their current system management tools, enabling the desktop team to preload the client as part of any existing image package or push the client to each endpoint device for quick, easy deployment and upgrading, if needed.

- ✔ Their team can test and approve any updates and upgrades to the client or agent before the vendor, an integrator, an MSP, or the desktop team themselves uploads or pushes those changes to the users' endpoints.

- ✔ They can vet and test any updates that the NAC solution makes to operating system or application patches, as well as antivirus or other anti-malware applications loaded on a user's device before they can manually or dynamically push those changes organization-wide.

In short, the desktop team can do its part to ensure that they can identify and eliminate any potential issues or incompatibilities before those issues occur and propagate in the actual environment, creating user panic and helpdesk nightmares.

Compliant with Compliance

The need to meet an increasing number of industry and government regulations and requirements faces most — if not all — of today's organizations, regardless of location or industry.

But meeting specific requirements set forth by industry bodies and government entities is just part of the problem that organizations today have to deal with. The other part of the problem involves the mandate that organizations *prove* their adherence to these government and industry regulations.

Adhering to (and proving adherence to) specific industry and governmental regulations places a tremendous burden on already-taxed network and security resources — both physical and human resources. Already stretched thin by being forced to do more with less, complying with industry or governmental regulations may stretch an organization's teams to the breaking point. We see it all the time.

So, we advocate that organizations create compliance teams (if they already haven't), either full or part time (based on your organization's needs). A compliance team has to

- ✔ Identify and fully understand the industry and government regulations to which the organization must adhere.

- ✔ Call out the various requirements and line items in each regulation that affect your organization and their business.

- ✔ Identify the means within the organization — the technology, processes, policies, and so on — that already exist or that you need to create to address the requirements in the regulations.

- ✔ Work with other teams (such as the networking team, security team, desktop team, and others) to ensure that the organization scopes, defines, and satisfactorily implements the necessary technologies, processes, and policies to meet the stipulations and requirements of the required industry and government regulations.

- ✔ Ensure that any compliance solutions (or solutions) capture and store any data pertinent to their organization's adherence to the industry and government regulations, and that the organization uses that data if the compliance governing body or regulatory agency requires an audit to prove the organization met the stipulations of the compliance regulations.

More and more organizations are turning to NAC to address their regulatory compliance requirements. NAC can address compliance requirements for the same reason you, the reader, may find it so difficult to get a NAC project approved, implemented, and deployed within your organization — NAC is ubiquitous. It touches on every aspect of daily networking and computing, as well as the users themselves.

NAC deals with and touches nearly every device (and every person) that attempts to connect or actually connects to a network:

✔ Endpoint devices (particularly if your NAC solution includes a client, or a persistent or dissolvable agent, to check on the security state of the device prior to the solution granting that device network access)

✔ Users (ensuring that the NAC solution authenticates and authorizes the user to access the network, as well as specific servers, applications, and data stored on the network)

✔ The network's policies (enabling an organization to define or redefine their security and access policies, and often allowing them to interact with existing or supplying new security, antivirus and anti-malware, patch management, and access control policies)

NAC can deliver network admission control based on specific authentication and authorization, specific actions and policies, identity-based network and application access control, and user roles. These identity-based admission and access control, authentication and authorization, and policy management capabilities, makes NAC ideal for regulatory compliance needs because of its ability to combine all of these capabilities into one solution, and leverage other network and security components to deliver regulatory compliance.

Regardless of your industry or the government regulations to which your organization must adhere, many industry and governmental entities mandate several common requirements in their regulations that organizations must meet.

Antivirus (and Anti-malware)

Nearly every compliance regulation requires that an endpoint device have at least antivirus software (and, in some instances, additional types of anti-malware software) resident, operational, and current before that device receives network access. Most NAC solutions can address this requirement through *endpoint security checks,* which check an endpoint device for antivirus or other anti-malware products, whether the user or their device has invoked the antivirus or anti-malware, and whether that software is current before the NAC solution allows the device to access an organization's network. A NAC solution may not grant devices that don't meet the base level of antivirus or anti-malware policy state for network access until they do meet the baseline. Some NAC solutions can quarantine a non-compliant device, and some of those solutions can bring the device into compliance with the baseline through manual or automatic remediation.

Authentication

Most industry or government regulations require that an organization authenticate all users before those users can be granted access to the organization's network. Many NAC solutions include the means to support user authentication. Some NAC solutions support different forms and types of authentication, which can include unique user names and passwords, two-factor authentication, token devices and biometric devices, and password encryption and management. Some NAC solutions interface with an organization's existing authentication database or data store, others require a secondary interface to existing authentication stores, and some require that the data store reside on or in the NAC device.

Identity

Some compliance regulations require that an organization identify a user or device by more than just an IP address because hackers and malevolent users can easily spoof IP addresses. These regulations require identity-based controls. Some NAC solutions already deliver access control that's user identity-based, others offer access control that's role-based, and some provide both. By enabling identity-based or role-based access control, an organization gets to know who's accessing their network and sensitive applications, and when.

Access control

Many compliance regulations require organizations to restrict access to sensitive data and information stored on the organization's network. Many NAC solutions can address this requirement, some more easily and quickly than others. Some NAC solutions are designed, from the ground up, to deliver network and application access control. Those solutions have the native ability to separate and secure network devices or network areas that store sensitive data so that no unauthorized person or device can access that data. These solutions virtually segment the network. If a user or device doesn't have the authorization to access the device or area that stores the sensitive information, the NAC solution denies that user or device access. This type of NAC solution enables an organization to not only meet and address regulatory compliance, but it also helps inoculate the organization against data breaches and ensure the credibility of the organization — because no organization likes to see themselves as the spotlight story on *60 Minutes* as the poster child for information breaches (or to put out a press release about and have to pay compensation to their customers for stolen personal information and data).

Encryption

Most compliance regulations include a requirement that data communicated or transmitted — usually outside of the network — remain secure. However, several regulations now expand this requirement to cover data communicated *within* the LAN, as well, because of the growing propensity for insider threats and security breaches, which now happen more frequently and cost more for an organization to fix than external breaches (not to mention the cost to the organization's reputation if the hacker, users, or even the compliance governing agency publicizes the breach).

Many NAC solutions provide a means to encrypt transmitted data when a user communicates that data outside of the network. Some NAC solutions utilize and leverage the IEEE's 802.1X standard for port-based network access control, which includes robust encryption that protects data and credentials transmitted from the endpoint to the network. Some NAC solutions provide another form of encryption — such as IPsec — to protect data communicated outside of the organization's network. A few NAC solutions go so far as to provide a means of encryption for data when a user transmits data over the network, from device to device.

Audits

Many compliance regulations require an organization to prove that they adhere to many of the requirements listed in the regulation. Some specific regulations require proof of adherence by authorized users, access to protected resources (such as stored sensitive data), and so on. NAC solutions can offer audit trails and logs, and some even include reports on network and application access, authentication, authorization, and so on. Some NAC solutions can export their logs to external devices, such as security information and event management (SIEM) products, which can correlate and analyze the log information; or to existing report-generation files and products. A few NAC solutions that deliver identity-based and role-based controls can correlate user identity and role information to network and application usage to provide detailed logs and reports, ready for regulatory compliance audits.

If the compliance team is involved in the NAC solution decision, they will likely want to understand how the NAC solution helps them address

✔ the appropriate compliance regulations to which they must adhere

✔ how the NAC solution addresses each one of the compliance requirements that they must meet (probably in detail)

✔ their compliance audit needs

Be prepared to discuss, in some detail, how your selected NAC solution addresses regulatory compliance and audits. Focus on how it can help the compliance team, and gain them as backers of your selected NAC solution, instead of having to deal with a compliance team that's opposed to the solution.

Other Players

Depending on your organization, you may have other teams or groups involved in various stages of your NAC decision-making process:

✔ **Telecommunications:** If your organization has equipped most users with BlackBerries, Treos, iPhones, or other mixed telecommunications and wireless access devices, or if the organization uses only Voice over Internet Protocol (VoIP) phones, you should (or will need to) include the telecommunications team at some point in the NAC solution decision process.

✔ **LAN and wireless networking:** Your organization may have split its networking team into LAN and wireless groups, each of which you want to involve in the NAC solution process or decision.

✔ **A third party:** Sometimes, organizations decide that they want to include a third-party organization — an integrator or a value-added reseller (VAR), for example — in the NAC solution process because the organization trusts this third-party company and values their input about technology products and their adoption.

✔ **Access:** If you have an access team, get them involved in the NAC evaluation and decision process, as well as the deployment of the selected NAC solution.

✔ **Remote access:** Your organization might have a granular approach to access control. For example, you might have a remote access team that's responsible for user and guest remote access, as well as remote security for the organization's network. This group would want to know how the NAC solution addresses or integrates with their existing — or new — remote access capabilities, such as IPSec or SSL VPN.

Build consensus for NAC within your organization, fostering understanding among your constituents, and internal groups and teams, then making them comfortable, and finally convincing them to adopt the NAC solution. NAC doesn't work if you shoehorn it into your environment, nor does it work if you force-feed it to any team involved in deployment and use.

1 + 1 = 3?

Some NAC solutions may not be a single solution. You may need two or more NAC solutions, in combination, to address your organization's security and access control needs.

So, how do you work with various teams on different NAC solutions that need to, in the end, integrate (or, at least, interoperate) so that you can ensure network access control?

Working with separate teams on separate NAC solutions that you need to intertwine in some way works pretty much the same way as a singular NAC solution:

1. **Try to build consensus for the NAC solutions within the different teams in the organization that you want to test and/or deploy the combined NAC solution.**

2. **Work with each team, allowing them to gain a better understanding of each other and their NAC needs.**

3. **Make each team comfortable when working with the NAC solution — and with each other.**

4. **Allow the teams to work together toward a combined NAC adoption.**

   Designate a point person from each team and have them work together, attend each other's meetings, and ensure that the teams can implement the different NAC solutions on time and in concert, seamlessly integrating them.

Integrating different NAC solutions requires more development time and interaction than working with a single solution. So, you may want to make the point person from each group that's deploying a NAC solution a representative of, or from development or engineering, someone who can make sure that all the pieces can come together and work. This approach ensures that at least some level of (technical) cross-pollination can occur.

If your organization is really large, then create a separate team geared for and with the goal of integrating the various NAC solutions to ensure that you have one team that can make it all work together seamlessly, and deliver your integrated, multi-vendor NAC solution on time.

Help! (Desk)

Although you probably won't have the helpdesk team actively involved in the evaluation of and decision making for a NAC solution, you will certainly need to involve them after you start testing, piloting, or deploying the NAC solution in a lab environment, in phases, or (gulp!) all at the same time on the organization's existing network environment.

Users see your helpdesk as the first line of defense, so naturally you should involve the helpdesk team in your NAC solution. If a user attempts and fails to access the organization's network, which they've been accessing successfully every day for several years, who do you think they're going to call? The helpdesk team.

Who do you think the CEO calls when the new NAC solution kicks his or her laptop off the network because that laptop's antivirus automatic protection is disabled or its operating system patches are out of date? He or she calls the helpdesk.

Get on the good side of the helpdesk team by lab testing or piloting the NAC solution first, and involving the helpdesk team in the process. Involve your helpdesk team by

- Setting up and deploying the solution

- Creating new or repurposing existing policies

- Knowing to stage, operate, and use the NAC solution of choice

- Staging and deploying the lab test or pilot of the NAC solution, so that they can observe the NAC solution being deployed and in action, and even become familiar with the NAC solution by using it.

If the helpdesk can't answer a user's question (for example, the question or issue requires greater knowledge or more in-depth investigation), the helpdesk team usually falls back on the subject matter experts (SMEs) in the various teams familiar with the device or service that's generating the questions or issues. So, if the helpdesk team isn't properly trained on or sufficiently comfortable with the NAC solution, not only can the breadth and depth of support calls from their user base easily overwhelm the helpdesk, but the teams involved in the NAC solution decision and deployment can expect to lose precious time helping the helpdesk team answer questions and solve issues that they are unable to answer — because the helpdesk team didn't receive proper training about the NAC solution.

The helpdesk can not only help users, but also the teams involved with the deployment. Make sure you get the helpdesk team involved in the NAC solution process!

Get an audit

You can ease the potential pain of the helpdesk team by initially deploying the NAC solution in audit mode. Most NAC solutions include an audit mode — although that mode may have a different name, depending on the solution. An *audit mode* simply is a way to implement NAC without turning on enforcement, which includes quarantine, remediation, or active enforcement (such as not granting a non-compliant device access). An audit mode can actively enforce only the authentication and authorization NAC functions, to ensure that only authenticated users can access the network or any protected resources.

Audit mode can really help users by easing them into the capabilities of network access control, revealing whether they and their endpoint devices are compliant or non-compliant with organizational security and access control policies, and showing how the NAC solution reacts if they or their device are out of compliance. Audit mode can help make the user comfortable with the deployed NAC solution.

Audit mode also helps the helpdesk. Instead of being deluged with calls from frustrated, screaming users who can't access the network or the network resources which they usually can, the helpdesk team can work directly with the users whose devices are the most out of compliance or who have the most issues when trying to access the organization's network with the newly deployed NAC solution. The helpdesk team can get those users' devices into compliance with policies and address the users' access issues. Deploying the NAC solution for an initial time period in audit mode can ensure that the NAC solution catches nearly all the endpoint devices connecting to the organization's network that are out of compliance with the organization's access and security policies, brings those devices into policy compliance without trauma or consternation, and exposes users to how the NAC solution will work going forward. Most NAC solutions provide users — and, sometimes, the helpdesk — with messages about why a user or device was non-compliant and how to remediate the device to bring it back into policy compliance. Some NAC solutions also notify the user and/or the helpdesk about what the user needs to do in the future to ensure the device remains compliant.

User-bility

Don't forget about the users.

The users in the NAC solution process are vital. They can make or break any NAC solution deployment. Ensure a smooth transition and ensure users will use and embrace any NAC solution deployment by initially deploying the NAC solution in audit mode. In this way, users can experience the NAC solution, how it works, and the messages that it provides — all without worrying about policy enforcement, or not being able to access their network or network resources.

Audit mode deployment — at least for a period of time at the start of the NAC solution deployment — can ensure the success of the NAC deployment after you turn on policy enforcement.

You can also establish training classes for users. Although a suitable NAC solution doesn't modify or change a user's procedure for accessing the network, you can make the users comfortable with the NAC solution by providing them with training about what occurs in a NAC deployment, the policies that they and their devices now have to follow to achieve network access, and what can happen if they or their devices aren't in compliance with organizational access and security policies.

Train users about situations such as quarantine or remediation. Be sure to explain to users that remediation can be manual or automatic — and which process will bring their device into NAC compliance, as well as why.

Users may have questions or concerns about accessing the network for the first time after you deploy a NAC solution. Work with the various NAC deployment teams and the helpdesk to provide as much electronic (or hardcopy — but try to be green!) information about how the NAC solution works and why your organization needs it, so that users can feel like they're part of the process.

Remote users

If your organization has remote users and/or telecommuters, try to work with them before you implement and deploy the NAC solution — even if you deploy it only in audit mode.

The remote users might be concerned by the different screens — depending on the NAC solution — that they see, the way or number of times that they may have to authenticate, and so on. Be sensitive to their needs because, unlike local users, they may access the network and its new protector, NAC, at times when the core team isn't available to answer questions, or walk or talk them through issues or concerns.

You should include remote employees and telecommuters as testers of the NAC solution, either in audit or full enforcement mode. Including remote users and/or telecommuters in the NAC evaluation and testing process can help both the NAC deployment teams — by ensuring that remote employees and users can access the network, with their compliance ensured via NAC, without issue — and the remote users.

The remote user or telecommuter may need a little more hand-holding and conversation about NAC and its use and deployment than on-site users.

Contractors

If your organization employs a number of contractors, or other guest-like users, notify these users of the impending NAC solution deployment. Even better, have several of these users test the NAC deployment, like the remote users. By employing contractors or other guest users as NAC solution testers, the organization can ensure that users vital to the ongoing success of the company — such as contractors, partners, and other outside users who require some level of network access to get their work done for the organization — can access the network after you deploy NAC, and can feel comfortable with the NAC solution.

The Cattle Corral

Just don't spring a new NAC solution on users on a Monday morning, with full enforcement invoked, because it could be a difficult day, for the user, the helpdesk, the NAC deployment teams, and the organization as a whole!

NAC is ubiquitous. It touches many different areas and components of the network, various teams throughout the organization, and every user. It affects every area of the network:

- ✔ NAC will not work if an organization, network, or environment is not ready for it or prepared for how NAC works.
- ✔ A NAC solution will not work if dictated as a mandate to employees that it be used.

It's up to you and your organization, including users, and specifically to any team involved in NAC solution deployment, use, and adoption, the level of success a NAC deployment can enjoy.

Chapter 8

Identifying Who's On My Network

In This Chapter
▶ Identifying your identity
▶ Mapping out your users

Grasping identity and folding it into your network-access-control–based network can move your network into the next generation. Tie your network to your *authentication servers* to create a detailed view of your network and who has access to what. This view gives you something that you can see and control!

Hey, It's Me

Three drivers make identity a must-have component of network access control (NAC):

- ✔ Regulatory compliance: Regulations such as HIPPA, Sarbanes-Oxley, and PCI (Payment Card Industry)
- ✔ Resource protection: Protecting your high value network resources
- ✔ Traffic auditing: Actually seeing what happens in the network traffic

Before you try to create a large, complex NAC deployment, start with identity at the center of your plans. Without a proper definition of user identity, you can't realize the full potential of a NAC-based infrastructure.

Before creating a complex NAC deployment, check for an internal identity stores that your NAC deployment can leverage and make a list of those identity stores before you try to create policies. Typically, you have to use several identity stores across your network to define complete policies that cover all users on your network. Identity typically isn't in the realm of your network infrastructure IT groups, and you may have to pull in your authentication IT group(s) to have a successful network access control deployment.

Most networks are built to connect users to resources. In the modern NAC view, both devices and users have identities. These identities can be either

✔ A user who has a user name and other information

✔ A device that has a location, hardware ID, or other information

Both users and devices have an identity that Network Access Control can leverage to control access.

Think of identity not just as a person with a name, but as a label for a user or device. You can create labels for any groups of users to give them identities on the network:

✔ Users

✔ Printers

✔ Fax machines

✔ Security cameras

✔ Barcode scanners

Identity Authentication

The policy engine is at the core of the authentication process for the NAC-based network. *Authentication* is a process of determining whether a user or a device (identity) is really what it claims to be:

✔ Identity *without* authentication is like a hostess at a restaurant asking for your name to ensure a reservation.

  Maybe you can lie and get away with it (until the real party of seven shows).

✔ Identity *with* authentication is like a police officer asking for your driver's license after a traffic violation.

  The officer and his network will verify your identity to make sure that you're who you say you are.

Many networks operate today as a network without identity, which isn't that much different than an open parking lot, where nobody checks who comes and who leaves. These networks connect the user or device to the network, and after the user or device is on the network, the enforcement point blocks access if that user or device has no credentials. Identity checks should happen a lot sooner, like putting a card-checking booth at the entrance to a parking lot.

With NAC, you can find out who the user or device is before you attach that user or device to the network.

Collecting identity

Although different NAC vendors support different methods of collecting identity, the typical first step in validating identity for access control is to collect the identity's credentials.

Your method of collecting those credentials must recognize whether the identity belongs to a user (human) or a device (non-human) for some very obvious reasons:

✔ Users have jobs to do (and feelings, too). They don't like being authenticated dozens of times during the day.

✔ Devices don't care how many times you authenticate them.

Although you can use several methods to collect user identity for NAC policy decisions, *how* credentials are collected can determine what the user experience is like when a user connects to the network (and the quality of the user experience is directly related to the number of complaints that come to your attention).

NAC gives you another level of authentication, on top of what users have to go through today. For example, a user might need only to plug into your current network to connect. With a typical NAC deployment, a user logs in to the network. After the network connection is complete, the user has to log in to Windows before he or she can start working. Users can start complaining pretty quickly because they don't like to have to log in twice before they can start their work.

Here's the generic process for most NAC authentications:

1. The user plugs his or her computer into the network.

2. The network detects the computer.

3. The network asks the agent on the computer for credentials.

4. The agent pops up a dialog box in which the user types his or her credentials.

5. The agent sends the user credentials across the network to the policy engine.

6. The policy engine verifies the user credentials against a backend authentication system (such as Microsoft Active Directory, LDAP, and so on).

7. The policy engine creates an access policy for that computer.

8. The policy engine allows the computer and the user on the network.

The key steps in this whole flow for user authentication are how the credentials are collected (Step 4) and what they're verified against (Step 6). Without a verified source to validate them against, you can't validate with user identity.

Essentially, the success of the user experience hinges on how the endpoint agent collects the identity. Some technologies can solve the sticky problems and make the user experience more seamless.

Web portal

A Web portal is the simplest form of identity collection, similar to a Web page to which you have to submit a user name and password.

For example, in your hotel room, you plug into the network and open a Web browser, and then the hotel asks you for your credit card number or your room number. This user experience is a *captive portal,* also called the hotel-room experience. In a NAC deployment, you plug your computer into the network and get an address that you can enter to access a Web page. After you log on by using your Web browser, the NAC solution sees that you aren't authenticated and redirects your browser to a login page, where you have to submit your credentials.

Using a Web portal for authentication has some benefits:

✔ It's the most cross-platform–friendly method of collecting credentials because it uses a Web browser.

✔ You don't need to have any endpoint software running on the endpoint.

Web portals have a couple of limitations:

✔ You have to open a Web browser to be able to log in. If the user opens an application such as Microsoft Outlook first, that user doesn't see a login page and can't connect.

✔ Network or enforcement point needs to give the endpoint and IP address on the network before the user is authenticated. The network needs to give some sort of limited access initially, and after authentication, the access for that user changes.

Web-portal–based authentication is suited for many use cases and is often used in conjunction with some other form of credential collection. For example, a deployment might use

✔ Agent-based collection for all managed corporate endpoints

✔ Web-portal authentication for any guest users who connect to the network

Agent-based

An *agent* is a software program that performs a set of tasks. In NAC policy, the agent is a piece of software that runs on the endpoint trying to connect to the network.

You can find two different types of agents: persistent and non-persistent. This section covers only the persistent endpoint agent that's installed on the connecting endpoint. Most NAC agents are designed to be persistent and start up with the computer when the OS loads. Agents give the NAC the most interaction with the connecting endpoint, and they allow agents to collect the connecting user's credentials in many different fashions.

The most popular agent-based methods of collecting credentials are

✔ **Dialog box:** During the process of authentication, the agent displays a dialog box to the user (sort of like a pop-up window) and asks for that user's user name and password.

✔ **Saved credentials:** The user has provided his or her credentials to the agent, and the agent is reusing those credentials.

Using saved credentials isn't the most secure method. If someone steals a user's machine, the thief wouldn't need to enter credentials to get directly on the network.

✔ **Windows GINA (Graphical Identification and Authentication):** This method uses a GINA plug-in that has the ability to collect credentials and log in the user to the network as a part of the Windows login process:

1. When the Windows' login screen appears, GINA steps in, starting all the network connections and logging in the user to the network.

2. After GINA completes its login process, the Windows authentication starts.

GINA gives a very seamless way to tie NAC to a Windows login.

✔ **Certificates:** The agent can collect a user certificate that was issued to the user who's logging in. The agent can use a certificate in conjunction with other credentials or a PIN that's configured for the certificate.

✔ **Smart cards:** Similar to certificates, except that the certificate is contained on a card that the user needs to put in a card reader.

✔ **Kerberos tickets:** Kerberos tickets allow agents to interact with the operating system so that they can piggy-back on available authentication sources. In a Windows environment, the agent can use the Kerberos ticket of the user to authenticate and get on the network.

The agent approach does have a downside — it's platform dependant. The access control vendor needs to write an individual agent for each platform that you might support, such as Windows, Macintosh, and Linux. The agent approach is the most popular because most of the devices connecting to the network are managed PCs that can have the agent preconfigured and installed before the endpoint tries to connect to the network.

Single Sign-On

When you want a clean user experience, Single Sign-On (SSO) can help clean things up a bit. In a typical login scenario, a user hits Ctrl+Alt+Del, which causes the windows login screen to appear, which the user uses to log into Windows. Most NAC agents start only after the user logs in to Windows. So, the agent asks for a user name and password immediately after the user types them into the Windows login screen. Single Sign-On helps alleviate this problem.

With Single Sign-On, double logins are a thing of the past. In a Windows Active Directory environment, a PC that's logged into the domain gets a Kerberos ticket as the result of a successful authentication. In some NAC solutions, the agent can take the Kerberos ticket and send it to the policy engine for verification, instead of asking the user for a user name and password again. The Kerberos ticket shows that a user has already submitted his or her credentials correctly. The policy engine then takes the Kerberos ticket and validates against Microsoft Active Directory. If the ticket is valid, the user successfully logs in to the network. The user isn't aware of this validation process — he or she sees only that the agent starts up and successfully logs in.

When you deploy your NAC solution, you probably use a blended solution that's made up of several types of authentication collection because each type serves a particular purpose.

Transporting credentials

Access control solutions communicate credentials between the agent and policy engine, or the endpoint and the policy engine, in some common ways.

If possible, look for an access control solution that leverages open standards for the communication process. (See Chapter 12 for more information on open standards.)

Several possible transports for authentication information exist. The transports discussed in the following sections are the most common.

802.1X

802.1X allows an access control solution to communicate the user credentials at a Layer 2 level before an endpoint is connected to the network. This method offers a benefit because you can authenticate a user before his or her machine is ever connected to your network, and it gets an IP address.

Pop authentication collection quiz

Start thinking about your network access control's user experience early because it can help determine how you want to collect credentials and shape the deployment by dictating the types of authentication that you can leverage.

Ask yourself these questions:

✔ What do you want the login to be like? Do you want it to request credentials many different times?

✔ What's the maximum number of times you want a user to have to provide his or her credentials?

✔ Do you want the login to be interactive, or would you rather the user to be logged in without any interaction?

✔ Do you want to use two-factor authentication for additional security?

✔ Do you want guest-access users to provide credentials?

Answering these questions early in the process helps to identify any possible issues you might encounter. The user experience may seem like a simple detail, but it can make or break your deployment, especially when users can't authenticate correctly or figure out how to log in to the network.

802.1X transport happens across a secure tunnel that policy engine sets up between the endpoint and the policy engine. The standards-based tunnel receives two different manners (as we talk about in Chapter 4 and 802.1X authentication). Here's how the 802.1X works:

1. The user plugs a PC into the network.

2. A switch that's configured for 802.1X asks for credentials at Layer 2.

3. The agent (also known as a supplicant) sends the credentials in an EAPoL (EAP over LAN) frame.

4. The switch takes the EAP payload containing the user credentials and repackages the payload in an EAP over RADIUS packet. The switch then sends the EAP over RADIUS packet to the policy engine.

5. The policy engine pulls the EAP message out of RADIUS to validate the user credentials.

Authentication is made up of several authenticating-data trips back and forth to and from policy engine. The simplest way to think of 802.1X is as a secure tunnel that runs from the endpoint that contains the agent to the policy engine. The switch, or access point in the middle, is a dumb device that passes messages between the endpoint and the policy engine.

One of the biggest benefits of 802.1X is that it gives access control the ability to communicate with a connecting endpoint before that endpoint has an IP address on the network.

The biggest drawback is that you have to have an agent (supplicant) installed on the endpoint for that endpoint to be able to communicate with the policy engine. If the user's machine doesn't have an agent, the user can't pass the credentials to switch or access point.

Secure Sockets Layer (SSL)

SSL is a proven method of transmitting information securely across networks.

When you log in to your bank's ATM machine, your information is transmitted across a secure tunnel and verified.

You can use SSL to transmit credentials in several places, such as

- **Using a Web portal (or hotel-room experience):** Typically done across SSL so that the credentials are protected when they're submitted

- **Communicating user credentials across SSL to the policy engine:** Typically not visible to the user because it happens when the agent is connecting to the network

You most often use SSL for a guest-access scenario that has no agent, so you want to leverage the Web browser as the agent for the endpoint.

The biggest drawback to relying on SSL for transmitting credentials is that the endpoint has to have an IP address on the network before the browser can establish an SSL connection with the policy engine.

Extensible Authentication Protocol (EAP)

EAP is a flexible framework for authentication used most often as an 802.1X-type access control deployment.

You can use EAP to pass credentials from the endpoint to the policy engine in additional ways that we don't cover in this book, but you can find them available from various vendors if you need to implement them.

You can pass credentials between the endpoint and the policy engine in several ways that we don't talk about in this book. Just like any technology, some access control solutions use proprietary protocols to communicate credentials. Use solutions that leverage standards, not proprietary solutions, if you can because you may need to tie your deployment into another solution tomorrow — say, when you merge with another company or office. But, then again, your network needs might be so unique that they require a proprietary solution. Think twice before you act.

Identity validation

Although the policy engine decides whether a user should have access to the network, it doesn't do the validation on its own. The validation is typically a coordinated effort between the policy engine and the authentication server on your network.

After credentials are collected on the endpoint and sent across the network, the policy engine uses those credentials to validate the user against the authentication server.

The policy engine has an important job that dictates whether endpoints can connect to your network, but it doesn't act alone in this process — it has an accomplice. Most of the time, when the policy engine receives the credentials, it validates them against an external authentication source, such as Active Directory, which sends a pass or fail back to the engine. If the credentials are valid, policy engine may also get back group info that it can combine with the policy engine policies to create complex NAC rules (for example, the user is validated, but only to this group and not on weekends or evenings).

Most policy engines can tie back to your existing authentication servers. Some of the existing authentication sources that you can use include

✔ **Lightweight Directory Access Protocol (LDAP):** LDAP gets wide use. It accepts authentication requests and also returns group information when users are classified into different groups:

1. The policy engine receives the credentials and verifies them against LDAP.

2. If the credentials are valid, the policy engine uses the group membership information from LDAP to map users to different access control roles.

✔ **Microsoft Active Directory:** Enterprise networks often use this authentication server because it accepts authentication requests and returns group information. Active Directory has three different interfaces:

• **LDAP:** Allows you to use Active Directory as an LDAP server

• **NTLM:** An authentication protocol by Microsoft

• **Kerberos:** Ticket based authentication system

Most companies have at least Microsoft Active Directory or LDAP already installed in their networks, so Microsoft Active Directory and LDAP are the most popular validation choices for tying access control together.

✔ **Remote Authentication Dial-In User Service (RADIUS):** For user-based authentication. It has only a limited ability to map users to access control policies in the policy engine.

✔ **Kerberos:** Based on a key distribution system, which uses a third-party key server to validate and create secure communication of credentials.

One of the most common uses of Kerberos is authentication of users against Microsoft Active Directory, which implements Kerberos-based Single Sign-On. The policy engine verifies the Kerberos ticket that's collected from the endpoint against the domain controller. Kerberos allows both authentication and group membership lookups.

✔ **Two-factor authentication:** Used to prevent passwords from being compromised. Two-factor authentication requires both

• A password

• A device that has a unique code

The combination of something that you know (the password) and something that you have (the code from the device) allows you to authenticate to the network.

If you use two-factor authentication in your company already, you should be able to leverage that deployment for your access control deployment.

✔ **Certificates:** Allow you to authenticate a device or a user based on certificates that the certificate server has issued. You typically use certificates in conjunction with technologies such as smart cards:

1. The user puts the smart card in his or her device, making the certificate available for authentication.

2. The policy engine checks whether the certificate is valid and not revoked.

3. If the certificate is valid, the policy engine then allows access.

You can do group membership validation in conjunction with something such as LDAP, based on an attribute in the certificate.

Whatever access control solution you evaluate should allow you to use multiple authentication servers. You don't need to build something new to make a NAC solution successful. You should leverage your existing authentication infrastructure for network access control. For example, you may already have authentication servers, and you may need to use more than one type of server.

Authorizing the Workforce

After you authenticate your users and receive a basic yes or no, pass or fail, on their credentials, what do you do? You're ready to authorize the workforce. Although you *did* just authenticate them, authorization allows you to take that information to the next level.

Pop quiz: Authentication

Now it is time to determine what source I can use for user authentication:

✔ What authentication servers are at my disposal?

✔ What portion of my user populous does auth server cover?

✔ Will I be missing any users?

✔ Does a central authentication server, which I can leverage for NAC, tie everything together?

✔ Can I add the extra authentication load to the authentication server?

With authorization added to authentication, you can take the authenticated user name that you receive, as well as the authorized group membership info for that user, and create differentiated access based on user identity.

For example, say that Bob connects to the network and types in his password. The agent sends his credentials to the policy engine, which verifies them against the Active Directory. The Active Directory confirms that his credentials are valid. But, so far, all you know is that the request gave Bob's correct password. Authorization allows you to dig deeper so that you can find out more about Bob.

If only authentication existed, everyone would end up on the same network with the same access because authentication is simply pass/fail. The policy engine requests more information about Bob and gets the group information for Bob. It turns out that Bob is a member of Finance and HR, so when the policy engine knows that he should have access to Finance and HR resources, it opens access accordingly.

The *role mapping* that NAC provides is critical for NAC's success. Role mapping gives you the power to control to what different groups of people have access. You can define the roles simply:

- ✔ Create your access control role in the policy engine.

- ✔ Create a mapping rule that says anyone who maps directly to the Active Directory group Finance receives the access control role Finance.

Your access control solution *must* allow you to differentiate between different user groups. It should also be able to merge access roles together so that when someone such as Bob works in both Finance and HR, he should get access to both finance and HR applications or resources.

Roles and groups with access are the most difficult thing for most network administrators to define because the administrators don't know this type of personnel info. Start mapping out a plan as soon as possible — you may have to involve people who can identify potential users and what those users do.

Chapter 9

Verifying that a PC Is Safe

Most organizations that deploy a NAC policy tend to group the NAC options into two key categories: user identity and machine security posture. This chapter deals with machine security posture, helping you answer the question of which machines you want to allow onto your network. Chapter 8 covers user identity.

The capabilities of NAC products certainly go beyond the questions of user identity and machine posture — many NAC products allow you to create policies based on location, time-of-day, wired versus wireless, and so on. Although these policies might seem more or less important to your deployment, depending on your deployment criteria, you need to determine your policies for these two primary categories first and foremost; therefore, these categories are of key importance.

Industry analysts, journalists, vendors, and enterprises fiercely debate machine integrity because many different schools of thought relate to how much security it adds to a network, and whether organizations should quarantine users or prevent them from accessing network resources as a result of machine integrity. Most organizations now have to simultaneously deal with ever increasing sets of user groups and machine types on the networks. IT departments in every major industry are opening up their networks to employees, partners, contractors, customers, and more. At the same time, these user groups want to access the networks by using machines other than their corporate-managed laptops or desktops — Macintosh and Linux machines are increasingly popular, and Solaris and Unix machines might exist on the network. More users have mobile devices — such as Windows Mobile, Apple iPhones, Symbian phones, and so on — because those users are becoming more mobile, so the importance of managing this barrage of new devices and ensuring that corporate data is safe on them increases over time.

This chapter takes you through some of the key factors to weigh when you're deciding which machines should have access to the network. It also outlines how remediation works and discusses some best practices around remediation and quarantine policies.

All PCs Are Not Created Equal

In recent years, the sheer number of device platforms that you can find in a typical enterprise network has mushroomed; Windows, Macintosh, Linux, Unix, Solaris, Windows Mobile, Apple iPhone, Symbian, RIM BlackBerry, Google Android, and more.

Different groups within the organizations have different reasons for their platform of choice, and nowhere has choice manifested itself more openly than with the enormous popularity of mobile devices. The question you have to ask yourself right now is, "How can I possibly keep our data secure with so many different types of devices on the network?"

Figure 9-1 shows several possible devices that a typical end user might use during the course of the day. Multiply this group of devices by potentially thousands of users, each with his or her own personal machine preference, and you end up with a very large list of devices on the corporate network that require access to e-mail, files, applications, and more.

Without help from a NAC solution, you definitely can't easily classify these different devices and gauge an appropriate security posture. Fortunately, most NAC vendors realize that today's modern organizations require choice and mobility, so product offerings are evolving to support more and more devices. After all, the first step in deciding whether a device can access the network involves determining what type of device it is.

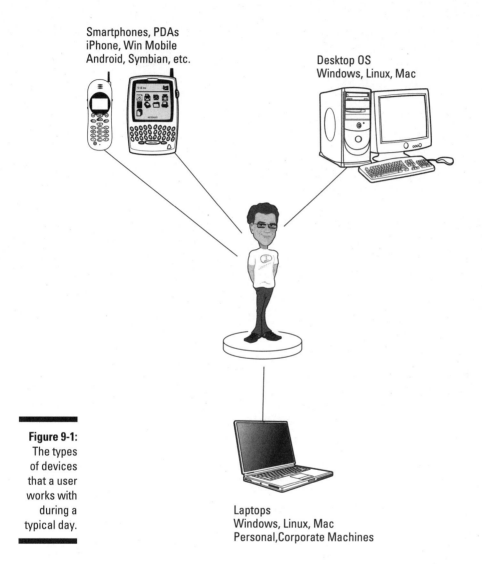

Smartphones, PDAs
iPhone, Win Mobile
Android, Symbian, etc.

Desktop OS
Windows, Linux, Mac

Figure 9-1:
The types
of devices
that a user
works with
during a
typical day.

Laptops
Windows, Linux, Mac
Personal,Corporate Machines

After NAC determines the device type, the question becomes what (if any-thing) the user should be able to access on the corporate network from that device. While the policy you use will vary with your organization's require-ments, here's a list of questions to ask yourself so that you can make this determination:

✔ Who's requesting access from the various types of devices, and what type of data do they need to access? For example, application developers may need to access sensitive databases and source code from Linux machines, which is their primary development platform.

In this case, you may want to allow them on the network so that they can do what your organization pays them to do — write code.

✔ Does your CEO request e-mail access from his or her Apple iPhone?

Although you might allow access based on this person's title, you can require that any data be encrypted on disk or restrict what the CEO can access from this device.

✔ Do salespeople want to access your customer database — which contains Social Security numbers, credit card numbers, and other sensitive information — from their personal laptops, which also double as gaming/hacking devices for their teenage children?

In this case, you probably don't want to provide access at all.

✔ Do you ever wonder when you can consider a device secure?

Different platforms and operating systems (OSs) come with different concerns regarding security. The Microsoft Windows platform, for example, is more likely to be attacked simply because it's the world's most common OS and many hackers go with the numbers. So, is Windows inherently less secure than Macintosh or Linux? Maybe, maybe not (though most seem to think that it is). You might decide to allow access to different types of information depending on the type of machine accessing that information, leading you to a device security policy that relates to which device can access what information. A device that's allowed to access sensitive financial records, for example, might require a more stringent security policy than a guest user's device that only accesses the Internet.

Regardless of how often users scream for device choice, you need to make security paramount before you open the network to any of the myriad mobile gadgets and computers that hit the stores every week. Also, figure out whether users really need to gain network access by using their new smartphones or Macs. Your job is to allow them to be as productive as possible while you maintain data security. Balance accessibility with security:

✔ A policy that goes too far to secure network assets might render important data unusable, leaving users who need access out in the cold, unable to do their jobs.

✔ A security policy that's too lenient might land your company on the front page of the nation's newspapers as the victim of the latest data theft incident.

Which Device Gets the Trust?

NAC vendors have responded to customer needs for endpoint security with a wide range of endpoint scanning functionality. Some solutions use agentless scans to check for known vulnerabilities, and other solutions include downloadable agents that take a more in-depth inventory of machine security. Before analyzing the advantages and tradeoffs between downloadable agents and agentless approaches, first, you need to focus on what you can look for on these machines.

Endpoint security applications

One of the most commonly used types of endpoint security policies are those that verify the presence, operation, and up-to-date nature of third-party endpoint security applications — ranging from personal firewall and antivirus applications to anti-spyware and disk encryption suites. Essentially, these types of policies ensure that endpoints connected to your network have the appropriate self-protection mechanisms in place. Not all NAC solutions are equal in their capabilities. Your NAC solution needs to do more than simply look at a registry setting or search for a file to ensure that the endpoint device has a certain antivirus package installed, for example. Your NAC solution should ensure that the endpoint device has active protection enabled.

Operating system

Operating system scans allow you to verify the operating system (OS), and potentially the service pack, of the incoming endpoint device.

This information can help you to verify which type(s) of additional endpoint security mechanisms you want to put in place. You might have a different endpoint security policy for a Windows XP SP2 device than you might have for a Windows CE or Macintosh OS device. Even within something like the Windows OS, you might have some differentiation — for example, you might have a different corporate standard personal firewall on Windows XP machines versus Windows Vista machines.

Ensure that a machine has appropriate service packs in place. If Microsoft introduces a new service pack for the OS that your company uses as a corporate standard, you may have reasons to not allow machines that have older service packs (or older versions of Windows) onto the network, ranging from security concerns to incompatibility with corporate applications.

Antivirus

Scanning for antivirus applications is one of the most common types of policy implemented for endpoint scanning in NAC environments. Organizations want to ensure that machines connecting to their networks have an appropriate level of protection, and most NAC deployments require the presence of an antivirus application when it comes to verifying endpoint integrity.

NAC can't simply scan the machine to ensure that it has an antivirus application installed — scanning for particular files or registry settings, for example, doesn't necessarily guarantee that the antivirus application is actively protecting the machine itself. Also, NAC may have problems looking at processes running in memory, even if you're verifying an MD5 checksum of the process, because modern antivirus applications may have several processes running at any given time. Without an in-depth knowledge of what each process does, it can be difficult to determine the processes that must be running for normal antivirus operation. Throughout normal operation, some processes might start at different times, making determining whether the AV is running a difficult task.

Most NAC vendors offer a solution that verifies not only that the machine has an antivirus application installed, but also that the application is running and up to date. Some of the available policies on the market include

- ✔ Verifying installation of a particular version or vendor of antivirus solution(s)
- ✔ Verifying that the system has real-time protection actively enabled
- ✔ Verifying that virus signatures are fully up to date or that they've been updated at some point in the recent past, depending on your policy
- ✔ Ensuring that the antivirus application has completed a successful full system scan in the recent past (within a number of days that you choose)

Depending on your organization's security policy, you might want to verify one or more of those attributes related to an antivirus application.

Your verification might vary, based on the user and machine in question. For instance, you might want to conduct a very specific scan when an employee comes onto the network with a company-owned and -managed machine, but when a contractor wants to access the network from an unmanaged machine, you might want to simply verify that the machine has an antivirus installed and running, instead of requiring a specific version or vendor.

Personal firewall

Organizations deploying NAC commonly check to ensure that a personal firewall is installed and enabled as an endpoint security measure. This scan ensures that the endpoint device has active protection enabled.

Make sure that you verify the personal firewall is actually running, not just that it's installed.

Disk encryption

With the number of highly-visible data-loss incidents in the news, disk encryption is becoming more popular by the day. These scans allow you to ensure that the sensitive data on a mobile device's hard disk is secured and encrypted.

Backup software

Scanning for appropriate backup software isn't necessarily a security mechanism, but it can help you verify, for example, that there is properly stored corporate data on a laptop in case the laptop is stolen, lost, or damaged.

Anti-spyware

NAC antispyware policies ensure that the machine has an anti-spyware application running and actively protecting the system, not only installed.

Peer-to-peer applications

Many organizations fear peer-to-peer applications because they can inadvertently download viruses or malware, and because the access could potentially allow an intruder to get into a machine. NAC products are increasingly beginning to scan for these types of applications so that you can verify their presence and, if necessary, shut them down before allowing the user to have full access onto the network.

You can most likely find a much more comprehensive list of policies for the Windows operating systems than you can for any non-Windows OS — including Macintosh, Linux distributions, and mobile platforms. Windows is the most heavily targeted OS and has the most known vulnerabilities. So, you find the largest selection of endpoint protection suites for Windows OSs. While other platforms gain or lose market share, you'll see an expansion or contraction in terms of the number of offerings for these devices. For example, the number of antivirus and personal firewall applications for Windows Mobile and Macintosh machines has increased significantly in recent years, mostly as a result of increased popularity of these systems, which leads to an increased likelihood that hackers will target these machines.

Figure 9-2 depicts a typical policy grid that you might enable on a group of devices in your network — managed devices, for example.

Figure 9-2:
A typical
policy flow
chart grid
that you
might create
on a white-
board.

Component	Policy	Result
Antivirus	Installed	Passed
	Up-to-date	Passed
	Real-time protection enabled	Passed
Personal Firewall	Installed	Passed
	Real-time protection enabled	Passed
Disk Encryption	Installed	Passed
	Active	Passed
OS Patches	Installed	Passed

Operating system and application patches

In today's world, new application and operating system vulnerabilities are discovered on a daily, even hourly, basis. Hackers are increasingly motivated by profit, rather than by fun and glory, so exploitation of these vulnerabilities happens alarmingly fast. As a result, you absolutely must appropriately patch operating systems, middleware, applications, and so on as often as possible.

Virtualization and data center management technologies allow the administrator to easily take machines offline, patch them, and then bring them back online with minimal user disruption.

Outside the data center, however, it's an entirely different ball game because of all the different types of devices on the average corporate network. These devices are often mobile in nature, coming into the corporate network at different times throughout the day. More frighteningly, the devices also connect to other, potentially insecure, networks. These devices might hold intellectual property, customer information, or sensitive financial data, so you need to both

✔ Scan these machines when they come onto the network (to protect the network and network assets).

✔ Ensure, at least on a periodic basis, that NAC can patch the device to protect against known exploits, thereby protecting the data on that machine.

To help solve this problem, many NAC solutions offer a mechanism that checks the endpoint machine for required patches *prior* to allowing it on the network. Because available patches change on a continual basis, NAC servers implementing this type of scan typically include some sort of update mechanism that allows them to stay up to date and dynamically enforce policies that scan for new patches.

For example, Microsoft sticks to a monthly release schedule for their new patches on what they call Patch Tuesday. After Microsoft releases these new patches, most NAC vendors publish new patch scans as soon as possible. The NAC vendor dynamically updates the NAC server, and then NAC enforces those new policies for new sessions or for policy re-evaluations.

But what to scan for? A fully loaded system might have dozens, or even hundreds, of applications available to the user. Do you need to ensure that every single application is fully patched and up to date?

- ✔ Most patches are classified by severity, so you probably don't have to scan every single one.

- ✔ When these patches are released, you might determine that the potential impact of some high-severity vulnerabilities is higher than others, so you want to make sure that all devices have these corresponding patches installed.

  For example, in the retail marketplace, your customer relationship management (CRM) software might have a critical vulnerability that the vendor recently patched. You want to ensure that endpoint systems have this patch installed, but you don't really need to worry about whether your endpoint machines have patched iTunes correctly.

If you go overboard with patch scanning, you might end up causing a bad end-user experience. Scanning for hundreds of patches on dozens of applications might take a long time to complete on an endpoint machine. During that time, the end user has to wait to get onto the network and do his or her job. Use caution — or, at the very least, assess performance implications — when you decide whether to implement scans for a large number of patches.

Machine identity: Who's on first?

Most organizations trust the machines that they own and manage more than foreign devices when it comes to accessing networks. Your organization can control the patch levels, software distribution, and (to some extent) who uses a managed device. As a result, you probably feel more comfortable providing access to sensitive corporate data from these machines.

If you find yourself in this boat, you might be looking for a programmatic way to identify your own machines versus others. You can make this identification easily enough when you can look at the PC and see your corporate asset tracking bar code or other physical identification, but your NAC solution may have problems differentiating between two seemingly identical Windows XP SP2 machines that have nearly the same installed software — only one of which is a corporate-managed laptop.

Over the years, we've seen customers use many different methods to accomplish this identification step, some of which are more secure than others. Because of the native, custom endpoint security scans that many NAC solutions provide, people have come up with these unsecured and easily bypassed tricks:

- **Registry setting identification:** Some administrators hide information in Windows registries to identify corporate assets. This information creates a method of security by obscurity — although end users can easily spoof this secret registry setting, the administrators assume that no one will likely come across this secret and identify it.

- **Secret files:** Similar to the registry setting, this scheme relies on security by obscurity, but instead of hiding information in the registry, the administrator hides a file somewhere in the file system where no one will likely find and delete it. The administrator then uses a custom scan to find this file and identify the machine.

- **MAC address:** This technique involves storing the MAC address(es) of a user's machine in the corporate directory or somewhere accessible by the NAC solution. When the user logs in, the NAC solution extracts the MAC address of the endpoint machine and compares that address to the one stored in the directory. If the addresses match, NAC considers the machine managed.

This approach raises two primary concerns:

- Users can easily copy or spoof MAC addresses (ask anyone who's cloned their machine's MAC address onto their home router to fool their ISP into thinking that they have only one system on their network).

- Most modern machines have multiple adapters, and therefore, multiple MAC addresses — so make sure that you have all these addresses categorized and available, if necessary.

  A machine that comes onto the network via a wired switch port has a different MAC address than that same machine connecting via your 802.11 wireless network.

Get your certificate

To move beyond these less secure options, many companies have begun using a more secure method of device identification — machine (or computer) certificates. If you're looking for a secure way to identify corporate assets, machine certificates might be your best bet.

Machine certificates are standard X.509 digital certificates, similar to what you might find on a Web server or for user identification (such as in a smart card or USB drive). The key distinction between machine certificates and user certificates, however, is that machine certificates are stored in the computer or machine on the endpoint device, and NAC uses them to identify the machine, not the user. So, for example, a Web browser doesn't present these certificates to the user as identification. NAC must have another mechanism in place to extract and validate the certificate.

Machine certificates use private key infrastructure (PKI), which is designed to protect against spoofing, man-in-the-middle type attacks, and other security concerns associated with authenticating a previously unknown third party. But many IT administrators don't feel comfortable with some of the PKI concepts and think that rolling out certificates can be difficult or costly. Vendors have made huge advances in certificate management tools so organizations can easily create, distribute, and manage certificates.

Known vulnerabilities

In many cases, you may not be able to have any type of software presence on a particular machine or device on the network:

- ✔ Some machines, such as printers, for example, can't have software added.
- ✔ Other machines might be outside of your organization's management control and completely locked down, making it impossible for you to install even simple Java or ActiveX dissolvable host-based scanning agents.

For these reasons, some NAC vendors allow remote vulnerability scanning — with no endpoint presence whatsoever. You can use two primary methods for remote vulnerability scanning:

- ✔ Some methods actually look at the PC itself — for example, scanning the Windows registry to determine which patches the device has installed.
- ✔ Other methods, such as Nessus and NMAP, take a more active approach by attempting various exploits against the endpoint device to determine how well it's patched.

Active scanning technologies may cause issues with different types of devices on corporate networks — particularly unmanaged devices, such as badge readers and HVAC systems. Take care when you plan a deployment that involves active scanning to ensure that you aren't inadvertently crashing sensitive network resources as a result of a scan.

Trusted Platform Module and the lying endpoint problem

Any security technology has strong solutions, and then even stronger solutions. Although machine certificates are much more secure than some other possibilities, some security professionals still question whether the machine certificate really is secure. The lying endpoint problem goes beyond just verifying machine certificates because a compromised machine might also, for example, state that it's healthy when it really isn't.

Luckily, most modern laptop and desktop computers are equipped with a special cryptographic processor known as the Trusted Platform Module (TPM). You can use TPMs, which the Trusted Computing Group (www.

trustedcomputinggroup.org) devised and made popular, for many functions — ranging from disk encryption to machine authentication to machine integrity verification. Because the TPM is hardware-based, it doesn't have the same vulnerabilities that might cause harm to an operating system or the applications running on that OS.

You can find a wealth of information on the Trusted Platform Module specification, systems containing TPM chips, and implementation of TPM for a wide range of secure operations online by doing a simple search on Google (www.google.com) or Wikipedia (www.wikipedia.org).

Custom policies

You might find yourself wanting to scan endpoint devices for certain applications, patches, or other types of information that the predefined list of applications provided by your vendor doesn't include. For example, instead of scanning for a known personal firewall, your organization might have implemented its own endpoint security application. Or you may want to scan for some endpoint security application that's available from an outside vendor, but for which your vendor hasn't yet provided a predefined policy. You don't have to stick with predefined parameters.

Many NAC vendors offer you the ability to create your own custom endpoint integrity policies, which allow you to scan for such attributes on a system as

- Presence or absence of certain files on the file system
- Whether a particular process is running on the endpoint

- ✔ The MD5 checksum of that process
- ✔ Particular registry settings

Taken in conjunction, these scans can provide you with

- ✔ A picture of whether a particular application is running on the system
- ✔ Customized information that you might find applicable to access control for your organization, as set forth in the corporate security policy

Third-party verification

Some NAC systems, by using either open standards or proprietary application programming interfaces (APIs), can provide an extensible mechanism that can use scan for additional types of endpoint security software that the native scans provided by the NAC vendor don't cover.

For example, your patch remediation system might have a client-side component that NAC needs to determine its operating system. Through these APIs, even if the NAC product doesn't have the ability to query the patch remediation client natively, NAC can still scan the client and use the results in the access control decision. In Chapter 13, we delve into NAC standards.

Help! My Machine Is Infected!

When endpoint security scans reveal that machines are out of compliance with security policies, you can deal with the issue in several ways:

- ✔ **Device remediation:** Includes any process that's designed to correct the issue on the machine before allowing that machine full network access
- ✔ **Device quarantine:** Describes processes that restrict access to the network — either wholly or partially — for either the duration of the session or until the machine corrects the issue

Most NAC solutions offer some form of remediation, as well as some form of quarantine.

Remediate

Remediation comes in two flavors:

- ✔ **Automatic remediation:** A NAC system's ability to repair or correct issues identified on an endpoint machine without end-user intervention

  Common types of automatic remediation include

  - Enabling a personal firewall

  - Updating an antivirus application

  - Applying operating system or application patches to an endpoint system

  When a NAC system uses these schemes, the system automatically fixes a machine when it's out of compliance, instead of burdening the end user with instructions about how to solve system issues.

- ✔ **Manual remediation:** Puts the task of correcting machine deficiencies in the hands of the end user.

  Although a successful NAC implementation should remove the end user from as much interaction as possible, you sometimes can't avoid it. In these cases, NAC vendors generally provide the tools necessary to make this task an easy one for end users. For example, many NAC tools allow you to customize messages that end users see when they're out of compliance. In addition to system-generated messages, you can use custom messaging to alter the message so that your group of end users can understand it.

Regardless of the remediation type that your NAC solution uses, the typical process involves requesting that the user wait until the NAC/NAC system remediates his or her system before he or she can access the network. In some cases, the user can access the network in quarantine (as discussed in the section "To quarantine or not to quarantine, that is the question," later in this chapter), until either automatic or manual remediation repairs the machine.

After a machine is successfully remediated, it's removed from quarantine, and the user gains full access to the network, according to his or her role restrictions. Keep this remediation time in mind when designing your NAC implementation. You probably don't want to force users to wait for 20 minutes while their antivirus applications perform full system scans of their entire file systems.

You can put issues that can resolve quickly, such as enabling a personal firewall, in the short-wait category. Other issues might call for another strategy — for example, if you want to do an antivirus full-system scan, you might be able to start the full system scan but not wait for the results before allowing the user onto the network.

Figure 9-3 shows a sample manual remediation instructions screen from a leading vendor's implementation.

Figure 9-3:
Sample
remediation
instructions
that a user
might see.

Make mine an automatic

Employ automatic remediation whenever possible because an end user can find the task of repairing or altering a machine complex and challenging. We've seen hundreds of end users who can't even identify the antivirus icon in their Windows System Tray, let alone get through the task of updating virus signatures or enabling real-time protection. For example, many NAC solutions can fix existing antivirus applications, but they can't deliver and install a new AV application if one doesn't already exist on the endpoint machine. So, someone must manually do the installation.

In general, your end users need only to get their jobs done, not know how to interface with complex NAC technologies. You have to ensure that a user's machine is patched and up to date. Fall back on manual remediation only when necessary — such as when a user's machine is an unmanaged, non-compliant device or when automatic remediation provided by your NAC vendor doesn't cover the issue in question.

To quarantine or not to quarantine, that is the question

This Shakespearian dilemma is one of the biggest questions facing IT professionals who want to roll out NAC in their networks, and it could be the single biggest decision you make when planning your implementation.

Security is essential, but not at the expense of user productivity. Implementing the wrong policy can leave your CEO locked out of the network, and you might find yourself locked out of the building.

Luckily, the NAC vendors provide you with options.

If repeated attempts at remediation fail, you need to decide how the inibality to remediate the system should affect the user's access to the network. In the most extreme cases, organizations lock these users out of the network altogether, keeping them from spreading infections, but at the same time potentially keeping them from their normal jobs. Here are your policy options:

- ✔ **Place the device in a temporary quarantine.** You might restrict access while the machine updates itself via a patch management server, for example. After the machine fully patches itself (hopefully after a very brief delay), NAC reevaluates the access control policy and grants the user full access.

- ✔ **Provide access, but in a more restricted fashion.** For example, an employee who accesses network resources from his or her corporate-owned laptop might have full access to e-mail, the intranet, and some sensitive financial data. That same employee coming in by using his or her Windows Mobile smartphone, however, might have access only to e-mail and the intranet, not the financial records.

- ✔ **Implement network security policies based on machine state.** For example, a contractor's machine might be in violation of your policies because it doesn't run an antivirus program. Because you don't own and manage this machine, you might not be able to add software to it. Instead, you might map this contractor to an access control policy that pushes all his or her traffic through an intrusion prevention system (IPS) device or a network-based antivirus scanning engine, which other traffic doesn't have to go through. This flexible type of policy allows workers to be productive without your network losing security.

These examples outline typical quarantine scenarios for different users in your network:

- ✔ **Compliant employee:** Shown in Figure 9-4, the user, who's a member of the Finance group, has passed all the host check policies. In this case, the user gets access to the Internet, as well as to all corporate resources, including the Finance servers.

- ✔ **Non-compliant guest:** Shown in Figure 9-5, the user is a guest on the network and has failed all host checks. This guest can access the Internet but can't access any corporate resources.

- ✔ **Compliant contractor:** Shown in Figure 9-6, the user is a contract employee who uses a machine that has passed all the host check requirements. This user can access the Internet, as well as some corporate resources, but not the Finance resources.

✔ **Non-compliant contractor:** Attempts to access the network, but his or her machine has failed the host checks. In Figure 9-7, the contractor has access only to the Internet and can't access protected corporate resources.

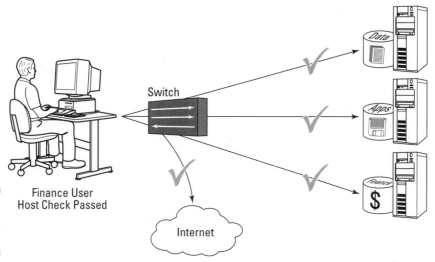

Figure 9-4: Scenario one.

Finance User
Host Check Passed

Switch

Internet

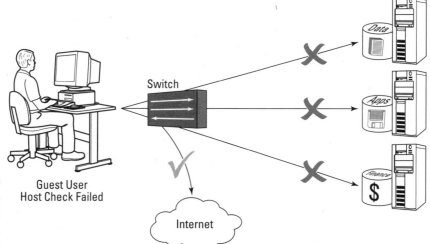

Figure 9-5: Scenario two.

Guest User
Host Check Failed

Switch

Internet

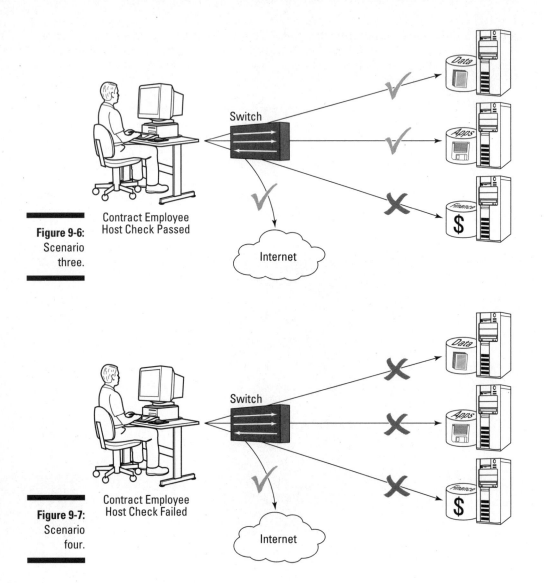

Figure 9-6:
Scenario
three.

Contract Employee
Host Check Passed

Figure 9-7:
Scenario
four.

Contract Employee
Host Check Failed

Get Scanned in Mid-Stream

Whatever your NAC implementation, consider using time-based scans or
event-driven monitoring that your vendor might offer:

- ✔ **Time-based scans:** Run periodically on the endpoint device, generally at
administrator-specified intervals

- ✔ **Event-driven monitoring:** Reports back to the NAC server as soon as it
determines that a machine has come out of compliance

Just because a machine meets the appropriate security requirements when it first joins the network doesn't mean that it necessarily maintains that same security posture throughout the duration of the user's session. Always scan the endpoint both prior to and throughout the session.

Regardless of the mechanism, post-authentication scanning ensures that these machines stay in compliance throughout the session and that users don't game the system — for example, by turning off their personal firewalls as soon as they gain access to the network.

Chapter 10

Deciding Where to Enforce

· ·

In This Chapter

▶ Identifying an enforcement mechanism for your needs

▶ Planning to leverage NAC-based enforcement

· ·

*M*any people start looking at network access control solutions because of NAC's ability to enforce policies on the network.

Enforcement gives network access control teeth. When you create policies, you're outlining rules that you want users and devices on the network to live by. NAC enforcement gives you the ability to create a policy, and then make devices adhere to that policy.

Operating Modes

Operating modes are different ways that the enforcement point can behave when controlling user access. NAC solutions can operate in two modes.

Evaluate only

The evaluate-only mode allows you to examine endpoints, create access policies, and log data without actually changing access to network resources.

You may find this mode useful for several reasons:

✔ **Regulatory compliance:** To meet regulatory compliance requirements, you may want only to log who has access to resources, when they log in, what software they have running on their machine, and so on. You can create an audit trail that meets several of the regulatory compliance stipulations. For example, you can log who had access to the datacenter, including the users' names and IP addresses. With some NAC solutions on the market, you can also log what traffic went to which server in the datacenter. If there's a question about a server or resource being accessed, you can refer back to the log data and identify the user, what machine he or she was using, and so on.

✔ **Learning your network:** See how NAC would change user access to resources without actually changing that access. When you start to deploy NAC, evaluate-only mode can let you figure out which users might have problems getting on the network before you actually break their network access. Using evaluate-only mode lets you locate all the access problems that your NAC configuration may create before you flip the switch and turn it on. This process takes a lot of risk out of initial NAC deployments.

Enforcement

Network access control flexes its muscles when it enforces policy. To use the full potential of NAC solutions, enable policy enforcement. Enforcement allows you to make devices and users adhere to a policy that you create.

For example, you can enforce a policy that controls access to a server in a datacenter. Create a policy that says all users who work in finance have access to the finance server. With this policy in place, enforce on a device in front of the datacenter to allow access to only users who are logged in and members of finance. Then, also log the traffic to create an audit trail of users who access the server. Enforcement lets you know that only finance users have access to the finance server. You can limit the number of people who can access certain data, which drastically reduces the risk of compromise for the data that exists on the network.

When you turn on enforcement, you can go from an open access network to a closed access network, which can greatly increase the security on your network.

Open access network

Some users on a network have open access to resources, such as servers. Users can typically access Active Directory and other resources directly over IP, without anything controlling access. Nothing has to authenticate you if you want to reach the resources. For example, a Web application may feature application authentication, such as a Web page that asks for credentials to log in, but you can reach the Web server without the network authenticating you. A datacenter may have a simple firewall that does some blocking, but access to resources is open and doesn't change.

The benefit to this type of a network is that you can access it relatively simply. A user typically just needs to get an IP address to reach the network's resources. If the user experiences access problems, it can usually troubleshoot those problems really easily. If the user has an IP address, the problems are usually simple, such as routing, switching, or firewall rules. Nothing changes the end-user experience, such as network login screens or required credentials to get an IP address.

An open access network has several problems:

- ✔ **Weak security:** In an open access network, all users typically have access to all resources. In this type of environment, you have to trust applications to protect themselves. If a user has access to a Web server that requires authentication to get access to the content, you have to trust the Web server to block access to anyone who doesn't authenticate correctly. Open access makes that server vulnerable to application attacks. If the Web server has a vulnerability, anyone on the network can exploit it and gain access to the server.

- ✔ **No user-based audit trail:** In most networks today, a firewall in front of an application has some sort of logging enabled, but if an attack happens, locating the offending user or machine is very difficult. DHCP makes this problem even greater. Because users get different IP addresses every time they plug into the network, you can find it hard to correlate an IP to a user or machine.

- ✔ **Static configuration:** Configuration in an open access network doesn't change when the networks and devices change. A lot of companies tried to deploy departmental firewalls to protect the datacenter access network problem. A departmental firewall would sit between resources, users, or business areas. These firewalls worked on the idea that if you create policies, you can limit what information or access can flow between the areas.

You most likely have departmental firewalls in your network already. If you do, make a list of where they're located. Determine whether the firewall policies are doing anything productive. After you look at the policies, ask yourself what you'd change. Do you want to control access to resources behind a particular firewall? If you do, you may want to add that firewall's location to your list of places whose network access control you want to evaluate.

Closed access network

Network access control allows you to create a closed access network. A *closed access network* is a network that blocks anyone from accessing anything by default. To get access to a resource, an administrator has to explicitly allow or create that access.

To illustrate the difference between open access and closed access, consider a grocery store and a military base. At the grocery store, anyone can go through the open door. At a military base, you have to show identification, and then the person at the gate decides whether you have permission to enter the base. If you receive access to the base, the gate person then tells you where you do and don't have permission to go.

A closed access network has several advantages:

- ✔ **Security:** When you have closed access, you can create a network that opens up access to resources under conditions that you control. In other words, you control what users can and can't see on the network.

  You may want to create a network that allows access to a finance server only after the user provides credentials proving that he or she works in finance. You can also create rules to further protect the finance server. You can add a policy that says the user has access only when he or she has an up-to-date antivirus client on his or her machine, which further protects the finance server. You can then sleep at night knowing that only finance users that have updated antivirus have access to the finance data — nobody else. You can then layer on traffic logging to create an audit trail so that if there's a data access violation, you can identify which finance user to talk to.

- ✔ **Risk mitigation:** With a closed access network, you can select what machines you want on your network. You can create rules that place potentially risky machines in one restricted, or quarantine, network. The machines that you decide are safe can get access to the corporate network. This quarantine process reduces your risk greatly because you separate your risky machines from the rest of the machines. Think of this security access method like preschool. If you know that one of the kids has lice, you don't want to put him or her with the other kids — you want to separate him or her, and get rid of the lice. When the lice are gone, he or she can then go play with the other kids.

A closed access network adds a lot of complexity to your network. Troubleshooting problems becomes difficult when you increase the complexity of your network. Simple problems, such as a user not getting an IP address, can suddenly become a lot more difficult. You now have to start looking at other causes for the problem. For example, do the users have valid credentials? Is the software that runs on the machine up to date? Is the endpoint agent on the device configured correctly?

In a closed access network, a user typically has to authenticate before he or she can access resources. Depending on the configuration, this authentication can make the user experience more cumbersome. In other words, if a user has to provide his or her credentials again before he or she can get on the network, you're adding one more step before a user can be productive. You need to reach a delicate balance between open access and closed access.

Decision making

If you're thinking about using NAC, you've likely decided that you want a closed access type of network. You need to decide how closed a network you want to create. By moving to a closed access network, you can create a network that's so closed it diminishes user productivity. You need to be very careful when you start taking away user access. You can actually go too far and make the network so restrictive that users can't get their day-to-day work done. NAC gives you great power. And as the saying goes, with great power comes great responsibility.

The log data that network access control gives you can usually help you meet certain regulatory requirement stipulations. If your organization has to follow important regulations, make sure that you add logging to your product evaluation plans. Logging for auditing purposes has the most value when an enforcement point can actually enforce it. If you use source IP-based logging or enforcement, that enforcement isn't 100-percent reliable. Malicious attacks, such as IP spoofing, can render this data inaccurate. If you need completely reliable logging and enforcement information in case of outside inquiry or investigation, you need to leverage an enforcement technology such as IPSec enforcement.

Make a list of the types of enforcement devices that you have in your network. You can most easily make this list if you have a network diagram of your network handy. While you go through the different enforcement mechanisms that your network has, check whether you can use any of them for NAC enforcement. After you identify all the places where you can enable enforcement, you can go through the pros and cons of each type of enforcement to figure out which enforcement makes sense for your network.

Not all enforcement mechanisms are equal. Each type of enforcement has a different function in network access control. You probably want to use a combination of at least two types of enforcement.

Technologies that NAC most commonly uses for enforcement are

- Inline enforcement
- Firewall enforcement
- IPSec enforcement
- Host-based enforcement
- 802.1X enforcement
- SNMP-based enforcement
- ARP-based enforcement

When you review a NAC solution, ask the vendor what technologies they leverage for enforcement. This information can help you narrow down which solution makes sense for your network.

Endpoint/Software Enforcement

Endpoint enforcement involves software on a connecting client that enforces policies. This kind of enforcement is similar to putting firewall software on an endpoint. In the firewall software, you can control with what the endpoint can communicate by using source IP, destination IP, ports, and protocol type of a nomenclature. That type of functionality is the most basic of endpoint enforcement. In the case of NAC, the policy engine controls the policies, instead of statically configuring those policies on the endpoint.

You can use endpoint enforcement for not only network enforcement, but also endless types of policies (including which software can be run).

Never use endpoint enforcement on its own in a NAC deployment. Because of the nature of an endpoint, if it's compromised and contains malicious code, you can't trust the software on the endpoint to do its job. In other words, if you're using endpoint enforcement to control what server or IPs the endpoint can reach, you put all your eggs in one basket. If the endpoint is compromised, malicious users can circumvent the software to reach the network. Always use endpoint enforcement in conjunction with another form of enforcement, such as 802.1X- or firewall-based enforcement. This extra enforcement adds an external check and balance so that if the endpoint becomes compromised, the firewall, in all likelihood, won't be compromised at the same time. Also, when the user terminates the endpoint agent, the endpoint may not have any endpoint enforcement in that state.

NAC can use two distinct types of endpoint or software enforcement: host-based and server-based.

Host-based

NAC host-based enforcement is a software-based approach that has its functionality bundled in the endpoint agent.

The functionality available in host-based enforcement differs greatly from vendor to vendor.

Network policy enforcement

Network policy enforcement is the most common of the policies that administrators use in conjunction with NAC. Network policy enforcement dictates with what the endpoint can communicate on the network, usually based on the five-tuple concept:

- ✔ Source IP
- ✔ Source port
- ✔ Destination IP
- ✔ Destination port
- ✔ Protocol

The simplest example is a policy that says a user can't reach the exchange server if he or she doesn't have an up-to-date antivirus program installed and running. The endpoint agent blocks any traffic that tries to reach that server by filtering packets on the network interface of the endpoint.

Don't use host-based enforcement as your only form of enforcement. If the machine is compromised, you could have malicious software on that machine that may be able to bypass the agent on the endpoint. This is not such a big deal if there is a network based enforcement point also enforcing the policy; it will still block the traffic.

Software or application enforcement

One of the biggest benefits of having an agent on the endpoint is that the agent can control what software the endpoint runs. By using NAC, you can create policies that prevent a user from running instant messaging software on the endpoint. The endpoint agent can't monitor whether the user attempts to run the instant messaging software, and it can't block the software or terminate the application. Therefore, you have the power to actually control what applications run on an endpoint that's connected to your network.

Virtual environments

A *virtual environment* is a temporary workspace on top of the existing desktop. A virtual environment protects the user, and his or her data, when he or she connects to the network.

Virtual environments are the least popular type of enforcement technology.

Server-based

Server-based enforcement deals with policies on an agent that's running on a server. This agent controls which users have access to a particular application or the server itself.

If possible, take server enforcement off of the server because enforcement can add additional strain or load to the server. But keep application authentication on the server for NAC because of audit trails. In some cases, you can tie your network access control into your application authentication infrastructure, which can allow your applications on the server to have Single Sign-On (SSO) functionality.

Inline Appliances

Inline appliances can add NAC functionality to your network. You can transparently layer these appliances on top of the existing network infrastructure, so you can very easily roll out NAC. When you add inline appliances you don't have to re-architect your network just to add NAC.

Inline appliances allow you to differentiate between different users and devices on the network, and enforce different policies for each user and device.

This example explains

All users are connected to the corporate network and receive an IP address in the same Layer 3 network. They all get addresses from DHCP and can see the datacenter. You need a way to differentiate between the different users in the same network — which is what an inline appliance enables you to do.

Inline appliances allow you to enforce different policies for different users who are in the same network. But the appliance needs to sit inline in the traffic flow between the user and the appliance (or resource) to which you want to control access. You typically place an inline appliance in front of a datacenter or server location.

You can use two main types of inline devices: A firewall or hardware-based enforcement device, and a NAC appliance.

Firewalls

A *firewall* is a hardware appliance that's designed to enforce network policies at high speed. This appliance sounds like a perfect device to use for NAC, doesn't it?

In the past, you'd use static policy based on the five-tuple policy (source IP, source port, destination IP, destination port, and protocol). By using network access control, you can make the policies *dynamic,* meaning that the policies change based on the users or devices connecting to the network. To add this type of intelligence, NAC extends the basic concept of a firewall policy. A firewall that supports doesn't just statically control network policy anymore. It now uses policy based on such data as network information, user identity, and endpoint state.

In this example, corporate users need access to a Web server in a datacenter. A firewall in front of the datacenter protects the Web server (which has the IP address 192.168.1.100).

✔ **Old firewall policy:** This is what the existing firewall rule for this Web server looks like:

   • **Source IP:** Any

   • **Source port:** Any

   • **Destination IP:** 192.168.1.100

   • **Destination port:** HTTP

   • **Action:** Allow

✔ **NAC firewall policy:** If NAC leverages the firewall as a part of your NAC infrastructure, you can

   • **User:** Valid Corp user authenticated against LDAP

   • **Endpoint:** Up-to-date AV, latest OS patches

   • **Source IP:** Received from the authenticated user

   • **Source port:** Any

   • **Destination IP:** 192.168.1.100

   • **Destination port:** HTTP

   • **Action:** Allow

The NAC policy can dynamically change based on user and endpoint information. The policy enforcement now ties directly to the IP address of the user who connects to the network, instead of providing general enforcement for everybody who connects. The NAC policy also opens access after the user provides valid credentials and authenticates to the network. The policy is also valid only if the software on the endpoint is valid and up to date. In the preceding example, you take a lot of the risk away from the Web server. You create a rule that allows only valid users who have compliant machines to have access to the server.

Firewall-based enforcement brings Layer 3 access control power to the table for NAC. Hardware-based firewalls are designed to enforce policies at high data rates, which you need for enforcement in front of network areas, such as data-centers, to which all your users need access.

NAC appliances

NAC appliances are NAC-solution devices that are designed to enforce poli-cies in the network. NAC appliances fall into two main categories — software-based appliances, and hardware- or application-specific integrated circuit (ASIC)-based appliances.

The performance of these appliances differs greatly when it comes to enforc-ing NAC policies in the network. This difference comes from the design of these devices.

Software appliances

Many vendors offer software appliances in the NAC space. These appliances can come in multiple forms. You can purchase software that the network administra-tor installs on x86 hardware to make a network enforcement point for NAC, or an appliance can come with software pre-installed to make that appliance a NAC enforcement point.

You need to consider several factors when you're evaluating NAC appliances that you plan to use as inline enforcing policies:

 ✔ **NAC Software:** Software-based NAC appliances are usually based on Linux with some customer software on them. These appliances can usually sit inline in front of a datacenter or resource that you want to protect or control access to. They typically use two network interfaces — one in and one out. The NAC appliance then does network filtering between the two interfaces.

  • **Pro:** Because the NAC appliance sees all the traffic, it can figure out a lot about a particular user by dissecting the packets. It gives you great flexibility because you can filter or block the traffic any way that you want.

  • **Con:** You now have another machine to maintain on your network. And this machine sits inline with all your network traffic.

> ✔ **Traffic limitations:** Only so much traffic can pass through an x86 machine. Discuss it with your vendor to make sure that an inline NAC appliance can scale to your datacenter's data rate.

Consider what happens when the NAC appliance locks, freezes, and needs upgrades so that when you're deploying it, you have plans to deal with all these contingencies.

Hardware appliances

Hardware appliances are devices built specifically for the special requirements of network-based enforcement. These appliances usually include ASICs, special network-based hardware that enables the appliances to process and enforce network policies with higher performance than a software-based appliance.

The functionality is usually very similar, but you can position a hardware NAC appliance in a network location that has a higher traffic volume.

Network Infrastructure

The network switch infrastructure allows you to closely control access to the network.

When you want to control users and devices that get on the network, the closer you position the policies to the user, the more control you can have. In the case of network infrastructure, you can directly control whether the user can even get on the network, as well as what network he or she can access.

In an effort to make the network as secure as possible, move to a closed access network. The more closed, the better. By using NAC, you can control the actual ports on switches, which means that you no longer need a network drop that's open to the network, available for anyone to plug into. For example, say that a stranger walks into your building and sits down at a network computer that has an open network drop. What would he or she be able to access? If you have NAC, you don't have to worry about that scenario because you know that the NAC solution controls what he or she can see.

It can control and enforce policy in your network infrastructure in several different ways. Virtual local area networks (VLANs) often segregate traffic and users. We take a deeper look at VLANs in the following section.

Two main technologies control the actual switch port:

> ✔ 802.1X
> ✔ SNMP

VLANs

In your typical Layer 2 switched environment, all user traffic happens on the same network. So, both compliant users and out-of-compliance machines use the same network.

Over the last several years, you may have noticed some trends in the security and resilience of networks. While vulnerabilities increase, they directly affect the resilience of networks. Simply said, while more malicious applications (such as worms, viruses, and spyware) have emerged, networks have experienced more downtime.

NAC has the goal of minimizing potential problems. For example, take viruses. If you know that a machine poses a potential virus risk, you don't want to put that machine on the network, where it can affect other machines and potentially put your network at risk. VLANs let you separate the two types of machines — compliant and non-compliant.

VLANs segment switches into multiple Layer 3 or IP networks. In a typical unmanaged switch that has no VLANs, the entire switch is one broadcast domain. When a broadcast happens, it's forwarded across all ports on the switch. VLANs allow you to segment ports virtually into multiple broadcast domains or virtual networks. If you have a 24-port switch, you can configure ports 1 through 12 as VLAN 1 and ports 13 through 24 as VLAN 2. This configuration, in essence, creates two networks on the switch. All devices in ports 1 through 12 see only each other. Devices in ports 13 through 24 see only their own broadcast traffic. You create two different IP networks, one on each VLAN:

- ✔ **Original unmanaged switch:** An unmanaged switch that has no VLANs behaves like this:

  - **VLANs:** None

  - **Ports membership:** Ports 1 through 24 (the default network)

  - **Layer 3 IP network:** 192.168.1.100

  - **Broadcast network:** The default network (ports 1–24)

  - **Switch configuration:** One IP network, one broadcast domain

  An unmanaged switch is the most basic of all switching configurations. It includes one network and one broadcast domain. Every device on every port has the ability to communicate with every other device on the switch. Broadcasts pass over the entire switch.

✔ **Managed switch with static VLANs:** A managed switch that has static VLANs behaves like this:

- **VLANs:** Two (VLAN 1 — Corp, VLAN 2 — Finance)
- **VLAN 1 ports membership:** Ports 1 through 12
- **VLAN 2 ports membership:** Ports 13 through 24
- **VLAN 1 Layer 3 IP network:** 192.168.0.0/24
- **VLAN 2 Layer 3 IP network:** 172.16.0.0/24
- **VLAN 1 broadcast network:** Corp network (ports 1–12)
- **VLAN 2 broadcast network:** Finance network (ports 13–24)
- **Switch configuration:** Two IP networks, two broadcast domains

This switch configuration behaves like two different physical switches, even though you really just virtually separate one physical switch. You can use this configuration to manually and statically segregate different ports into different networks.

✔ **Managed switch with VLANs that dynamically uses it for NAC:** A managed switch with VLANs behaves like this if the switch dynamically uses it for network access control:

- **VLANs:** Three (VLAN 1 — Corp, VLAN 2 — Quarantine, VLAN 3 — Guest)
- **Ports membership:** Ports 1 through 24 (VLAN 3 — Guest)
- **VLAN 1 Layer 3 IP network:** 192.168.0.0/24
- **VLAN 2 Layer 3 IP network:** 172.16.0.0/24
- **VLAN 3 Layer 3 IP network:** 10.0.0.0/24
- **VLAN 1 broadcast network:** Corp network (no ports)
- **VLAN 2 broadcast network:** Quarantine network (no ports)
- **VLAN 3 broadcast network:** Guest network (ports 1–24)
- **Switch configuration:** Three IP networks, three broadcast domains (the Corp network and Quarantine network are closed by default)

You can use VLAN tagging to share VLANs across multiple switches:

1. **Configure your switch network so that VLANs span multiple switches.**

   You accomplish this configuration by using VLAN tagging.

2. **If you have an uplink interface that connects your access layer switch to your distribution layer switch, enable VLAN tagging on the uplink interface.**

3. **Select which VLANs' traffic you want to add as tagged traffic on the port.**

You can choose from several standards when you configure VLANs. The most common standard used in enterprise networks is the IEEE standard 802.1Q. 802.1Q is an open standard that defines how it tags traffic with VLAN identifiers so that when that traffic passes between switches, it transfers the VLAN information.

Ports configured for normal access that have a VLAN configured for them are called *untagged ports*. These ports send out packets to the host that doesn't have an association with the VLAN, but the ports are configured as members of the VLAN to which the network assigns them. When the network dynamically uses NAC with managed VLAN switches, like in the list earlier in this section, the network statically configures the ports for VLAN 3 (the Guest VLAN). All devices that connect to that port join the Guest VLAN by default. By using NAC, you can also dynamically change which VLAN assigns to a particular port, in essence, moving the endpoint that's connecting to the network between different networks (in the form of VLANs).

The network can use two main methods of dynamically changing the port VLAN membership: 802.1X and SNMP.

802.1X

802.1X is a standard that provides port-based authentication for switches and access points. You need several components to make 802.1X work (as shown in Figure 10-1):

 ✔ Supplicant (endpoint agent)
 ✔ Authenticator (switch or access point)
 ✔ Authentication server (RADIUS server)

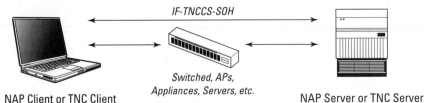

Figure 10-1: The components of 802.1X.

IF-TNCCS-SOH

NAP Client or TNC Client

Switched, APs, Appliances, Servers, etc.

NAP Server or TNC Server

Supplicant

The supplicant is generally a part of the endpoint agent. The supplicant communicates authentication information and, in some cases, endpoint integrity information across a network at Layer 2 to authenticate the user, all before the endpoint even has an IP address. This transport is called Extensible Authentication Protocol over LAN (EAPoL). This adds to NAC because you can pass authentication and endpoint integrity information across a Layer 2-only network before the endpoint receives an IP address.

A supplicant makes the most sense for managed corporate machine access to the network. In some situations, you may be able to leverage other supplicants, such as supplicants built into the operating system. Look for a NAC solution that allows you the flexibility of doing both.

Authenticator

The *authenticator* is the switch or access point that you leverage for 802.1X. The authenticator is a dumb device in the 802.1X world of authentication — put very simply, the switch (authenticator) needs only to collect authentication information sent from the endpoint (EAPoL data), and then send that information to the authentication server over RADIUS. It collects the Layer 2 EAPoL auth data, takes the EAP payload out, and puts it in Layer 3 IP RADIUS transaction (EAPoRADIUS). The authenticator acts as a go-between, moving EAP between the Layer 2 transaction and the Layer 3 IP transaction. The traffic across this 802.1X authentication transaction is encrypted and not in the clear.

The authenticator also has to satisfy several other jobs:

- When a client connects to the network, it sends an authentication request to the authenticator so that it can start the 802.1X auth process.
- If the endpoint authenticates successfully, the authenticator needs to open up access for that endpoint.
- If the endpoint doesn't have a supplicant, the authenticator doesn't get a response to the start of 802.1X, so it needs to time the port and perform an action. It might perform an action as simple as continuing to block the endpoint, or it may move the port to an unauthenticated VLAN.

The switch can open up access for an endpoint by performing one of several actions. When you use 802.1X, the port is closed (unauthenticated) if it doesn't have an endpoint connected to it. When an endpoint plugs into the port and authentication happens, the system can take many possible actions. In the simplest form, it can change the port from *closed* (blocking and unauthenticated) to *open* (forwarding and authenticated). In this case, the switch just starts forwarding traffic to whatever VLAN the system has statically configured the port.

IETF Request for Comment (RFC) 3580 allows the switch to also consume a set of RADIUS attributes that contain actions the system can perform on the switch port. The most common of these actions is to return a VLAN number to the switch. With this functionality, the switch can open the port and then change the VLAN to which the system is connected. This feature gives you the most control over network segmentation and access control when the system uses 802.1X.

A switch that supports VLANs, 802.1X, and RFC 3580 combine to create a powerful tool for switch-based enforcement. Find out whether your switches support these protocols. If they do (and most switches do), you can use them as a part of your NAC solution. If you already own them, you don't even have to buy them and can use them as enforcement points!

Authentication server

The authentication server is the brains behind the whole 802.1X operation. An 802.1X authentication uses a RADIUS server as the authentication server. In most NAC solutions, RADIUS service is built into the policy engine, and you need to configure this RADIUS server on the switch. To configure your switch to use this server, you usually need the IP address of the authentication server and a shared key that you use as a part of the authentication process.

MAC authentication

Not every endpoint or device that connects to your switched network can run a supplicant and authenticate over 802.1X. These endpoints need to use MAC address-based authentication.

Switch dependence

MAC address authentication is a switch-dependent feature. When a device connects to the network, the switch asks it for credentials by using a Layer 2 802.1X request. If the device doesn't have a supplicant, it doesn't respond to the authentication request. The switch then waits, based on a configured timeout value. It then takes the MAC address provided by the device that's trying to connect and sends that address to the RADIUS server as the user name and password in an attempt to authenticate the device. If the RADIUS server has the MAC address in its database, it can pass the authentication and return an accept to the switch, which then opens up access. It can also return any RFC 3580-based attributes at the same time, in the same way that it can for a regular 802.1X transaction.

The difference between MAC-based authentication and 802.1X authentication is that the switch acts as both the supplicant and the authenticator in a MAC-based authentication. You can use this functionality with any unmanaged devices, such as printers, fax machines, badge readers, and any other device that can't run an agent or supplicant.

Unauthenticated VLANs

You can use unauthenticated, or guest, VLANs when using 802.1X. If a device doesn't have an agent or supplicant, you may choose to connect that device to the network and then provide a capture portal or Web page for authentication by using an unauthenticated VLAN. This feature, which depends heavily on a switch, is unfortunately called a different name by each switch vendor.

When a device plugs into the network, the switch asks for the endpoint to authenticate over Layer 2. The device doesn't respond, either because it doesn't have a supplicant or the supplicant isn't correctly configured. The switch then automatically opens up the switch port in an unauthenticated VLAN after a configured period of time. After an endpoint gains access to this network, it can authenticate to a Web portal or even have the supplicant installed.

SNMP and CLI

SNMP (Simple Network Management Protocol)- or CLI (command line interface)-based control of the switch is an option. Instead of using an open standard for control of the switch, several vendors have cobbled together control mechanisms for switches that are based on management technologies.

In this scenario, the switch is configured in the SNMP control-based policy engine, with the policy engine as a SNMP trap server. When an endpoint connects to the network, the switch sends a SNMP trap to the policy engine that says the port on the switch came up. The policy engine connects back to the switch to get the MAC address of the device connecting to the switch. If the policy engine determines that the device should have access to it allows the device to have access, the policy engine then does a SNMP write or runs a CLI command on the switch to change the configuration of the port, usually changing the VLAN configuration. The policy engine changes the static configuration of the switch, and the device can now get access to the new VLAN.

SNMP and CLI NAC approach has some downsides:

- **Inconsistency:** SNMP or CLI is based on changing static switch configuration, and it lacks the security-based approach of 802.1X. Because of the static configuration, the actual switch configuration and what the policy engine thinks the switch configuration can be vastly different. This can allow open or mis-configured ports to bypass the security of your NAC solution. Because policy engines also modifies configuration on the switch all the time, you can't enable switch configuration change control on your network. A lot of inconsistency can show up down the road. You think your network is configured one way, but it's actually running a whole different way.

- **Dependency:** CLI and SNMP device control depends very highly on the device or switch involved. Different versions of software on the switch can make or break SNMP- or CLI-based control of the device. Version monitoring becomes very important in these types of NAC solutions.

Other Enforcement

You can leverage protocols and standards for NAC enforcement in new or unique ways.

DHCP

The Dynamic Host Configuration Protocol (DHCP) is the method that most enterprises use to assign IP addresses to endpoints that connect the network. When a host or endpoint connects to the network, the endpoint sends out a Layer 2 broadcast (called a *DHCP request*) that asks for an IP address. The DHCP server on the network then responds to the request with an IP address from its database for the endpoint to use so that it can connect to the network.

DHCP makes assigning IP addresses dynamic and prone to change. An endpoint may get a different IP address each time it connects to the network, which makes audit trails for traffic difficult to follow. Without DHCP in the network, all endpoint machines would need statically configured networking, which would create a deployment and management nightmare. This process doesn't scale for large environments.

Certain NAC vendors can use DHCP to control network access for endpoints:

1. When an endpoint connects to the network, it requests an IP address.

2. The NAC solution, rather than the DHCP server, responds to the DHCP request.

3. If the endpoint doesn't meet the corporate security policy or the user isn't authenticated yet, the NAC DHCP server sends a quarantine IP address back to the endpoint.

This quarantine IP address differs from the normal IP addresses that corporate machines receive. DHCP enforcement separates user traffic by using a different IP address range on top of the same Layer 2 network. So, if two different machines — the first a regular corporate user and the second a quarantined user — reside on the same network, they can't communicate with each other over IP. Their different IP addresses don't route between each other, so DHCP separates them at Layer 3, even though they're on the same Layer 2 network.

The biggest drawback to DHCP enforcement is that it's security by obscurity. It doesn't really separate users, and it can circumvent it easily. For example, say that two users are coworkers, and one is quarantined but the other isn't. The quarantined worker can't reach the network properly, so he calls over the cubicle wall to his coworker and asks her for her IP address. The quarantined worker sees that his IP address is different than his coworker's, so he decides to change his IP address to something similar to his coworker's. When the worker changes his IP address, he bypasses the DHCP enforcement and can get on the network.

DHCP enforcement can easily separate users, but it's not the most secure solution, so use it cautiously.

IPSec

When data integrity is critical, IPSec comes to the rescue. Some NAC solutions offer IPSec as a form of enforcement. *IPSec* is a collection of protocols designed to secure IP-based traffic by adding authentication and encryption for each packet that's sent across the network.

IPSec is well suited to handle several types of use cases, including protecting traffic going to business-critical applications or servers. For example, when users gain access to critical financial data on a finance server, IPSec can add encryption to the users' traffic so that the data stays private. To make this encryption work, two parts are required:

✓ **The IPSec client:** The client is usually a part of the NAC endpoint agent.

✓ **The IPSec termination point:** This point can be an IPSec concentrator or a device such as a firewall.

The policy engine dynamically provisions IPSec policies to the endpoint client and the termination point so that when a user tries to access the resource, the traffic triggers the IPSec tunnel, which encapsulates and encrypts that traffic.

Encryption provides data privacy for user traffic, which you may find useful if you're concerned about the privacy of information traveling across the corporate network. In a way, IPSec adds an authenticated transport across the network. IPSec enforcement can typically run in two different modes:

- ✓ **Encapsulation only:** You can use this mode when you're concerned about man-in-the-middle types of spoofing attacks on the network. By leveraging IPSec, you can ensure that the traffic is genuine. The endpoint brings up the IPSec tunnel in a null encrypted mode, which allows the traffic to be in the clear but still encapsulated in IPSec so that agent can still sign it to guarantee authenticity. If you have intrusion detection systems on your network, you can usually inspect this traffic because it's still in the clear. Null encryption or encapsulation only adds a tamper-resistant seal to the data.

- ✓ **Encrypted:** If you're concerned about the privacy of your data, you can add data encryption on top of data encapsulation. Administrators leverage encrypted IPSec in most types of implementations.

    You may also find encryption very useful when an endpoint connects across potentially risky parts of the network, including any location where guests or contractors connect and you want to access secure information.

If you're considering leveraging IPSec enforcement, you need to decide what you're more interested in:

- ✓ Protecting against spoofing attacks on the network
- ✓ Adding data privacy to protect against network-based sniffing

In most NAC solutions, you can leverage either configuration, depending on which makes sense for a particular situation. These configurations usually don't operate in an all-or-nothing way, and you can turn them on or off as necessary, or configure them however you want.

ARP

Address Resolution Protocol (ARP) is the foundation of network communication. Network devices use ARP to create bindings between the Layer 2 address (the MAC address) and the Layer 3 address (the IP address) of machines that attempt to communicate on the network.

Pop enforcement quiz

Start thinking about your NAC solution's enforcement potential in your network.

Start asking yourself these kinds of questions:

✔ How close to the user do you want to enforce policies?

✔ Do you consider any resource on your network mission-critical?

✔ Do you want to segregate users from each other?

✔ Are you willing to replace network infrastructure?

✔ Can you logically plan enforcement phases? Where should you start (for

example, would enforcing user access to the datacenter be most important)?

Answering these questions can help you narrow down what you want from an enforcement technology, which can dictate how much you're willing to pay for your NAC solution. In other words, what can you leverage in your current network without spending additional money, and what do you need to add or replace in your network to enable NAC? Remember, the cost of your NAC solution includes not only the capital investment of purchasing equipment, it can also include costs associated with reconfiguring existing infrastructure to enable NAC.

A network has two devices. Device 1 wants to communicate with Device 2, but it hasn't communicated with that device before. Device 1 sends a broadcast message — the *ARP message* — out over the network asking for the MAC address of Device 2's IP. Device 2 responds, and it creates an entry on both devices that features a table of IP-to-MAC address correlations, called the *ARP cache.* The two devices now have the basic network information that allows them to communicate.

ARP-based enforcement involves the manipulation or modification of the ARP cache on devices on the network. A NAC solution that uses the ARP table as a method of enforcement sends ARP messages on to the network that changes the IP-to-MAC address binding tables on devices. For ARP enforcement to work correctly, NAC must modify the ARP tables on all devices. If the ARP table of a device includes any static ARP entries that NAC can't modify, communication with another device whose ARP table does change therefore breaks.

You can use ARP-based enforcement to

✔ Break or block communication.

✔ Trick devices' traffic so that it goes forward to a captive portal or Web page, where it can log into the network.

ARP cache manipulation can cause networking problems for some devices on the network. If you want to use ARP cache manipulation as an enforcement mechanism, make sure that you thoroughly test it before you deploy it in your network.

Pop quiz: Sizing enforcement

While you consider enforcement, think about what size and scale you'll need to make the NAC solution work for your deployment.

Decide where you plan to enforce:

✔ **At a datacenter:** How many users will need to get access to the datacenter and resources? What throughput will you likely see for users accessing the datacenter?

✔ **At the access layer:** How many switches do you want to enforce access on?

How many concurrent users do you plan on having? How many are managed users, guests, unmanaged devices, contractors, and so on?

Chapter 11

Flipping the Switch

*Y*ou need a properly planned and executed deployment to have a successful access control implementation. No matter how well you determine the
appropriate policies for your organizational needs, and regardless of whether
you partner with the best possible vendor, a poor rollout upsets your end
users, harms productivity, and leaves wagging fingers pointed at you.

In this chapter, we explore how to plan for a successful NAC deployment. We
take you through proof-of-concept testing, piloting, and initial rollouts that
focus on evaluation rather than enforcement — these NAC deployment steps
give you a sense for what will happen when you fully implement NAC and
control who can get on your network.

Gearing Up for the Deployment

Follow several incremental steps to appropriately ensure that the chosen
vendor's solution meets your needs and that the full rollout will go smoothly.
In our experience, most organizations follow a typical four-point deployment,
as shown in Figure 11-1:

1. Proof-of-concept test

2. Pilot implementation

3. Larger scale rollout focusing on evaluating policies, rather than enforcing them

4. Full deployment of the NAC program

Figure 11-1:
Steps to a
successful
NAC imple-
mentation.

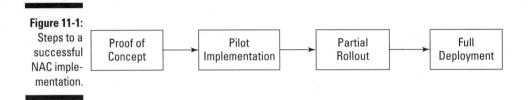

Figure 11-1:
Steps to a
successful
NAC imple-
mentation.

Your company may use a slightly different phased deployment, but understanding what goes on in each phase can help you form your own plan, even if you don't use the deployment steps that we detail in this chapter.

The proof is in the pudding

You typically first do a proof-of-concept test on a vendor's equipment. This test lets you determine major roadblocks that you might run into when you move forward into the deployment. In this phase of testing, you want to work with key stakeholders in the organization to ensure that the proposed NAC solution meets their needs:

- ✔ **Network architects or designers:** They want to ensure that the NAC solution meets the security objectives set forth in the policies.

- ✔ **Network administrators:** These stakeholders want to ensure that the system is manageable and user-friendly, and that it offers the appropriate level of visibility into events and traffic on the network. They also want to ensure that any software-based agents work on standard corporate machines, and other potential endpoint systems, such as those belonging to guest users that might be connecting to the network.

- ✔ **Helpdesk personnel:** They want to make sure that they have access to the appropriate troubleshooting tools, as well as logging and auditing capabilities. In addition, they want the system to appear seamless to the end users, thereby minimizing incoming helpdesk calls.

- ✔ **End users:** The entire cast of people involved in the proof of concept should realize that end users just want to get their work done. They want easy access to the network — they don't want to deal with loss of connectivity, figure out how to patch their machines, or worry about the intricacies of network access control!

Do a proof of concept on a small scale, making many of the policies and configurations similar to what you plan to eventually roll out across the organization. You want to assess the solution at a high level and identify potential product gaps or redesigns that you need to do before moving on to the pilot implementation.

You can frequently do the test itself in conjunction with your vendor or systems integrator. Don't be afraid to leverage these folks for information about how to conduct a proof of concept or how to design the solution. They deal with these products on a daily basis and have a lot of in-depth deployment knowledge that you can tap into. In many cases, because they also provide equipment and facilities for the proof of concept, they're already involved, so use the opportunity to take them for a test drive. You can ensure that they really offer the support that they promise, and at the same time, you can validate the marketing claims that they made during their sales pitch.

The pilot implementation

After the successful selection of vendor and proof of concept, you're ready for the pilot implementation.

The pilot implementation involves a larger group of users. It's the final test of the design and implementation before you roll out NAC to the rest of the organization.

Keep the same set of stakeholders that you involved in the proof of concept when you move on to the pilot implementation, but also open the test to a larger group of end users so that you can get their feedback.

The size of the end-user group that participates in the pilot implementation depends on the number and diversity of end-user systems and groups across the organization.

You may find selecting the appropriate group of end users challenging — they don't really have a lot to gain by participating in the pilot, and they don't necessarily know enough about NAC technology or the goals of the stakeholders to provide adequate feedback. Follow these guidelines when choosing end users for your pilot implementation:

✔ Choose end users that have the time and willingness to participate.

Don't try to force end users to participate in the pilot. Requiring participation frequently gives you end users who don't cooperate.

✔ Choose end users who know enough about technology to provide valuable feedback. They do not need to be technical experts, but those with a base level of technical knowledge, such as

 • A working proficiency with PCs

 • Some level of networking or security knowledge.

✔ Select a group of participants who represent the broadest possible cross-section of endpoint devices, operating systems, and corporate-application and data-access requirements.

✔ Provide adequate training for the pilot participants for these reasons:

  • To increase the likelihood of a successful pilot because end users know what they're testing and why

  • To get a chance to refine training tools and delivery before you roll out NAC to the broader end-user community.

After you choose the participants, you can begin the pilot test in much the same way that you start the proof of concept (as discussed in the preceding section). When you design the pilot test, you must identify the testing methodology and the critical success factors:

✔ When you begin the pilot, carry forward any findings from the proof-of-concept testing.

  You might learn, for example, how

  • Certain policies will require you to change software on your endpoint devices.

  • Changes need to be made to your corporate directory to support the role-based policies that you want to create when rolling out NAC.

✔ Document any potential problem areas uncovered during the pilot so that you can ensure they're tested thoroughly during the controlled pilot environment. For example, say that the NAC solution you're testing includes an 802.1X supplicant. You encounter installation issues with that supplicant on a machine during proof-of-concept testing, so you need to ensure that the issue doesn't persist on multiple machines when you roll out the pilot to the test group.

Some of the questions that you might want to answer during this phase of the deployment testing include

✔ Does the proposed vendor's solution work with your existing network and security infrastructure? If not, what type of upgrades might you need in order to fit NAC into your environment?

✔ Does the vendor's client software consistently work with the types of systems and machines that you have running on your network?

✔ Is the end-user interaction smooth and trouble-free? Do non-technical end users have any problems getting on the network? Does automatic remediation of the endpoint device work with minimal end user interaction?

✔ Do all your end users get access to the appropriate data and applications that they need to get their jobs done?

✔ Does your intended NAC solution properly account for guests, partners, contractors, and any other third parties on the network?

✔ Does the solution meet your needs in relation to both threat prevention and threat containment/control? Can it properly mitigate attacks on the network from authorized users?

✔ What type of reporting capabilities does the NAC solution offer? Can you easily provide key reports to management and other interested parties?

✔ Does the solution properly log end-user access in accordance with the company's compliance (such as Sarbanes-Oxley, HIPAA, and PCI) needs? Are the logs granular enough to allow you to conduct proper trouble-shooting and network-event analysis?

✔ Does the NAC solution tie in with your existing network management and analysis tools?

Use the questions in the preceding list as a starting point, but generate a list of questions specific to your organizational needs and environment. We've seen Requests for Proposals (RFPs) that include hundreds of questions that each NAC vendor needs to answer about how a NAC solution fits.

Always keep in mind the current environment, your end users, and your administrators. The impact of NAC on each of those three categories can mean the difference between success and failure for your NAC implementation.

Sample pilot test plan

Regardless of the format that you choose, the test plan document becomes a key communication vehicle that indicates how you plan to run the test, who's responsible for what, time constraints, and key success factors. Given this huge task, the pilot test plan is crucial. To give you an idea of what your pilot test plan might look like, we provide a sample test plan in the following sections.

The following test plan is basic — probably more basic than the one that you need to create — but it gives you an idea of the key elements that you should incorporate into your plan.

Executive summary

This pilot test plan outlines the scope, goals, and deliverables for the For Dummies, Inc. network access control implementation. Upon successful completion of this project, For Dummies, Inc. plans to move forward with an enterprise-wide production implementation of network access control from XXXYYYZZZ Networks.

The overarching goal of the network access control project is to provide a much stronger level of network security on the For Dummies, Inc. network than currently exists. While our workforce becomes more mobile and our network opens to a broader set of devices and users, implementing identity-based access control has moved from a nice-to-have feature to a must-have component on our networks. After we complete the project, NAC will authenticate all users on the network and check those users' machines for an appropriate security posture before allowing access to any sensitive information on the network. If a user fails any of these checks, the NAC solution will quarantine him or her, and provide extremely limited access only to non-sensitive network resources and the Internet.

This pilot involves stakeholders from across the organization who, with assistance from the vendor, will refine the proposed implementation and ensure that the NAC solution will meet the needs of For Dummies, Inc. Table 11-1 shows the targeted stakeholders that will be involved in the implementation. Because the NAC implementation involves coordination across so many groups within For Dummies, Inc., a successful pilot will involve not only a technology readiness assessment, but also an organizational readiness assessment — ensuring that each team can work closely with the others.

Table 11-1	Typical Pilot Test Stakeholders		
Role/Title	**Department**	**Number of Users**	**Responsibility**
CSO	Corporate IT	1	Final approval of NAC implementation
Security architect	Corporate IT	1	NAC architecture design
Network administrator	Corporate IT	5	NAC implementation in test network
Network administrator	Each business unit (units A, B, and C)	3	Business unit liaison/implementation in business unit network
Helpdesk personnel	Corporate IT	4	Troubleshoot user issues, evaluate tools and end-user impact
End users	Business units A, B, and C	30	Test and evaluate end-user impact
Sales engineer	Vendor	1	Design and implementation support
Support engineer	Vendor	Multiple	Vendor support liaison

This document describes the project, timelines, and goals of the For Dummies, Inc. Network Access Control deployment, and isn't intended to be a full description of the pilot configuration and NAC technology. Those details should be documented elsewhere in the appropriate design documents and vendor descriptions, and should go hand-in-hand with this pilot test plan description.

Pilot test plan goals

The goals of the pilot test are to ensure that

- ✔ The chosen network access control solution can adequately protect against insider threats, which are outlined in the requirements of the For Dummies, Inc. corporate security policy document.

- ✔ Implementation of this technology will have minimal impact on For Dummies, Inc. end users. End users shouldn't have significant barriers to full network access, nor should they need to interact often with the chosen technology.

- ✔ End-user training and support methodologies are refined prior to a full-scale deployment.

- ✔ The needs of every business unit within the organization are met.

- ✔ The helpdesk can appropriately field questions and troubleshoot issues raised by end users.

- ✔ The management tools provided by the vendor meet the needs of the For Dummies, Inc. network administrators.

- ✔ The cross-functional team chosen to lead the NAC implementation can work together successfully, despite their differing goals and objectives.

- ✔ The chosen access control, logging, and reporting tools meet the Sarbanes-Oxley Act compliance requirements for both control and auditing.

Pilot team interaction

The pilot team, with the exception of the end users, will meet on a weekly basis to review schedules and milestones, discuss past and current issues and progress, and ensure that the entire pilot team has adequate cross-functional communication. An e-mail alias (`NAC_pilot@fordummiesinc.com`) will provide an outlet for end-user feedback and intra-team e-mail.

Prior to the start of the pilot test, the network administrators will fully train end users in how to use the draft training materials created by corporate IT. The administrators will also bring end users up to speed on the goals of the NAC implementation, the goals of the pilot, and key areas in which feedback is most valuable. End users will document all feedback via e-mail to the NAC team e-mail alias or in trouble tickets when they open helpdesk tickets. The pilot team will summarize the results of this feedback and present it prior to the weekly pilot team meeting.

Network deployment

The pilot implementation will be conducted on a non-production network for the duration of the test. Pilot testers will use a second wireless network deployed for this purpose. This wireless network requires successful authentication into the NAC solution via 802.1X before the user is granted any access onto the network. No non-pilot end users can access this network — For Dummies, Inc. will force them to stay on the production network. The network administration team has staged vendor gear, in addition to all other required network equipment and software, for deployment onto this network, with the goal of replicating the production environment as closely as possible.

Pilot assessment/schedule

The pilot test is scheduled to last three months from start to finish, with an aggressive deployment timeline thereafter. If, after three months, the pilot NAC implementation hasn't successfully reached its major goals, the pilot team, including the Security Architect, will re-evaluate the solution, with final sign-off on forward plans conducted by the CSO. If either the vendor or For Dummies, Inc. considers the existing challenges insurmountable, the team will explore alternative solutions.

Table 11-2 shows the proposed timeline for the various milestones that are targeted for the pilot implementation.

Table 11-2	Typical Assessment Milestones	
Requirement	**Responsibility**	**Completion Date**
End-user recruitment	Business unit network administrators	One month prior to pilot
Network equipment procurement	Network administrator (Corporate IT)	One month prior to pilot
NAC pilot equipment procurement	Sales engineer (Vendor)	One month prior to pilot
Test design plans	Security architect	Two weeks prior to pilot
End-user training	Network administrator (Corporate IT)	One week prior to pilot
Pilot go-live approval	All stakeholders	Day 0
User feedback	End users	Continuous

Requirement	Responsibility	Completion Date
Helpdesk feedback	Helpdesk personnel	Continuous
Operational feedback	All network administrators	Continuous
Status review meeting	All stakeholders	Weekly
Mid-pilot milestone review	All stakeholders	Week 6
Pilot end		Week 12
Final recommendations	All stakeholders	Week 13
Production rollout approval	CSO/all stakeholders	Week 14

Evaluation Before Enforcement

When you expand your NAC deployment and begin requiring user authentication and endpoint inspection over a huge number of end users, you don't want the NAC system to block the CEO from accessing her e-mail simply because her machine isn't adequately patched or her antivirus software is out of date.

After you finish the proof of concept and pilot test, both of which involve only a limited number of end users, you need to push the proposed NAC policies to the rest of the organization so that you can truly assess the impact of NAC across the production environment. If you don't know what's going to happen when you flip the switch, do a broad test run. Many organizations simply don't have a firm grasp of the overall state of the machines on their networks. In many cases, multiple groups are responsible for desktop management, each with their own organizational policies and management tools. In other cases, a large number of partners, contractors, and customers run unmanaged devices on the network.

People really become nervous when they don't have the appropriate strategy in place to *keep* their machines updated. Follow the processes outlined in this chapter, and throughout the entire book, and you will have nothing to worry about when rolling out NAC!

Even if you're confident about how well the rollout will work, best practices dictate a slow introduction of NAC into your corporate network.

Luckily, NAC vendors have responded to the need to verify how well their users and network will respond to NAC policies in advance by offering an evaluation mode that allows you to more seamlessly transition over to NAC. First, run your NAC deployment in an evaluation-only mode prior to the initial rollout so that you can see what type of situation you really have related to desktop management. During this phase, answer these questions:

- ✔ Are the organization's managed devices patched and up to date?

- ✔ When machines are out of date, do the appropriate manual and/or automated remediation mechanisms fix any issues?

- ✔ Have you chosen the appropriate managed machine policies for endpoint integrity to serve the entire range of machines on the network?

- ✔ How many unmanaged machines run on your network?

- ✔ Can these unmanaged machines pass the acceptable endpoint integrity policies that you intend to put into place?

- ✔ What policy will you enforce for unmanaged machines that aren't in compliance?

- ✔ Do manual and/or automated remediation mechanisms work for these unmanaged devices?

- ✔ Will any machines out there (such as mobile devices) not work properly with the NAC solution that you're evaluating?

- ✔ How does the chosen solution allow network access for devices that have no user involvement, such as a printer, networked HVAC system, or video-conferencing system?

Take a deep look at the reporting and logging capabilities available within your NAC solution. Knowing these capabilities can help you determine whether the native capabilities of the NAC solution are sufficient to meet your needs or you need additional functionality through a third-party tool.

NAC solutions vary in the number of pre-defined reports that are provided in order to meet requirements, such as compliance, management reports, and technical challenges. In general, however, NAC solutions tend to fall into one of two categories:

- ✔ Include a full, integrated reporting engine

- ✔ Have no native capabilities but can offload to other third-party reporting engines that can provide this functionality.

Evaluate-only mode

Evaluating before enforcing means that you install the NAC solution in some or all areas of the network and have the agreed-upon policies running, but NAC doesn't take actions on end user sessions if the devices do not meet the policy requirements.

For example, if you're scanning to find out whether endpoint machines have the appropriate operating system patches, antivirus applications, and personal firewalls, create those policies in the system but take no action if they fail. Later, when you actually begin enforcing these policies, you might decide to start taking actions, ranging from automatically remediating the endpoint software to using quarantine or network restriction mechanisms that alter resource access on the network.

You can run evaluate-only mode for any amount of time, depending on what the organization needs and the amount of work that you have to do in order to get the various components NAC-ready for fully enforced deployment. Your company might already have fully managed machines that are patched and running the appropriate software. In that kind of situation, evaluation mode lasts a very short amount of time. In other cases, a wide range of different types of devices might be on the network, and each device has a different security posture. If that's the case, you might want to spend more time either correcting machine issues or working to deploy a more consistent strategy for desktop management.

Whatever kind of NAC solution you have, be sure to get the appropriate level of visibility. When you evaluate policies, avoid sorting through thousands of log entries to determine how many of your machines are failing planned NAC policies by leveraging the provided reporting tools. These reporting tools, whether part of the NAC solution or provided through a third party reporting tool give you an at-a-glance view of the overall network health, as well as an easy way to identify out-of-compliance machines.

What Are Your Best Practices?

You can plan a NAC rollout in many ways, but in each case, the best recommended practice involves careful planning, phased deployment, and leveraging experts in the field to ensure a smooth and successful project.

On location

You can phase in your NAC solution by location. Select a certain office, floor, or area where you can deploy NAC piece by piece, systematically rolling it out across your entire organization. This approach allows you to work with manageable segments of the user groups, network infrastructure, and end-point machines. A location-based phase-in also allows for a kind of extended pilot — the user group simply grows over time.

Organizations that have attempted to roll out NAC to all their users all at the same time have often backtracked to roll out in smaller parts of their network before providing NAC to the whole user community. This allows the organizations to test and refine how they plan to roll out NAC with a smaller group of users before enforcing policies for everyone.

You can take a similar approach to this type of deployment by deploying NAC in public areas, such as lobbies and conference rooms, prior to deploying in the rest of the network. Figure 11-2 illustrates an approach that allows for gradual, controlled guest-user access in public areas, providing protection where the company is most vulnerable because of an absence of physical access controls (such as badge readers, security guards, and so on).

Phase 1 – Months 1–2	
Corporate HQ – Lobbies, Guest Areas, Conference Rooms	Wired Ports
Corporate HQ	All Wireless

Phase 2 – Months 2–4	
Branch Locations 1–10	All wired, wireless

Phase 3 – Months 4–6	
Branch Locations 11–20	All wired, wireless
Corporate HQ	remaining Wireless Ports

Figure 11-2: A location-based rollout plan.

Role playing

Most organizations have certain data that's more sensitive than other data on the network:

- ✔ A public company might have financial data that the Sarbanes-Oxley Act requires them to protect.
- ✔ A software company might need to securely protect its source code.

In these cases and countless others, some data has a role in the organization that requires better protection than other corporate data. As a result, treat protection of this data with a higher level of urgency. Figure 11-3 shows this process.

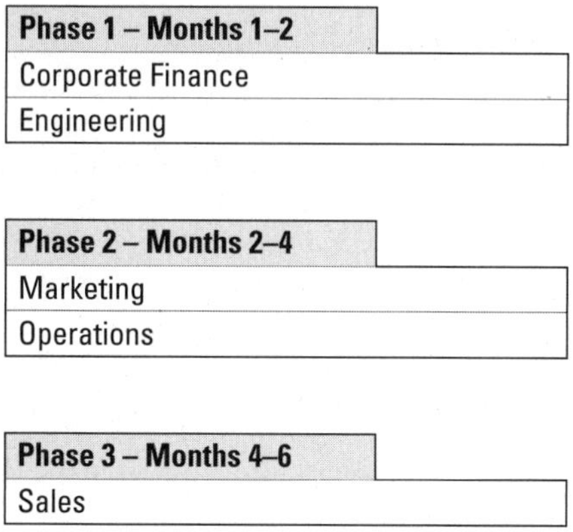

Phase 1 – Months 1–2		
Corporate Finance		
Engineering		

Phase 2 – Months 2–4		
Marketing		
Operations		

Figure 11-3:
A role-based
rollout plan.

Phase 3 – Months 4–6		
Sales		

In these cases, the preferred deployment might involve providing access controls that require authentication of only those people who access this sensitive data. Many NAC solutions offer a deployment model that allows you to place an enforcement point in front of certain key resources, requiring authentication and endpoint assessment only when the user wants access to the system.

For example, all employees in a corporate network have relatively open access to the LAN, which lacks access control enforcement, but to access the sensitive financial data, user authentication and endpoint assessment through NAC must occur. After the company has solidified the NAC deployment for this use case, they can expand the scope of their NAC deployment to include the rest of the network.

Wireless, rather than wired

Many organizations have targeted their wireless infrastructure as most sensitive, and therefore, that infrastructure most urgently needs the protection provided by NAC. A wired port can more tightly control who can access the network; its physical infrastructure separates authorized users from non-authorized users. Wireless connections don't have that distinction — a user can access a wireless connection within buildings, outside buildings, in parking lots, in common or public areas, and so on. So, you might want a NAC deployment that first spans your wireless infrastructure when you start to phase in NAC.

Function first

Many of the early adopters of NAC technologies have phased in their NAC deployment via functionality, rather than by location or user group. For instance, your organization might want to use NAC for both user authentication and endpoint assessment, but you decide to start by enabling one or the other first, and then working with the rest of the functionality after you gain experience and confidence.

First concentrating on user authentication and guest access can help you figure out who's on your network and whether they're members of your organization who need access to potentially sensitive corporate data.

After you successfully roll out user authentication, you might then add granular access control within your internal groups. For example, in addition to authenticating employees, you might layer in access control lists (ACLs) or other types of network controls that segment traffic and access by user groups — allowing users in the Engineering group to access engineering data only, while at the same time allowing users in the Finance group to access finance data only. Both groups might have access to the intranet and other common corporate resources that guests can't access.

When user authentication has been fully deployed, you might decide which machines can access which resources, and you might also add endpoint integrity to the policy and control engine for your NAC solution. Machine-based access control is the next logical step in the deployment progression. For example, at this point, you might decide that users on mobile devices or their own un-patched machines can gain only very limited access to corporate data, whereas the same users on an appropriately patched corporate-owned machine get full access.

Professional Services and Consulting

NAC is much more than a simple drop-in appliance or product. More than any other security technology that you've worked with in the past, NAC spans your entire infrastructure (depending on the extent to which you choose to deploy it), and it requires a tight coordination between many elements of the network and (just as importantly) many different teams or stakeholders.

Because customers often perceive a NAC deployment as complex, many value-added resellers, consulting firms, managed service providers, and security professionals have developed practices around deployment of NAC.

You might decide to outsource some or all of your NAC deployment to these professionals, which gives you access to their professional experience with deploying NAC.

The extent to which you involve these professionals depends on how comfortable you are with the various phases and tasks associated with the NAC deployment:

  ✔ You might take on a consultant to deal with only NAC agent deployment on your desktop systems.

  ✔ You might require consulting services to help design your policies for access control and endpoint assessment.

Regardless, working with a NAC specialist ensures that your deployment goes smoothly and cost-effectively, with as little impact as possible on the end user and the internal teams who are designing and managing the NAC solution.

Part III
NAC in the Real World

In this part . . .

This part reveals what you really need to know about NAC architectures, standards, and extensions. It's like the form you have to fill out for eHarmony before you get to the dating process.

Read carefully, or you may waste your time with several awful dates.

Chapter 12

NAC Architectures

*N*AC vendors build most NAC solutions on a foundation by using an architecture or framework. Although you can find a number of architectures and frameworks for NAC, this chapter covers three core NAC architectures:

✔ Cisco Network Admission Control (Cisco NAC)

✔ Microsoft Network Access Protection (Microsoft NAP)

✔ The Trusted Computing Group's (TCG) Trusted Network Connect (TNC)

These frameworks and architectures have only a few differences and many similarities. These frameworks and architectures have different points of focus; for example, placing additional emphasis on the client side instead of the server side.

Most of this chapter is very technical. If you're still a little unsure about how NAC works or what it does, you might go over some earlier chapters until you have a firm enough handle on general NAC strategies and goals to be able to get through the technical details. Fasten up, we're going deep into Acronym Land.

Also, we have made forays into several of these NAC solutions, frameworks, and architectures working together, which we present after the descriptions of the main NAC architectures and frameworks. And finally, this chapter briefly discusses a few other NAC architectures and frameworks to give you a well-rounded view of the system.

Cisco Network Admission Control (Cisco NAC)

Announced by Cisco in 2004, Network Admission Control (NAC) is one of the graybeards of network access control. Cisco NAC was a pioneer in NAC architectures. Although other companies had been circling the NAC flame for a couple of years, Cisco was one of the first to pull together a framework for NAC. It was also one of the points at the end of the spear for LAN security management.

At a high level, the goal of Cisco NAC — and, really, any other NAC framework — is to prevent unauthorized or compromised endpoint devices from gaining network access. Among other things that Cisco NAC does and can do, it assesses the security state of an endpoint device prior to allowing that device to access a network, much like other NAC architectures, frameworks, and solutions.

Cisco has stated in promotional materials that the Cisco NAC framework is suited for various use cases or scenarios, including protecting a network from infected endpoint devices, whether the infection was unintentional or intentional; securing access to networks for business partners; and enabling and managing network access for guests.

The Cisco NAC framework empowers different types of devices used in a typical network — including switches, routers, and even wireless access points — to collect user authentication and device security state data from endpoint devices. The system can use the information gathered by these network devices to decide the access fate for a particular user and device.

With Cisco NAC, an endpoint device can send user authentication and security state information to the network devices that gather that data before a user accesses the network (before the user and device are assigned an Internet Protocol [IP] address by the network). This action is similar to how the IEEE 802.1X standard for port-based network access control acts; Cisco NAC includes core components of the 802.1X standard.

Cisco NAC then verifies the authentication and security state data communicated, and based on those results, it can control the network access for the user and device. Cisco NAC makes its access control decision when the system toggles LAN switch ports or the system directs user access to different virtual LANs (VLANs), based on the security and access control policies and procedures established by the organization implementing Cisco NAC. Cisco NAC, via the network devices with which it interacts, can deny users or devices network access, limit their access, or quarantine the devices until the system can *remediate* it — until the system repairs whatever makes the device non-compliant with an organization's policies.

To really begin to grasp how Cisco NAC works, you need to understand the various components that comprise the Cisco NAC framework. Refer to Figure 12-1 while reading the following sections if you need a little visualization help.

Cisco Trust Agent (CTA)

The CTA is the agent that resides on an endpoint device and gathers the user authentication and endpoint device security state data for Cisco NAC. The CTA interacts with third-party security and anti-malware applications on the device to collect data about the device's security posture, which can include operating system patch levels, antivirus updates, and so on. The system collects this data by using Cisco NAC–compatible third-party plug-ins, sometimes referred to as *posture plug-ins,* that either Cisco or the third-party provider has created. Depending on who created the plug-ins, either Cisco integrates them with CTA or the third-party provider deploys them as part of its application.

The CTA communicates the authentication and device security state information to network devices — including routers, switches, and wireless access points — which Cisco calls Network Access Devices (NADs). The system collects the authentication and security data in a Cisco NAC–compatible package and communicates it to the appropriate network devices by using a Cisco NAC–aware Extensible Authentication Protocol (EAP). However, the NADs aren't the only stop for the gathered authentication and security state data. The system also shares that information with the Cisco Access Control Server (ACS).

Cisco Access Control Server (Cisco ACS)

Cisco originally conceived and promoted ACS as a Remote Authentication Dial-In User Service (RADIUS) server. Over time, Cisco ACS has also become the policy manager for Cisco NAC.

Cisco ACS, whether deployed as server software or as a Cisco appliance, interfaces with the various third-party policy servers (such as antivirus policy servers) and third-party management servers (such as audit servers and vulnerability management servers) to ascertain whether the system should grant the device network access or restrict it in some manner, based on the security posture data gathered and communicated by the CTA. Cisco ACS also retains its ability to perform as a RADIUS server, interfacing with authentication databases and data stores (such as Microsoft Active Directory or Lightweight Directory Access Protocol [LDAP]) to determine whether the user is allowed access to the network based on the authentication information gathered by the CTA:

1. When the Cisco NAD receives the authentication and security state information from the CTA, it passes that information on to the Cisco ACS server or appliance.

2. Cisco ACS then interfaces with and checks the device security state data against third-party policy servers, based on an organization's predefined security and access control policies.

3. It interfaces with and checks the user's authentication information — gathered by CTA — against third-party directory servers.

4. Based on the responses received by the Cisco ACS server or appliance, it defines an access control directive for the specific user and endpoint device, referred to as an *access control list (ACL),* and communicates that ACL to the NAD that communicated the user's and endpoint device's information in the first place.

Network Access Device (NAD)

A NAD is simply a Cisco switch, router, wireless access point, or even a VPN server that the system has outfitted to support Cisco NAC, as well as the 802.1X standard. A NAD acts as the initial communication point with the CTA, receiving the user authentication and device security state information, passing that data through to the Cisco ACS. And NADs are the enforcement points for the access control rights granted (or denied) by the Cisco ACS and policy servers, based on the data that the system pass through from the CTA.

Third-party servers

Third-party servers that interface and interact with Cisco NAC include third-party policy servers, such as antivirus management servers, patch management servers, and other anti-malware servers. These third-party policy servers communicate with Cisco ACS, determining whether the security state data received by Cisco ACS (from the NAD, via CTA) adheres to an organization's security or access control policies, predefined on and with the third-party server. The third-party servers communicate an endpoint device's compliance or non-compliance to the Cisco ACS, which implements appropriate actions based on that communication.

Cisco NAC can interface with third-party servers such as vulnerability management servers or audit servers. These servers, after Cisco ACS communicates with them, may scan an endpoint device to determine its vulnerability state or to audit its security state. Based on the outcome of their scans, these servers communicate with Cisco ACS whether the endpoint device is in compliance, enabling Cisco ACS to take appropriate action — grant, deny, or limit network access for that user and endpoint device, or quarantine the endpoint device until the system has remediated the device.

Finally, Cisco ACS interfaces with third-party directory servers, databases, or data stores that contain authentication data to determine whether a user is authorized to access the network based on the authentication data supplied by CTA (and communicated through the appropriate NAD). If, after interfacing with the directory server (or database or data store), Cisco ACS determines that the user is authenticated and authorized to access the network, the system allows that user to access the network — if, of course, his or her device passes security and access policy muster. If the user isn't authenticated, then he or she isn't authorized to access the network; Cisco NAC doesn't allow the user, or his or her device, onto the network.

Figure 12-1 shows all the various components of Cisco NAC that we talk about in this section and the preceding sections.

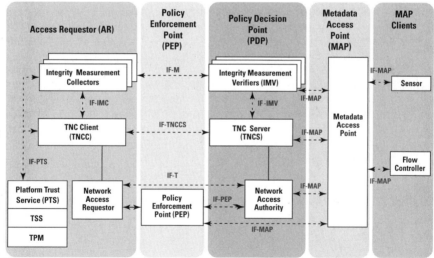

Figure 12-1: The Cisco Network Admission Control (NAC) framework.

How Cisco NAC works

When an endpoint device attempts to access a network protected by the Cisco NAC framework, the CTA on the endpoint device invokes the various third-party plug-ins (posture plug-ins) embedded within CTA or already preloaded on the endpoint device by third-party anti-malware or security applications. These plug-ins collect the endpoint device's security state information and provide that data to the CTA.

The CTA also gathers the user's authentication data, packaging the collected security state information and authentication data, and then communicating that package to the appropriate NAD (such as a Cisco switch, router, wireless access point, and so on) by using an EAP method (EAP over UDP).

After the NAD receives the packaged authentication and security state data, it passes that data through to the Cisco ACS by using a typical 802.1X communications method, EAP over RADIUS. Cisco ACS accepts the authentication and security state data, parsing out the user authentication data from the endpoint device security state information.

Cisco ACS compares the user authentication data against directory servers, such as Microsoft Active Directory or LDAP, to authenticate the user and determine whether he or she has authorization to access the network. Cisco ACS then separates the endpoint device security state data and sends the state data to each appropriate third-party policy server. The system compares the collected endpoint device security data to the policies that the organization predetermines on the policy servers for each of the third-party applications.

If the system authenticates the user and the endpoint device's security state adhere to the organization's policy, Cisco ACS communicates the appropriate access rights to the original NAD. That NAD, acting as the policy enforcement point, allows the user and device access to the network. However, if the system authenticates the user, but his or her device doesn't pass the policy check, Cisco ACS sends a message to the original NAD (again, which serves as an enforcement point) to either deny network access to the user and device, limit the network access for the user and device, or quarantine the device until the system can remediate it and bring it into policy compliance. How the system handles network access for a non-compliant endpoint device depends on the policies of the organization. If the system can't authenticate the user, the system usually denies that user (and his or her device) network access.

Microsoft Network Access Protection (NAP)

Microsoft developed Network Access Protection (NAP) to ensure that networks remain free of malware and any vulnerability potentially delivered and distributed by endpoint devices that have antivirus applications with outdated signature files or operating systems that haven't been updated.

Microsoft NAP controls network access based on authentication and the security and access control policy compliance of users and endpoint devices. How Microsoft NAP controls a user and endpoint device's access depends on that user's identity, and associations or group membership, as well as the device's level of policy adherence. Not only can Microsoft NAP make sure that an endpoint device is healthy enough to access an organization's network, it can also quarantine and aid in the remediation of non-compliant endpoint devices.

Microsoft utilizes a health theme with NAP; therefore, they refer to the health of a computer or other endpoint device when discussing it.

Microsoft NAP comes as part of Microsoft Windows Vista, Windows Server 2008, and Windows XP Service Pack 3. It validates the security state and general state of health for a personal computer (PC) or device that runs Microsoft Windows Vista or Windows XP Service Pack 3 (or other operating systems that have third-party Microsoft partner support) while that device attempts network connection. NAP can also ensure devices are compliant with security and access control policies. NAP can automatically update noncompliant computers and devices, or even change their configurations through management software, such as Microsoft Systems Management Server (SMS). And if NAP deems a computer or device that includes Microsoft NAP non-compliant, an organization can reduce the exposure of its network by simply limiting the areas of the network that the non-compliant device can access or restricting the amount of time that device may access the network. But, although Microsoft NAP can help to protect a network against access by non-compliant devices, it (like most NAC solution architectures and frameworks) can't protect against access by malevolent users bent on wreaking havoc to a network.

Microsoft NAP's extensible framework encompasses a number of components.

Microsoft NAP Agent

The Microsoft NAP Agent is embedded in Microsoft Windows Vista and Windows XP Service Pack 3. The NAP Agent aids the flow of data between other NAP components, including the Microsoft NAP enforcement clients (ECs) and System Health Agents (SHAs). Depending on the enforcement method for Microsoft NAP, the NAP Agent can be involved in the enforcement process by serving as a supplicant or 802.1X client.

System Health Agents (SHAs) & System Health Validators (SHVs)

System Health Agents (SHAs) are client-side components that monitor system security and, in general, the health state of the Windows computer or endpoint device that attempts to access the network. Windows Vista and Windows XP Service Pack 3 both include an SHA for the Windows Security Center (WSC), which checks and tracks changes in the state of the WSC. This SHA is in addition to other SHAs. Third-party vendors can develop SHAs through the Microsoft NAP application programming interface (API). Allowing third-parties to develop SHAs on their own via the NAP API enables Microsoft NAP to interoperate with virtually any third-party vendor application for which the vendor has developed an SHA. It also enables NAP to leverage the data collected by that SHA on the computer or device on which it's installed, as well as using the application for which the vendor developed the SHA in the access control decision-making process.

System Health Validators (SHVs) are the yin to the SHA's yang. SHVs are the server-side components against which an SHA compares the security and health state data it collects from a device and that device's specific application. SHVs validate the compliance of the device to predefined organizational security and access control parameters. An SHV for the WSC comes in Microsoft Windows Server 2008, which corresponds to the WSC SHA found in both Windows Vista and Windows XP Service Pack 3. And, like SHAs, third-party vendors can develop SHVs through the Microsoft NAP API, enabling Microsoft NAP to further integrate with most third-party vendor applications for which the vendor developed an SHA and SHV.

Microsoft NAP enforcement components

The Microsoft NAP framework includes a number of enforcement components.

Enforcement clients

Microsoft NAP enforcement clients (ECs) are part of the client-side components of Microsoft NAP. The NAP ECs are eponymous, providing client-based enforcement based on compliance to security and health requirements. NAP ECs are necessary ingredients in addressing various NAP enforcement methods, which are based on specific network access and internal communications types and standards. (We describe all these in the following sections.) Either Microsoft or third-party vendors may provide NAP ECs.

Enforcement servers

Microsoft NAP enforcement servers (ESs), like NAP ECs, are eponymous: NAP ESs, part of Microsoft NAP server components, deliver server-based enforcement of security and health rules determined by an organization. NAP ESs are part of the *NAP server,* which is an access device resident on a network — such as a switch, router, VPN appliance, NAC-specific appliance, and so on. NAP ESs can limit or deny network access for computers and other devices that are non-compliant with the security and access control policies of your organization. NAP servers, in conjunction with their resident NAP ESs, enforce these access control policies. And, like NAP ECs, the system needs NAP ESs to address the different available NAP enforcement methods.

Enforcement methods

Microsoft NAP enforcement methods are network access and communications methods for which NAP can control network access. You can find support for the following NAP enforcement methods in Microsoft Windows Vista, Windows XP Service Pack 3, and Windows Server 2008; you can use these NAP enforcement methods individually, in sets, or collectively to restrict or even deny network access for non-compliant PCs and other devices:

- Internet Protocol Security (IPSec) traffic
- IEEE 802.1X networks
- Remote access/VPN connectivity
- Dynamic Host Configuration Protocol (DHCP) configurations
- Terminal server gateways

IPSec NAP enforcement

One of the most stringent forms of NAP-based enforcement, *IPSec NAP enforcement,* allows only compliant computers to communicate with other compliant computers, protected by IPSec. Microsoft NAP can limit this level of IPSec communication by IP address or TCP/UDP port number. Microsoft NAP's IPSec enforcement method requires

- A network device on the organization's network, running Microsoft Windows Server 2008, to serve as a Health Registration Authority (HRA)
- That an EC (IPSec Relying Party EC) resides in the supported Windows platforms, as well as in Windows Server 2008

After the system deems a NAP-enabled system or device compliant with security and health mandates, the HRA gathers a certificate of health from the compliant system or device. When two compliant computers begin to communicate, protected by IPSec, these same certificates authenticate them as compliant NAP client devices.

802.1X enforcement

Microsoft NAP's 802.1X enforcement enables a computer (or other device) that complies with an organization's health requirements — as established by and in Microsoft NAP — to receive network access via 802.1X compatible switches, wireless access points, or other access devices. Microsoft NAP 802.1X enforcement actively monitors a device's health state, so it can monitor a device both pre- and post-admission. Computers and other devices that aren't compliant, or which fall out of compliance post-admission, find their network access limited by a restricted network access profile, originated by Microsoft NAP and enforced by 802.1X-compliant access devices. The restricted access profile can identify and direct a non-compliant computer or device to a specific VLAN or particular IP packet filters, thereby limiting network access. Microsoft Network Policy Server (NPS), resident in Windows Server 2008 (replacing Internet Authentication Service [IAS]) acts as the policy server for Microsoft NAP. The system needs NPS, as well as an EC (EAP Quarantine EC) to use 802.1X NAP enforcement. Microsoft Windows XP Service Pack 3 installations require separate ECs for wired and wireless 802.1X access.

Enforcement over a VPN

Microsoft NAP's enforcement over a virtual private network (VPN) insists that a computer or other device comply with device health policies before it grants that device remote network access over a VPN. IP packet filters limit network access over a VPN for computers that aren't in compliance, whether the system determines non-compliance before or after granting remote network access; Microsoft NAP's VPN enforcement actively monitors the health state of the device. Microsoft NAP enforcement via remote access/VPN requires Microsoft NPS and an EC (Remote Access Quarantine EC).

DHCP enforcement

Computers that are compliant with network security and access policies may obtain an IPv4 address configuration from a DHCP server that provides unlimited network access. But computers that don't meet policy under Microsoft NAP's DHCP enforcement method receive a restricted IPv4 address configuration, limiting their accessibility to the network. Each time a DHCP client leases or renews an IP address configuration, it validates or revalidates device health. Active monitoring of the computer's health and adherence to policy dictates the open or limited nature of its network access. Microsoft NAP DHCP enforcement requires a DHCP ES (included as part of Windows Server 2008's DHCP Server service) and a complementary EC (DHCP Quarantine EC). The system considers this DHCP enforcement Microsoft NAP's weakest form of NAC enforcement because a user who has appropriate access rights can easily compromise or subvert it.

Microsoft Network Policy Server (NPS)

Microsoft Network Policy Server (NPS) is Microsoft NAP's policy server, where your organization can define your network security and access baseline — which Microsoft calls system health requirements — and where SHVs developed by third parties can reside, individually or collectively. NPS determines and validates a client device's health state. If a device doesn't comply with the health requirements set by your organization, NPS can also deliver remediation instructions for the non-compliant device. Microsoft NPS is the replacement in Microsoft Windows Server 2008 for Microsoft Internet Authentication Server (IAS), which was found in Windows Server 2003. And, like its predecessor, Microsoft NPS is also a RADIUS server, delivering authentication, authorization, and accounting (AAA) capabilities. NPS verifies user and device credentials — also referred to as network credentials — against Microsoft Active Directory for devices attempting local network connectivity via 802.1X or remote connection via VPN. The system can use NPS's duties as the NAP policy server, and its AAA and RADIUS capabilities, separately or together — for example, with Microsoft NAP 802.1X or VPN enforcement.

Third-party remediation servers

Third-party remediation servers include servers or other resources that update antivirus signatures, update software versions, or provide patches for applications or operating systems. They provide non-compliant computers and other devices with an organization's system health requirements, as defined and enforced by Microsoft NAP. These servers also supply the services and resources to bring those non-compliant devices back into policy compliance. The system can assign the SHAs developed by Microsoft and third-party developers, which you can find in Microsoft NAP, to communicate with either the remediation server or the application software installed on the device.

Third-party policy servers

Third-party policy servers can include antivirus management servers, patch management servers, and nearly any other anti-malware application servers. Policy for specific, third-party security applications are defined on these servers. These policy servers interface with Microsoft NAP via an SHV, typically developed by a third party — commonly the application developer — by using the Microsoft NAP API. Also, each policy server likely also has an associated, complementary security application that has a third-party SHA with which it communicates to Microsoft NAP and which matches the policy server's SHV.

How Microsoft NAP Works

Each organization structures and populates their network based on their networking needs and requirements. Microsoft designed NAP to work within different, heterogeneous network environments. Also, because Microsoft NAP supports various enforcement methods, the configuration of and operation for each NAP enforcement method differs somewhat.

The core operation of Microsoft NAP remains virtually the same, regardless of enforcement method:

1. The Microsoft NAP client sends a reading of the health state of the computer or other endpoint device as part of another, enforcement method-specific function (such as a DHCP request message or as part of an initial IPSec communication) or on request (like NAP's 802.1X and VPN enforcement methods do).

2. The system determines the health state of the computer or other device by checking a Statement of Health (SoH) that it gathers from all SHAs (each of which monitors a specific application), as well as from the WSC SHA that's part of Microsoft Windows Vista and Windows XP Service Pack 3.

   The system provides the SoH to the EC, which communicates the health state of the endpoint device to Microsoft NPS. The ESs, either resident on the NPS or located elsewhere on the network (for example, in the HRA in NAP's IPSec enforcement method), communicate the endpoint device's security state to Microsoft NPS. Microsoft NPS, as the policy server for NAP, validates whether the endpoint device complies with the system health requirements predefined by the organization.

3. If the system deems a computer or other device compliant with all organization-defined system health requirements (and, in the case of 802.1X and VPN NAP enforcement methods, Microsoft NPS and Active Directory have authenticated the user and/or device credentials), then the system either

   • Grants the device network access (802.1X and VPN enforcement methods, after sending the all-clear message to the appropriate 802.1X access device or VPN concentrator, respectively)

   • Allows the device to begin IPSec-protected communications with other compliant devices (IPSec enforcement method, after sending the health state data back to the NAP client, and the HRA receiving a health certificate from the NAP client)

   • Provides the device with an IPv4 address configuration that allows it network access (DHCP enforcement method)

Microsoft NAP, in both its 802.1X and VPN enforcement methods, checks user and/or device credentials for valid authentication prior to passing health state data to the ESs or Microsoft NPS. If the user and/or device credentials are invalid, the system terminates the network connection attempt by the user and device.

If the system deems the device's health state non-compliant with the system health requirements of the organization, the system directs the device to a necessary remediation server or servers. How Microsoft NAP accomplishes this depends on the NAP enforcement method used:

- **IPSec enforcement:** The HRA doesn't receive a health certificate from the NAP-enabled client device, so the device can communicate only with remediation servers.

- **802.1X enforcement:** The 802.1X access devices receive notification from the NPS that the device is limited to the remediation VLAN and can interact only with remediation servers.

- **VPN enforcement:** The system fulfills the VPN connection request of the non-compliant device, but by using IP packet filters, the system can access only the restricted network and communicate only with the remediation servers.

- **DHCP enforcement:** NAP, acting as a DHCP server, sends the device an IPv4 address configuration that has access to only the restricted network, and although the DHCP message exchange is completed, the device can interface only with the remediation servers on the restricted network.

After a non-compliant device has been remediated, however, the client device updates that device's health status, resubmits it, and (if it passes muster), the system grants the device access to the network.

Trusted Network Connect (TNC)

Trusted Network Connect (TNC) is a Work Group (WG) of the Trusted Computing Group (TCG), a not-for-profit organization established in 2003 with a charter to develop, define, and promote open standards for hardware-enabled trusted computing and security technologies across multiple platforms, peripherals, and devices. TNC is also an eponymous open standard and architecture for NAC and network security. Many members of the TCG actively participate in the definition and specification of the TNC's open NAC standards and architecture.

What is the TNC architecture?

TNC is an open, standards-based set of standards and architecture for device authentication and platform integrity measurement. Initially published in 2004, the TNC architecture serves as a framework for developing open-architected, standards-driven, interoperable NAC solutions. The TNC architecture and standards define open, standard interfaces that enable components from different vendors to securely interoperate to create a standards-based NAC solution that leverages existing installed equipment and operates across heterogeneous networks.

Identity and integrity are the core tenets of the TNC standards and architecture. Constructed on existing industry standards and protocols widely supported by networking equipment vendors (including 802.1X, RADIUS, IPSec, EAP, and TLS/SSL), TNC defines new open standards as needed to enable non-proprietary and interoperable solutions within multivendor environments.

The TGC has built the TNC architecture on top of a standard network access architecture, and TNC leverages many of the components of this architecture. The TNC architecture includes a client-side Access Requestor (AR); a server-side Policy Decision Point (PDP); and an enforcer for access control decisions, a Policy Enforcement Point (PEP). Figure 12-2 shows an example.

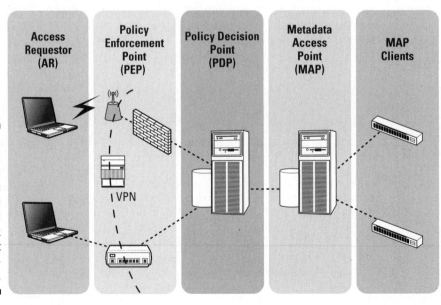

Figure 12-2:
The Trusted Computing Group's (TCG) Trusted Network Connect (TNC) architecture.

The *Access Requestor (AR)*, as its name suggests, is an element that requests network access. An Access Requestor can be a software client, hardware component, or other entity that initiates a network access request: An 802.1X client or supplicant, a VPN client, or even a Web browser that establishes SSL connectivity can serve as an Access Requestor in a TNC-based NAC solution.

Another component of basic network access architectures is the *Policy Decision Point (PDP)*. The server-side PDP is decision control central for network access. The PDP makes the determination, typically by using information supplied by or from the AR, whether an endpoint device gains admittance to a network. It can also decide the appropriate level of access that the endpoint device receives.

The TNC architecture also includes a *Policy Enforcement Point (PEP)*. A PEP enables or restricts access to a network. It's the bouncer of the network access architecture, enforcing the network access decisions determined by the PDP. A network device or access appliance (such as a switch, wireless access point, firewall, or VPN concentrator) may serve as the PEP.

All three of these entities work and interface seamlessly with one another in the TNC architecture: The AR supplies the data to the PDP to make the access control decision, a decision which the PEP then enforces.

 The components and interfaces that comprise the TNC architecture aren't physical, like most of the parts of the Cisco NAC and Microsoft NAP frameworks. So, the TNC architecture's parts aren't particular or vendor-specific software, devices, or services. Instead, they're open guidelines and specifications published by the TCG — and it encourages the inclusion and interoperability of vendor-agnostic entities and components.

Integrity and identity

The TNC architecture is extensible. It expands on a standard, identity-based access control architecture by adding additional layers to accommodate endpoint device integrity, as well as posture assessment and checks; extends the reach of access control support deeper into the network by leveraging additional and existing network devices; and broadens the scope of entities that can request access.

Figure 12-3 shows a diagram the TNC architecture.

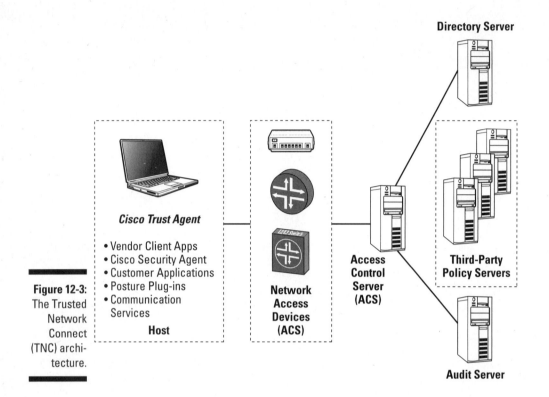

Figure 12-3:
The Trusted
Network
Connect
(TNC) archi-
tecture.

In the AR, the TNC architecture adds layers to pre-existing access control
architectures:

✔ **Integrity Measurement Collectors (IMCs):** Software components that
  measure and capture the state of security, anti-malware, and other applications, products, and services on an AR.

  Third parties develop IMCs by using an open, published TNC specification, and IMCs can include collectors for any number of applications,
  products, and services — such as

  • Antivirus status

  • Firewall parameters

  • Application and/or operating system patch levels

  • Anti-malware application versions

  Third-party applications, services, and other products may preload
  IMCs on an endpoint device. Multiple IMCs may coexist and interoperate
  on an AR.

✔ **TNC Client (TNCC):** An element (software, hardware, or browser-based) that runs on or interfaces with an AR and amasses the state data that IMCs collect, assisting the Network Access Requestor (NAR) in communicating through the PEP to the PDP. The NAR may be

- An 802.1X client or supplicant

- A VPN client

- A Web browser that initiates an SSL connection

The TNCC starts an endpoint integrity check on the endpoint integrity check on the endpoint client or device attempting to access the network.

The PEP remains constant as an access control enforcement point.

✔ **Integrity Measurement Verifiers (IMVs):** The matched set to the IMCs; IMVs check and validate the integrity and state of the information supplied by the IMCs about the AR or device requesting access against the policies for a specific application, service, or product determined by the organization. An IMV corresponds to each IMC on the client.

Third parties develop IMVs, like IMCs, by using an open, published TNC specification. After the IMV checks integrity and state, it formulates an action recommendation, which it communicates to the TNC Server (TNCS).

✔ **TNC Server (TNCS):** The conduit that provides the IMVs with the integrity and state data and measurements that the AR communicates. It also delivers and receives messages to and from the IMVs, including their action recommendations. The TNCS combines all the IMV action recommendations it receives into its own recommendation for action (which it bases on the baseline security and access control policies predetermined by an organization) and communicates that recommendation to the Network Access Authority (NAA).

✔ **Network Access Authority (NAA):** Might be either part of or a complete AAA and/or RADIUS server; but it doesn't need to be. The NAA is the decision-maker with regard to network access; it determines whether the AR receives network access based on the information and recommendations that the TNCS provides it. The NAA works with the TNCS to determine whether the integrity and state measurements supplied by the AR and verified by the IMVs comply with the predefined security and access control policies of an organization. The NAA communicates the final action recommendation — whether it should grant the Access Requestor network access — to the switch, wireless access point, firewall, or other device that serves as the PEP for enforcement.

Open interfaces

The TNC architecture publishes a number of open specifications for communication interfaces between logical components of the TNC architecture. For example, interface specifications can specify standard methods for

- Gathering device integrity, posture, and state measurements from IMCs (IF-IMC)
- Delivering the gathered measurements to IMVs (IF-IMV)
- Prescribing standards for messaging and communications between IMCs and IMVs (IF-M)

These specifications can also describe a standard for information exchange between the TNCC and TNCS (IF-TNCCS), as well as how the exchange should take place through tunneled EAP methods (IF-T). Finally, they can use RADIUS as a communications vehicle between an NAA — which may be a AAA and/or RADIUS server — and a PEP (IF-PEP).

Working with the TNC Architecture

In the TNC architecture, the TNC Client (TNCC) gathers the collected information about an endpoint device's security, integrity, and posture state from the various Integrity Measurement Collectors (IMCs) which monitor specific applications, products, and services on the endpoint device. The TNCC transmits this captured data via the 802.1X client or supplicant, VPN client, Web browser that initiates an SSL connection, or other method that serves as the Network Access Requestor (NAR).

The NAR communicates the data — usually through a tunneled EAP type — to the switch, wireless access point, firewall, or other access device that serves as the Policy Enforcement Point (PEP). Then — and again, typically through a tunneled EAP type — the PEP communicates the collected data on the endpoint's security state and integrity to the server-side Network Access Authority (NAA).

The NAA passes the captured state and integrity data through the TNC Server (TNCS) to the Integrity Measurement Verifiers (IMVs), which check and verify the integrity and state information provided against the policies for a specific application, service, or product, as determined by the organization. Based on these checks, the IMV formulates an action recommendation, which it communicates to the TNCS. The TNCS takes the received IMV action recommendations and, based on the organization's pre-defined baseline security and access control policies (defined in the TNCS), combines the IMV action recommendations with its own action recommendations, thus creating the TNCS action recommendation. It communicates its TNCS action recommendation to the NAA. The NAA determines whether TNC-based NAC solution, via the NAA, can admit the endpoint device to the network based on the information and recommendations that it receives from the TNCS, as well as the policies provided by the organization. For example, your organization may decide to limit network access based on certain state or integrity criteria, and deny network access completely based on other criteria.

The NAA makes the determination and communicates the final action recommendation — whether it should grant the endpoint device network access — to the switch, wireless access point, firewall, or other device that acts as the PEP for enforcement.

Extensibility and architectural options

Although the TNC architecture defines a published, open standard for NAC, in 2008, the TCG added two new optional architectural components, as well as an associated optional protocol interface that extends the existing TNC architecture to encourage and support in-depth, interoperable, coordinated network defense leveraging heterogeneous, vendor-agnostic environments. Many network security components — such as firewalls, intrusion detection systems (IDSs), intrusion prevention systems (IPSs), data leakage prevention (DLP), and so on — don't interface with one another. They're independent systems, limited in their ability to share information for network or traffic visibility and monitoring. These TNC extensions deliver a standards-based method of addressing real-time network protection. For example, they can use devices that change security state post-admission or endpoint devices that your organization doesn't manage (such as endpoint devices from guest users, contractors, partners, or others).

The optional, standard interface — the *Interface for Metadata Access Point (IF-MAP)* — is a client-server protocol that defines access to an optional, new component called a Metadata Access Point (MAP) server. *Metadata* is real-time information about network devices, policies, status, states, behavior, and relationships between network devices and systems (including security events, network identity, network location, and so on) that it can share. The optional MAP server stores the metadata information, and the optional IF-MAP standard protocol provides identifiers and data types for the metadata, as well as defining the processes by which it may publish or search the stored metadata. Systems and services that monitor the network, behavior, or traffic (such as IDS or DLP) may serve as MAP clients, using IF-MAP to report strange or dubious behavior to the MAP server. The MAP server alerts the PDP to implement appropriate enforcement actions, in conjunction with the PEP. Some MAP clients may even be able to parse and interpret information from IF-MAP, fine-tuning their own detection rules. IF-MAP aids network security by enabling security devices to share identity information.

Therefore, your organization can leverage your existing network investment in AAA; NAC solutions; IDS/IPS; DLP; firewalls; and other security, authentication, access, and other network devices — not to mention endpoint security systems — so that those investments focus on securing and protecting your network through a coordinated, vendor-agnostic security response across heterogeneous network deployments that involve multiple products and product types. Your organization can also use better reporting and more easily integrate data — regardless of device or vendor — into logging and reporting systems, such as security event management (SEM) and security information and event management (SIEM) systems.

The TNC architecture also broadens the scope of components and entities that can supply information to an Access Requestor or request access on their own. Another TCG standard, the *Trusted Platform Module (TPM),* can interface with the TNC architecture as an added factor in the access control decision process. The TPM (a microcontroller that stores keys, passwords, and digital certificates) can be found attached to the motherboard of most new notebook and desktop computing systems, and you can find TPMs in other endpoint devices, as well. Information stored on a TPM is secure from software attack or theft. Use of a TPM in the TNC architecture is optional; a TPM isn't a required component of the TNC architecture. But, if your organization takes advantage of the security and protection that a TPM's keys, passwords, and certificates provide, you can easily accommodate this process and involve it in your endpoint-device integrity and posture checks, and access control decisions. It provides a hardware root of trust from the endpoint device into the network. It also addresses the hairy problem of rootkits. When it uses TPM and TNC together, it forms a solution to a critical NAC problem — the lying endpoint. A *lying endpoint* is a corrupted endpoint device that sends all-clear messages from various security and malware applications when, in reality, device security has been compromised and malware is running rampant on the endpoint device. By incorporating the TPMs in computers and many other devices into an adopted TNC architectural process, you can have a secure method of ensuring that endpoint devices are trustworthy and delivering actual, true security and access control measurements in the access control decision-making process.

Internet Engineering Task Force (IETF) Network Endpoint Assessment (NEA)

The Internet Engineering Task Force (IETF) is a widely recognized and sup-ported standards body. It has developed many of the standards in use today on the Internet. In October 2006, the IETF created the Network Endpoint Assessment Working Group (NEA WG). IETF has chartered the NEA WG with providing an open, neutral forum for vendors to come together so that they can collaboratively develop and produce a standard client-server interopera-tion for endpoint assessment, which is an integral NAC component.

Many different vendors and components need to come together to create the NEA standard, so it needs cooperation, collaboration, and interoperability. Any member organization in the IETF NEA WG can come together with it to agree on these standards, as well as how products can interoperate in this space.

The TNC Work Group of the TCG and Cisco are active participants in the IETF NEA WG, with representatives from each company serving as co-chairs of the IETF NEA WG. The IETF NEA WG focuses on creating and driving the success of the NEA standard, and any other standard or standards that the NEA WG develops and produces.

Although the IETF NEA WG hasn't published an official specification (at least, as of the writing of this book), they have published draft specifications. Fortunately, the NEA draft specifications are based almost entirely on the open, standards-based TNC specifications, which should ensure a smooth transition of the TNC standards from the TCG's vendor consortium to more traditional standards bodies.

For the sake of clarity, here are the differences between the IETF NEA WG and the TNC effort:

- ✔ **The IETF NEA WG:** Its charter and focus is to work solely on require-ments and standards for client-server interoperability for endpoint assessment.

- ✔ **The TNC:** Focused on defining and delivering open standards and interoperability for NAC overall, including client-server protocols, but also dealing with specifications that extend NAC, APIs for client and server-side plug-ins, enforcement mechanisms, and so on.

Working Together

Interestingly enough, although Cisco, Microsoft, and the Trusted Computing Group promote their frameworks and architectures, they also work together to provide greater interoperability. These varying types and levels of interoperability can deliver many strategic benefits to your organization.

Microsoft NAP–Cisco NAC framework

Microsoft NAP and Cisco NAC frameworks can interoperate. This interoperability between frameworks allows organizations to protect their investments in network and security infrastructure. With a combined, interoperable framework, it can use a single agent — the NAP Agent in Microsoft Windows Vista. So, it doesn't need the Cisco Trust Agent (CTA), which is part of a non-integrated Cisco NAC framework. Also, it can use a single API to develop any necessary client- and server-side components to support the interoperable frameworks.

The integrated Cisco NAC–Microsoft NAP framework can use several of the Cisco NAC framework components and many of the Microsoft NAP framework components. (We describe these components in the section "Microsoft Network Access Protection [NAP]," earlier in this chapter.) It reuses and repurposes some of these components, so you should know their function and how they work together in the combined framework.

The Cisco NAC Appliance isn't part of the Cisco NAC–Microsoft NAP integrated framework.

A computer or other device that runs Microsoft Windows Vista Service Pack 1 or Windows Server 2008 should have the necessary Microsoft NAP Agent preloaded. The device needs the NAP Agent because it uses that Agent — as well as other NAP client-side components — to communicate its health and security state to the server:

1. The computer or other device attempts network access by using the 802.1X standard through an 802.1X-compatible Network Access Device (NAD).

   The compatible NADs may include

   - An 802.1X-enabled switch or wireless access point, connecting via RADIUS to a Cisco Access Control Server (ACS)

   - A router that has the ability to send a connection request to the Cisco ACS via Extensible Authentication Protocol (EAP) over User Datagram Protocol (UDP)

2. After receiving the endpoint device's connection request via the NAD, Cisco ACS sends a request back to the endpoint device asking for a Statement of Health (SoH).

3. The relevant *System Health Agents (SHAs)*, the client-side components that monitor system security and health state of the device attempting network access, continue to gather that specific information about the device.

   It needs a NAP EAPHost enforcement client (EC) because that client facilitates the network access request; the NAP Agent service negotiates the communications between the SHAs and EC.

4. The NAP Agent packages the device's health and security state, as well as the network credentials for authentication, into an SoH and communicates that SoH to the Cisco ACS through a specific EAP method — Extensible Authentication Protocol–Flexible Authentication via Secure Tunneling (EAP-FAST), a Cisco-developed, publicly available tunneled EAP type that uses the 802.1X standard.

   The NAP Agent packages the health and security state data, along with the network credentials (user and/or device credentials), in the SoH and communicates them to Cisco ACS through an 802.1X-compatible NAD that uses RADIUS messaging.

5. After receiving the network credentials via EAP-FAST, Cisco ACS validates the network credentials against a Microsoft Active Directory authentication data store. If Cisco ACS can authenticate the user and device, it forwards the SoH — which contains the device's security and health state data — on to the Microsoft Network Policy Server (NPS) via Host Credential Authorization Protocol (HCAP).

   HCAP, which you must deploy with Microsoft NPS, enables the interoperability between the Microsoft NAP and Cisco NAC frameworks by enabling Microsoft NPS to perform 802.1X authorization, which includes enforcing the Microsoft NAP health policies, while Cisco ACS performs the necessary AAA functions, including user and device authentication.

6. Microsoft NPS validates the device's security and health state; it reports back to Cisco ACS via HCAP. Cisco ACS provides the NAD with the specific network access action that it should take, including a network access profile (predetermined by the organization) that it applies against the specific NAD port on which the device runs.

7. Cisco ACS sends an SoH Response (SoHR) to the NAP Agent by using RADIUS and EAP-FAST. The SoHR, based on the device's level of compliance with security and health policy (as determined by the Microsoft NPS response), either provides the device with network access if it's compliant with policy or directs it to the non-compliant VLAN if it's not compliant.

Cisco NAC may restrict non-compliant devices from accessing the network until it remediates those devices, at which time Cisco NAC re-verifies their compliance with policy — and re-authenticates their network credentials. If a device passes both the new policy check and re-authentication, Cisco NAC grants the user and device network access.

Microsoft NAP and TNC

The Trusted Computing Group (TCG) and Microsoft Corporation (a TCG member and active participant in TCG standards development) have made their respective NAC frameworks — TNC and NAP — interoperable. The interoperability between these two leading NAC frameworks delivers easy-to-use, cost-effective, scalable endpoint integrity and NAC to organizations. It also provides investment protection, enabling organizations to leverage their existing investments in network equipment and endpoint software while future-proofing their investments in NAC. And it lowers implementation costs and deployment time, as well as offering a consistent, single NAC software client.

Microsoft contributed its Statement of Health (SoH) protocol to the TCG, which published it as a new TNC specification, IF-TNCCS-SOH. Published by the TCG and available for download or implementation, IF-TNCCS-SOH is an open-standard client-server protocol that reports the health and security state of an endpoint device prior to granting it a network connection. The IF-TNCCS-SOH protocol complements the TNC's IF-TNCCS protocol. These protocols define two alternative methods for the exchange of information between the TNC Client (TNCC) and the TNC Server (TNCS), and they serve as the protocols usually invoked for those sorts of checks.

When an endpoint device requests network access, it must share with the Policy Decision Point the state of security and health of the endpoint device, as well as whether that device is operating in a network protected by a TNC architected NAC solution or a Microsoft NAP framework solution. The device communicates this security and health information by using an SoH. If the endpoint device meets the required, predefined security and endpoint health policies — which the PDP in the TNC architecture defines and validates — it grants the device the appropriate network access, based on user authentica-tion (identity) and the device security and health check (integrity). If it finds that an endpoint device's state of security and health is non-compliant with the predefined security and endpoint health policies, it directs the device to a quarantine network. The quarantine network gives that device limited net-work access until it has remediated the device (bringing it into policy compli-ance), rechecks its security and health state, and possibly re-authenticates it. If the endpoint device meets policy after remediating it, the endpoint device — depending on the policies that the managing organization administers — gains appropriate, relevant network access.

The interoperability between the TNC architecture and the Microsoft NAP framework occurs at three different points in the NAC framework: at the endpoint device, at the PDP in the TNC architecture, and at the Policy Enforcement Point (PEP) in the TNC architecture.

When an endpoint device requests network access, it communicates its captured security and health state, as well as network credentials (such as user and/or device credentials), to a PDP in the TNC architecture's interoperable TNC-NAP framework by using the IF-TNCCS-SOH protocol. When an endpoint device uses this standard protocol, that device can be either a NAP client or a TNC Client. In fact, it can use a mix of NAP clients and TNC Clients with any vendor's NAP server or TNC server, as long as it uses the IF-TNCCS-SOH protocol.

The PDP determines the level of network access to grant the endpoint device after it authenticates network credentials (user and/or device credentials) and compares the security and health state of the endpoint device to the predefined security and access control policies of your organization. For endpoint devices that don't comply with policy, the PDP in the interoperable TNC-NAP framework provides remediation instructions to those devices through the IF-TNCCS-SOH protocol and access control instructions (via RADIUS protocols) to the PEP. In this situation, your organization needs only a single PDP server, regardless of whether it's a NAP server, such as the Microsoft Network Policy Server (NPS), or a TNC server. However, if your organization chooses to implement and use multiple PDP servers, maybe to leverage existing infrastructure or to copy an organizational blueprint, you can do it, as well.

Depending on the access control instructions that the PDP provides after it authenticates network credentials, and analyzes and evaluates a device's security and health status, the PEP (in the form of a switch, access point, router, gateway, or firewall) may grant the endpoint device full or limited network access, or may deny it network access altogether, depending on your organization's policies. If it quarantines the endpoint device and requires remediation, the device may have limited network access — such as being restricted to a remediation server — until it remediates, re-authenticates, and re-checks it for its security and health state.

As Figure 12-4 shows, the interoperability and co-mingling of the TNC architecture and NAP framework — as well as Microsoft's contribution of SoH to the TCG, and the subsequent release of the TNC's IF-TNCCS-SOH open, published protocol — enables NAP servers (such as Microsoft NPS) to perform security and health checks on TNC clients without additional software. Also, TNC servers can perform security and health checks on *NAP clients* — endpoint devices running Microsoft Windows Vista or Windows XP Service Pack 3 — without needing to add software.

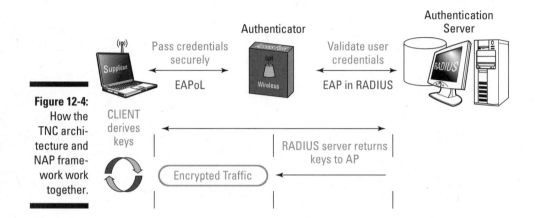

Figure 12-4:
How the TNC architecture and NAP framework work together.

Chapter 13

The Role of Standards

*I*n technology, the term standard has a single meaning: A *technology standard* is an agreed-upon set of guidelines, requirements, or specifications that may be adopted or approved universally or by a large group of like-minded parties.

Technology standards are typically designed to work with other technologies. Some standards even integrate other industry standards:

✓ **Open standards:** A set of interoperable guidelines made available and easily accessible to the public without any obstructions or restrictions (which includes any restrictive licensing or use fees), which anyone may use by accessing, adopting, and implementing the standard.

When we talk about technology standards, we're usually talking about concepts that encompass and capture the ideas of the *concurring many,* which are transcribed in granular detail and specified. These specifications serve as rules, and can strictly or leniently adhere to or enforce these rules in the implementation or adoption of usable technology, to which must apply the concepts and constraints of compatibility, interoperability, and agreement. Many times, open standards in technology are created to address a particular issue or set of issues, or to solve a specific problem.

✓ **Proprietary standard:** A guideline or requirement that's owned privately (by a company or organization).

Although an independent group or standards body may not have approved or certified a proprietary standard, or the standard may not be publicly accessible without restriction (for example, users may have to pay a license fee, use fee, or other monetary or non-monetary cost), an industry widely accepts or follows that standard.

Making the Case

A standards-based NAC solution, whether industry-based or based on proprietary standards, can help to simultaneously integrate existing or new technologies and products, leveraging them to control device security and network access, as well as those organizational groups and disciplines that manage and deploy those technologies and products.

- ✔ A standard can emphasize or ensure interoperability between existing or new network components.

- ✔ When you use an interoperable standard with other technologies and products, it can help to assure that any new technology or product selection that your organization makes works seamlessly with the standard and existing deployed products.

You and your organization need to determine what value a given technology or product, whether it uses industry or proprietary standards, offers to your business. The following sections give you the considerations that you must make to determine whether to use a standards-based solution.

Costs

Standards enable technologies to be open and accessible, and they can provide you the ability to choose from several different vendors. So, a NAC solution based on open industry standards, as discussed in this book, can decrease total cost of ownership, while at the same time enabling you to choose the product or technology that you want to use and integrate.

Integration

NAC solutions integrate user-, device-, and network-related security and access control technologies. These technologies include

- ✔ Authentication, authorization, and accounting (AAA)
- ✔ Endpoint device integrity and security
- ✔ Network policy management and enforcement
- ✔ Quarantine and remediation

A NAC solution that leverages industry standards can usually facilitate the integration and interoperability of disparate- or like-technologies. This can decrease the total cost of your NAC solution.

Organization linking

A NAC solution links within an organization various departments or disciplines that manage different aspects of the network and internal infrastructure. For example, a NAC solution may link the teams within an organization that manage and administer

- Network operations and administration
- Security operations
- Desktop management
- RADIUS or identity management
- Compliance

Filling the roles

Many open, industry-adopted, market-proven standards can play integral roles in your NAC implementation and deployment.

You also can find burgeoning open standards for NAC, as well as several proprietary standards in the NAC market.

Industry standards

NAC solutions may include industry standards that deliver robust authentication capabilities:

- **Remote Authentication Dial-In User Service (RADIUS):** In use extensively in networks worldwide for its powerful authentication abilities.

  RADIUS is a standard that the Internet Engineering Task Force (IETF) created and approved first for use in dial-up networks. Dial-in networks used to be prevalent, and anyone who wanted to communicate with another person by computer had to either

  - Connect to an electronic bulletin board or CompuServe.
  - Send e-mail by using a modem on their PC from which they dialed into a modem pool via a Telnet or other access telephone number at their Internet service provider (ISP).

- **Simple Network Management Protocol (SNMP):** Assists in the challenges of network management and provides a communications vehicle between networked devices.

  Some NAC solutions use SNMP to deliver access control.

✔ **Dynamic Host Configuration Protocol (DHCP):** Used to deliver the configuration parameters that enable endpoint devices to operate over an Internet Protocol (IP) network.

A basket of standards

Some open standards are a collection of standards and technology protocols combined by the standards organization to address a specific issue or problem.

For example, Internet Protocol Security (IPSec) is a collection of different open standards that IETF has created by combining Requests for Comments (RFCs), delivering a set of protocols that enable protected communications over an IP network.

Leveraged standards

Open industry standards leverage other standards to deliver a complete solution to a problem.

The 802.1X standard is for port-based network access control. The 802.1X standard integrates RADIUS, as well as a secure, flexible framework that ensures the secure passing of data between the components of an 802.1X-compliant network from the IETF, named the *Extensible Authentication Protocol (EAP)*.

In a network based on the 802.1X standard, RADIUS and EAP provide port-based network access control that has strong, durable authentication and security.

Groupies

Some standards have been created and approved by groups of individuals or organizations who agree that the defined specifications or guidelines address a specific challenge or solve a particular problem, such as network access control and network security:

✔ The Trusted Computing Group (TCG) — a not-for-profit organization created to develop, define, and promote open, accessible standards for trusted computing and security technologies — formed the Trusted Network Connect Work Group (TNC-WG) for this purpose.

The TNC-WG of the TCG has created and continues to develop an open set of standards and an architecture that serves as the foundation for open, standards-driven, interoperable NAC solutions.

✔ The IETF's Network Endpoint Assessment Working Group (NEA WG) has the charter of developing standards for network access control.

IETF Standards

Key standards drive NAC implementation. This section takes an in-depth look.

RADIUS: Completing the circle

RADIUS is the acronym for Remote Authentication Dial-In User Service, an IETF standard originally designed for use in dial-up networks. One of the main purposes for the RADIUS standard is to provide authentication.

RADIUS is a client/server security protocol that has been (and, in some cases, continues to be) used to authenticate, authorize, and account for dial-up users. But NAC vendors extended RADIUS for use in today's enterprise switching infrastructures.

Wireless networks also use RADIUS heavily, and although it wasn't initially intended to be a wireless security authentication method, it improves and strengthens the weak Wired Equivalent Privacy (WEP) encryption key standard. However, the real mettle of RADIUS is in its robust user authentication capabilities.

In RADIUS, user authentication is based on network credentials, not device information or other data. RADIUS centralizes the management of network credentials and authentication data. Already a widely deployed standard, RADIUS servers can either store network credentials, and authentication data or attributes; or they can access external credential data stores and databases, such as those based on Lightweight Directory Access Protocol (LDAP) or Structured Query Language (SQL), as well as Microsoft Active Directory, to name just a few examples. RADIUS can use and access many other types of back-end data stores and databases.

The RADIUS standard is very useful in a NAC solution, particularly one that implements or leverages the Institute of Electronics and Electrical Engineers (IEEE) 802.1X standard for port-based network access control. As shown in Figure 13-1, the authentication server in an 802.1X network receives RADIUS messages and uses those messages to authenticate the user, and his or her device. The authentication server makes the authentication decision — whether the authentication server can authenticate a user for access to the network — and communicates that decision to the authenticator, usually an 802.1X-capable device, such as a network switch or wireless access point, which enforces the authentication decision.

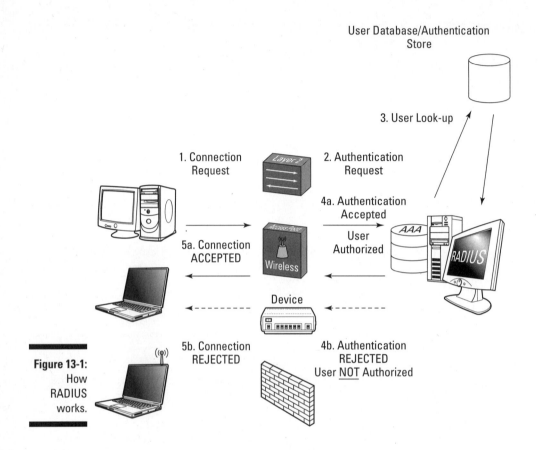

User Database/Authentication Store

3. User Look-up

1. Connection Request

2. Authentication Request

4a. Authentication Accepted
User Authorized

5a. Connection ACCEPTED

Wireless

Device

5b. Connection REJECTED

4b. Authentication REJECTED
User NOT Authorized

Figure 13-1:
How RADIUS works.

The simplicity of SNMP

Simple Network Management Protocol (SNMP) was designed to exchange device management information between network devices, called *elements*. Many network devices still primarily use SNMP for this information exchange. It allows administrators to gather information or change settings on a network device.

Although SNMP was originally designed for use with routers, other network elements (such as printers, switches, access points, and software) now include SNMP capabilities.

Inside SNMP

Two components make up SNMP:

✔ **Agent:** Resides on a network element (a device). The agent gathers network element status details and communicates them to a manager on request, or when network element status meets a specific condition or threshold.

SNMP's condition-based communications are called *alerts* or *traps.*

✔ **Manager:** Also known as a Network Management System (NMS). *NMS* is a centralized system that proactively monitors network elements, which can include polling an agent for information about the network element where it's installed, or

receiving alerts or traps. You can program the NMS, and it can take a specific action based on the results of its monitoring. Actions can include notifying an administrator by e-mail, text message, or other means so that he or she can address a current or potential issue, or take other preventative actions.

The NMS needs to be aware of the configurable information on a network element; this information is stored in a text file known as a management information base (MIB), and network management systems typically access MIBs by using SNMP. The SNMP's IETF standard defines the format for an MIB. If the MIB is in the appropriate format, an NMS should be able to communicate with the associated network element.

One . . . two . . . SNMP three

SNMP provides a very simple mechanism that allows you to monitor and configure a network device by using a centralized manager.

Although SNMP is readily available and simple to work with, it does have some limitations concerning the three versions of SNMP that you can deploy:

✔ The two older versions of SNMP don't employ strong security mechanisms, which can leave them open to unauthorized access, such as snooping or eavesdropping:

• **SNMP version 1 (SNMPv1):** The original version of SNMP that continues to be a standard protocol for the Internet.

• **SNMP version 2 (SNMPv2):** Offers enhancements to SNMPv1, such as additional protocol operations. SMNPv2 was replaced to address several security concerns, including authentication and privacy.

✔ **SNMP version 3 (SNMPv3):** Includes message authentication and packet encryption.

SNMPv3 employs security mechanisms that include authentication, message integrity, and encryption. SNMPv3 delivers a more secure architecture to ensure that passwords don't travel over a network in open, clear text. SNMPv3 also provides for an optional, encrypted data stream that can protect the data between devices in an SNMP architecture.

Managing SNMP

SNMP wasn't built to provide security. You must ensure that you correctly configure and deploy your SNMP-based NAC implementation.

When employed in a NAC solution, the SNMP standard can serve as a notification mechanism, enabling the solution to monitor the behavior and state of endpoint devices via alerts and traps on SNMP-enabled network switches. If your network has an ill-behaving endpoint device, a trap on an SNMP-enabled network switch sends an alert to the NAC solution.

The NAC solution may also dictate diverting the endpoint device that tripped the alert to a virtual local area network (VLAN) with limited or no access to the network and other services. You can also invoke this enforcement mechanism by using SNMP if both the network switch and VLAN are SNMP-managed. You may need to limit network access before you provision or access overall resources with a NAC solution that leverages the SNMP standard, depending on the solution and implementation. Figure 13-2 shows how SNMP accomplishes quarantine or network restriction.

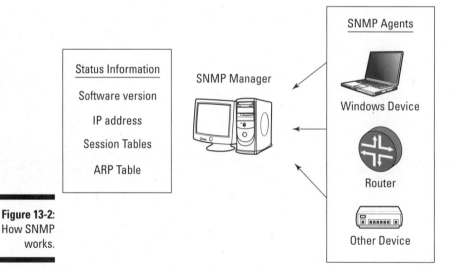

Figure 13-2:
How SNMP
works.

The lowdown on DHCP

The Dynamic Host Configuration Protocol (DHCP) is built on a client-server model and automates the configuration of devices on a Transmission Control Protocol/Internet Protocol (TCP/IP) network. By using DHCP, devices can automatically obtain the configuration parameters that can enable them to operate on the TCP/IP network.

DHCP can reduce the challenges associated with device administration, provisioning, and configuration over a TCP/IP network. It also enables organizations to simply and quickly add devices to a network.

Configuration data delivered by DHCP can include

- IP information on or about local area networks (LANs)
- Gateways and Domain Name Systems (DNSs)
- TCP/IP stack configuration parameters
- IP addresses for printers and other servers

Originated from the *Bootstrap Protocol* (BOOTP, the first mode of dynamic delivery of IP addresses to network devices), the DHCP standard has two components:

- **Protocol:** Defines the mechanism for delivering device-specific configuration parameters for any IP device (routers, servers, or other devices) on a network from a DHCP server or workstation (which is also a device) that runs the application or service which is supplying the parameters to IP devices.
- **Method:** A means to automatically assign and distribute IP addresses to devices on the network

When a DHCP application or service monitors network traffic and sees a request for DHCP, it responds with an IP address. It can also provide additional configuration parameters. The DCHP server can allocate or assign ranges of available or appropriate IP addresses to devices as they join the network.

The client-server structure on which DHCP is built can automate the process of adding devices to a TCP/IP network. DHCP uses and supports three different ways to provide IP addresses to requesting devices. You can use these methods alone or together on a network:

- **Automatic allocation:** The DHCP standard can assign a permanent IP address to a specific device.
- **Dynamic allocation:** The DHCP standard can assign a limited-time IP address to a device; or it can assign the IP address to a specific device until the device surrenders the IP address.
- **Manual allocation:** DHCP simply acts as the delivery mechanism for an IP address that an administrator or other individual in authority has manually assigned to a specific device.

Allocated and delivered IP addresses should be unique, not duplicated.

A NAC solution based on DHCP might include a DHCP proxy device placed between the centralized DHCP server and network switches:

- ✔ After an endpoint device connects to a switch port, the DHCP proxy device replies to the endpoint device.

- ✔ After it sends a reply and assigns an IP address to the endpoint device, the NAC solution (which can be on the same device as the DHCP proxy device, or the solution can actually serve as the DHCP server) could take over the access process and direct the endpoint device to launch a Web browser (and login page), begin assessment of the endpoint device, or take another action.

When you use DHCP as a NAC enforcement mechanism, as shown in Figure 13-3, it can enforce a situation in which the NAC solution provides an endpoint device that fails an assessment check with a configuration that restricts the device from communicating with other devices on the network.

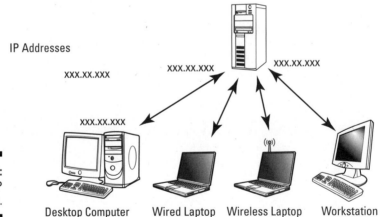

DHCP Server

IP Addresses

XXX.XX.XXX   XXX.XX.XXX   XXX.XX.XXX

XXX.XX.XXX

Figure 13-3:
How DHCP
works.

Desktop Computer   Wired Laptop   Wireless Laptop   Workstation

1 see 1PSec

Internet Protocol Security (IPSec) is a compilation of other protocols and standards that enables secure communications over an Internet Protocol (IP) network by intertwining cryptography and security.

IPSec delivers

- ✓ Data privacy (by using encryption)
- ✓ Message *integrity* (ensuring that a message doesn't change during transmission)
- ✓ Protection from certain attacks

IPSec also facilitates the negotiation of necessary security algorithms and security key handling processes, addressing IP network security needs.

Although a number of NAC solutions use IPSec, IPSec itself doesn't provide the means for network access control, nor is it a method of providing NAC. However, NAC solutions do put the IPSec standard to good use.

IEEE Standards

IEEE creates some popular standards for networking.

The 411 on 802.1X

The IEEE standard for port-based network access control, the 802.1X standard, is part of IEEE's 802.1 group of networking protocols. Originally designed for use in wired networks, but adapted to address WLAN security concerns, 802.1X delivers a robust, extensible security framework, as well as powerful authentication and data privacy capabilities.

The 802.1X standard securely exchanges user or device credentials and prevents virtually any unauthorized network access because it completes authentication *before* it assigns a network IP address.

The 802.1X standard provides a sturdy foundation for many NAC solutions because of its strong, durable security and authentication. The fact that the 802.1X standard has been in the field, and market-tested and deployed in many 802.1X wireless networks, has helped speed NAC adoption and ensure stable interoperability.

A secure 802.1X network needs only three components:

- ✓ **Supplicant:** A software client loaded on an endpoint device that supplies the client side of the 802.1X standard. The supplicant can be part of a wired or wireless environment, and it requests network access.

✔ **Authenticator:** A device, which sits between the endpoint device and the network infrastructure, that performs user or device authentication. Authenticators can include devices such as network switches and wireless access points.

✔ **Authentication server:** These servers can receive RADIUS messages and use the information from a RADIUS message to check user or device authentication credentials against a data store, database, or other data receptacle that contains authentication data. Some examples of data stores or databases that store authentication information include Microsoft Active Directory, LDAP, vendor-specific data stores, other directory stores or databases, or even RADIUS or a RADIUS proxy.

EAP — we've been framed

To support and ensure the secure passing and validation of user or device credentials, NAC needs a secure, flexible authentication framework. This framework needs to simplify the creation and maintenance of additional authentication methods. So, enter the IETF-developed Extensible Authentication Protocol (EAP) standard. The EAP standard allows network and security vendors to create and use extensible access protocols on a framework that enables flexible, expandable network access and authorization.

You can choose from many EAP types, but typically the authentication, or back-end data store or database, dictate the EAP type that you need to deploy and use.

The 802.1X standard works with powerful, robust EAP types, including tunneled types such as EAP-Tunneled Transport Layer Security (EAP-TTLS) or EAP-Protected Extensible Authentication Protocol (EAP-PEAP). Both EAP-TTLS and EAP-PEAP can provide a secure EAP overlay, which you can wrap around other, non-tunneled EAP types or other authentication protocols for additional protection and interoperation. The non-tunneled EAP types that communicate through the EAP tunnel (provided by EAP-TTLS, EAP-PEAP, or another tunneled EAP type) may be carrying user or device credentials, or other relevant user or device data (such as device security state information). Tunneled EAP types, when EAP uses them to communicate user or device credentials and other data between a device and a network, add insurance that the data they're carrying is protected and private, and that security is maintained.

EAP-speak

After you implement an EAP type, both the supplicant and the authentication server need to communicate in that chosen EAP type if you want to make a connection. They need to talk the same language to communicate effectively, and a dialect of EAP is the language.

An IEEE 802.1X standard network works pretty much the same way, regardless of whether you deploy it over a wireless or wired LAN, or in a NAC solution. An 802.1X-compliant network requires

✔ A supplicant and an authenticator that both support the IEEE 802.1X standard

✔ An authentication server in the environment, which completes the network connection

You can probably credit the popularity of the IEEE 802.1X standard to its combination of powerful security and authentication with simple on/off network access control.

The supplicant, authenticator, and authentication server follow this process:

1. A supplicant passes the credentials that the user enters, or that it collects from the device, to an authenticator on the edge of the network.

   The supplicant and authenticator communicate by using an EAP type that's on the Layer 2 of the Open Systems Interconnection (OSI) model, and is specified by the IEEE 802.1X standard EAP over LAN (EAPoL).

2. The authenticator (in the 802.1X compliant network) first verifies the network connection, and then passes the user or device credentials on to the authentication server.

   That communication uses EAP in RADIUS, a Layer 3 (OSI model) communications means that allows an authenticator and authentication server to securely pass authentication messages.

3. After the authentication server validates the user or device credentials against a database or a data store, a network port on an Ethernet switch or a wireless access point (serving as the authenticator) opens (or, in engineering parlance, the switch port closes, creating an open connection and allowing information to flow), allowing the user or device to access the network.

   If the authentication server doesn't find the credentials or those credentials aren't correct, the server can't validate the credentials for whatever reason, or it doesn't have credential verification available, it may deny the user network access.

If your organization wants to allow only limited network access to users or devices that have inappropriate, invalid, or unchecked network credentials, you can accomplish this quarantine by using VLAN tagging or routing, which the authentication server, such as a network switch or access point (see IETF RFC 3580), must support.

Putting it all together in 802.1X

NAC requires a secure, flexible framework for authentication, access management, network security, and data privacy — and the IEEE 802.1X standard can deliver. A typical IEEE 802.1X wireless network typology is shown in Figure 13-4.

The IEEE 802.1X standard allows you to create a powerful network perimeter defense through robust admission controls that refuse users or devices network access unless they comply with specific policies defined by your organization. The 802.1X standard also gives NAC solutions a durable, easily applied and integrated authentication process, guarding a network against improper access and use. Completing user or device authentication *before* a network IP address is assigned ensures that NAC can stop unauthenticated or unauthorized devices (which may carry malware or other threats) before those devices can spread their malicious payload to a network.

When you use the IEEE 802.1X standard as part of a NAC solution, it also

- ✔ Empowers the NAC solution to interoperate with new or existing standards-based network components. This interoperability can help your organization leverage your existing network environment, helping to hold costs down.

- ✔ Enables a NAC solution to work with and oversee a number of different network components, protocols, and methods. This can assure access control in heterogeneous networks, independent of vendor or environment.

- ✔ Simplifies the deployment and integration of other 802.1X-based components into an existing network that has a diverse platform environment.

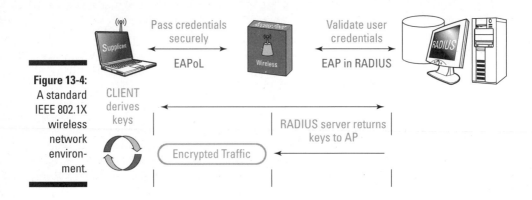

Figure 13-4:
A standard
IEEE 802.1X
wireless
network
environ-
ment.

The 802.1X standard does have some downsides:

- ✔ For 802.1X to work, each endpoint device must have a supplicant (or 802.1X client) deployed.

- ✔ Although supplicants are common and readily available — such as those included with a number of operating systems and software, provided with some endpoint devices, and available as part of a NAC solution — you still need to set up and implement that supplicant, which can be time-consuming.

- ✔ Network switches and wireless access points that you want to use as 802.1X authenticators need to support the 802.1X standard. Although most switches and access points now being sold likely include 802.1X capabilities, existing network switches and access points may not.

Each individual organization needs to decide which standard to use in their NAC solution, based on what they have currently deployed in their network environment and what they want to achieve — and protect their organization from.

In addition to industry standards, such as RADIUS, DHCP, SNMP, and 802.1X, you also can find open standards that like-minded groups interested in securing and controlling network access wrote and ratified, building them to control network access.

Open NAC Standards

Open NAC standards include the Trusted Network Connect (TNC) and the Network Endpoint Assessment (NEA) from the IETF. Many vendors actively implement TNC as part of their shipping NAC solutions, and NEA's standards body is, while we write this book, in the process of finalizing it.

Trusting TNC

The Trusted Computing Group (TCG) is a not-for-profit organization that was formed in 2003 to develop, define, and promote open standards for hardware-enabled trusted computing and security technologies across multiple platforms, peripherals, and devices. The membership includes some of the world's more recognizable brand names; emerging leaders; and successful vendors and developers of components, software, systems, and network and infrastructure. These companies and other organizations have joined forces to develop, define, promote, and approve open, accessible standards for trusted computing and security technologies.

Trusted Network Connect (TNC) is both a TCG Work Group and a TCG eponymous open standard and architecture for NAC and network security. Many of TCG's membership actively participate in the definition and specification of the TNC's open NAC standards and architecture.

The TNC Work Group has created an open, standards-based set of standards and architecture for device authentication and platform integrity measurement, which is a foundation for developing open-architected, standards-driven, interoperable NAC solutions. The TNC architecture and standards define several open, standard interfaces that enable components from different vendors to securely interoperate together, while creating a standards-based NAC solution that leverages existing installed equipment and heterogeneous networks. It builds on existing industry standards and protocols widely supported by networking equipment vendors, such as 802.1X, RADIUS, IPSec, EAP, and TLS/SSL (which we cover in sections "IETF Standards" and "IEEE Standards," earlier in this chapter), and defines new open standards as needed, with the objective of enabling non-proprietary and interoperable solutions to work together within multi-vendor environments.

Here's how the TNC open standards and architecture extends NAC beyond pre- and post-admission checks:

✔ Its foundation of industry standards and protocols enable organizations to incorporate the TNC standards and architecture, leveraging their existing infrastructure investments without sacrificing interoperability or their freedom of choice.

✔ The TNC's open specifications encompass the definition of software interfaces and protocols for communication among endpoint security components, as well as between endpoint hosts and networking elements.

✔ The TNC architectural framework provides for interoperable solutions from multiple vendors and offers you greater choice when you're selecting the components best suited to meet endpoint integrity and network access control requirements.

✔ The TNC architecture

  • Delivers a guideline for the interaction between various network components

  • Measures the state of a device that attempts network connection

  • Communicates the device state to other network entities, such as systems, appliances, and servers

The TNC specifications and architecture allow your NAC system to authenticate the user and assess the device's compliance to a minimum baseline of security policy, as set by you and your organization, as well as the determination of the network's reaction to a request for access. The TNC standard and architecture makes establishing a level of trust certain, before a TNC-based NAC solution allows a user and device to connect to the network.

In the know on NEA

In October 2006, the IETF created a Network Endpoint Assessment Working Group (IETF NEA WG). The IETF NEA WG provides an open, neutral forum for vendors that allows them to work together and arrive at a standard client-server interoperation for endpoint assessment, which is a core component for NAC solutions.

Many different components from various vendors need to come together to form NEA, so interoperability is vital. Any member organization or vendor of the IETF NEA WG can come together in the IETF Work Group to agree on these standards and the interoperation of products in this space.

The TNC Work Group of the TCG and Cisco are playing active roles in the IETF NEA WG, with representatives from each entity serving as co-chairs of the IETF NEA WG. The IETF NEA WG is focused on creating and driving the success of the NEA standard, and any other standard or standards that the NEA WG produces.

Here are the differences between the TNC and the IETF NEA WG:

- ✔ The IETF NEA WG charter and focus is to work only on requirements and standards for client-server interoperability for endpoint assessment; specifically, ensuring both client-side interoperability for endpoint assessment in heterogenous environments.

- ✔ The TNC focuses on defining and delivering open standards and interoperability for NAC overall, including

  - Client-server protocols

  - Application programming interfaces (APIs) for client- and server-side plug-ins

  - Enforcement mechanisms

Chapter 14

Extending NAC

● ●

● ●

Think for a moment about the absurdly huge number of network and security devices that are currently deployed across your network — what do they all have in common, and how does that similarity relate to NAC?

These devices all collect information about what your users do on your networks. A lot of information. That information might simply go into log file archives, where no one will ever view it again. Leveraged properly, this information can provide you with insight into user behavior across your network and allow you to use that information to change access control decisions on the fly.

Those devices that collect user-behavior information are strategically placed across your network for optimal visibility. In many cases, you can use this placement as an additional overlay enforcement scheme that allows you to drive user and machine identity into every policy on your network.

In this chapter, we discuss how you can expand many NAC systems beyond what the manufacturer provides so that you can coordinate NAC with a much broader range of systems, devices, and applications across your network.

Learning from Your Network

NAC truly is the first solution that allows you to coordinate the information available on all your many network and security elements into one single location so that you can establish access control policies based not only on user identity and endpoint security posture, but also on each user's behavior while he or she is attached to the network.

New standards, such as the TNC's IF-MAP protocol (discussed in Chapter 13), have opened the doors to this level of coordination. While these standards take root and an increasing number of vendors adopt them, you'll have access to many new types of enforcement and policies, allowing you to extract additional value from your NAC implementation through extension to other products. The following sections discuss some examples of how your NAC deployment can benefit from extension to include other products.

IDP/IPS integration

Intrusion detection and prevention (IDP), or intrusion prevention systems (IPS), have become increasingly popular in recent years, especially when vendors respond to early challenges in the NAC market, such as perceived deployment and usability difficulties. Many large organizations have now fully deployed IDP/IPS, but prior to NAC, those solutions were somewhat limited in their abilities to prevent new attacks from occurring against the corporate network. You can configure all IPS sensors to drop malicious or otherwise unwanted traffic on the network. For example, if a particular endpoint launches an attack against an application server in a corporate datacenter and the IPS detects that traffic as malicious, the IDP/IPS can respond by dropping the traffic as configured in its policies. Although that response is sufficient, for certain situations, you might want to go even further in order to prevent future attacks on the network. NAC can help you to take information from your IDP/IPS device, and use it to take action on end user access as a result of attacks or other unwanted behavior.

If you have your IDP device fully integrated with your NAC solution (some solutions on the market can do this level of integration), the IDP continues to perform its core function — detecting network traffic and dropping unwanted packets. The NAC integration, however, allows the IDP/IPS to forward details of the unwanted traffic (including severity, IP address of the user, and attack signature) to the NAC solution. When it receives this information, NAC can take action on the associated end user or endpoint. NAC might respond by placing the user in quarantine, disabling the user's session, or even disabling the user's account (depending on the policies set by the administrator). Figure 14-1 illustrates how a NAC and IDP/IPS combined solution might look in a corporate network.

The type of integration shown in Figure 14-1 allows for a full coordination between a NAC solution that has a great deal of visibility into user and device identity and an IDP/IPS solution that has a great level of visibility into traffic and behavior on the network.

NAC/IPS Integration

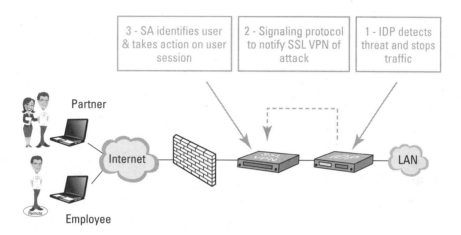

3 - SA identifies user & takes action on user session	2 - Signaling protocol to notify SSL VPN of attack	1 - IDP detects threat and stops traffic

Partner

Internet

LAN

Remote

Employee

Correlated Threat Information	Coordinated Identity-Based Threat Response	Comprehensive Threat Detection and Prevention

• Identity
• Endpoint
• Access history
• Detailed traffic & threat information
	• Manual or automatic response
	• Response options:
	  • Terminate session
	  • Disable user account
	  • Quarantine user
	• Supplements IDP threat prevention
		• Ability to detect and prevent malicious traffic
		• Full layer 2-7 visibility into all traffic
		• True end-to-end security

Figure 14-1: An example NAC/IPS integration.

Security incident and event management integration

Security incident/information and event management (SIEM) products have become more popular in recent years, and many vendors have entered this market. These products can coordinate a wealth of information from devices on your network, making a SIEM product a very logical integration or extension point for your NAC deployment.

A SIEM product can collect logs from a variety of devices, correlating that information so that it can effectively determine events, attacks, or other anomalies on the network. A SIEM product provides information that allows IT administrators to investigate these events and potential vulnerabilities further, possibly taking corrective action to solve issues before hackers exploit those issues. SIEM products leverage tools such as flow and event correlation in order to provide threat and vulnerability analysis that network administrators and security personnel can view.

Just like with IDP/IPS (discussed in the preceding section), SIEM products are limited in how they can prevent detected attacks from continuing to occur after the products discover the attacks. NAC can come to the rescue by offering the ability to protect against further unwanted behavior, extracting more power and value from your SIEM investment. With the appropriate integrations, you can funnel events from your SIEM directly into the NAC policy server. By combining with NAC, you can take similar actions with SIEM that you can with IDP/IPS. Depending on the severity and type of attack, you might take actions ranging from temporary end-user quarantine to disabling the end user's account so that he or she can't log in again until after the administrator conducts further investigation. The combined solution gives you a much more powerful combination than the two solutions standing on their own.

The full extent of the integration depends on the willingness of the SIEM and NAC vendors to work together to support the same standards or APIs that enable the exchange of this information. Because NAC is becoming increasingly popular, many SIEM vendors will likely realize the potential of these types of integrations and begin developing products that support these standards.

Figure 14-2 shows the flow of how such an integration might work in your network.

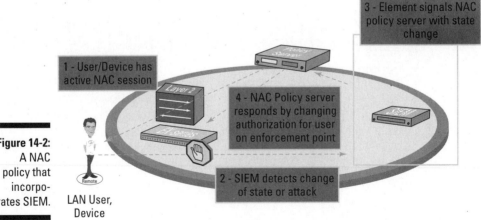

Figure 14-2:
A NAC
policy that
incorpo-
rates SIEM.

Network antivirus integration

Extension of NAC to your network antivirus gateways might make sense for your organization due to the popularity of antivirus in corporate networks. The network antivirus continues to view traffic on the network, scanning for viruses and performing cleaning if and when necessary.

Extending NAC to your network antivirus gateways has made both standalone gateways and gateways that are integrated into other multi-function network and security devices popular for customers in nearly every vertical industry.

But, if the antivirus gateway can react by not only dropping traffic, but also signaling back to the NAC implementation, your organization can accomplish a reactive infrastructure that learns how to adapt to user and machine behavior:

- ✔ For example, the NAC system might quarantine or disconnect users, as shown in Figure 14-2.
- ✔ The NAC system could take a more subtle approach, such as initiating an antivirus scan on the endpoint itself.
- ✔ The NAC system could also ensure that all future traffic from that endpoint be pushed through the network antivirus gateway before it's directed to its destination.

Network inventory/device classification integration

Network inventory is a key piece of many NAC deployments, primarily because so many devices in a given corporate network can't necessarily run required NAC software or authenticate properly into a NAC environment.

Figure 14-3 illustrates how network inventory or device classification solutions might fit into a typical NAC deployment. As shown in Figure 14-3, the policy server in most NAC solutions can adequately handle most managed devices. These devices can typically run some form of NAC software, and the NAC system can scan and authenticate them properly, such as with 802.1X. Typical devices in this category include

- ✔ Desktop and laptop computers that run various operating systems
- ✔ Smartphones
- ✔ PDAs
- ✔ 802.1X-enabled VoIP phones

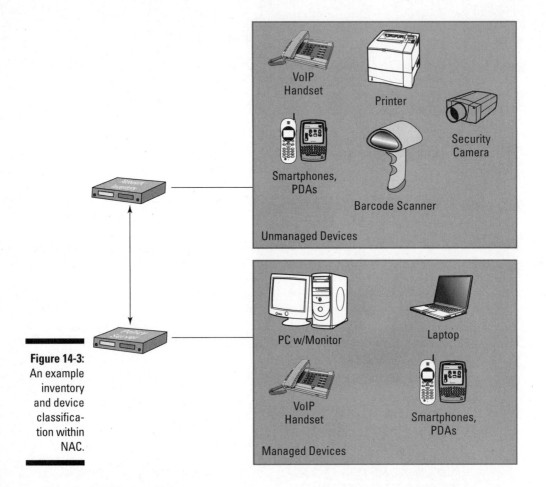

Figure 14-3:
An example
inventory
and device
classifica-
tion within
NAC.

Network inventory solutions come into play when your organization needs
to deal with devices that haven't been built to integrate into a NAC solution.
Depending on the type of organization you work for, these devices can even
outnumber the managed devices in your network. These kinds of devices
include older, less advanced

- ✔ VoIP phones and PDAs
- ✔ Printers
- ✔ Scanners
- ✔ Security cameras
- ✔ Video-conferencing equipment
- ✔ HVAC systems
- ✔ Medical equipment

Many IP-enabled devices on a large corporate network don't have the appropriate software to enable a full NAC authentication.

The network inventory solution has to discover these devices, profile them to determine what type of devices they actually are, and then report to the NAC solution its findings so that NAC can make a decision about what level of access it will give the device on the network.

The inventory system absolutely must be able to determine the difference between a true unmanaged device and a managed device posing as an unmanaged device. For example, an unscrupulous user might try to circumvent NAC policies by mimicking a printer on the network if the user knows that NAC gives printers permissive access to the network. The person might mimic a printer by cloning a known printer MAC address, for example. A good network inventory system has the ability to monitor that machine's behavior and classify it as a laptop rather than a printer, meaning that the device won't get on the network until the user has authenticated properly, ending the threat of that user circumventing the NAC policies and skipping the crucial step of authentication and device classification.

Extending NAC Enforcement

Because NAC has matured in the marketplace, and new APIs and standards have become available, you can choose from an expanding number of possible enforcement models.

The following sections discuss some of the many potential policy enforcement points that you can use in a NAC environment containing some of today's leading NAC solutions. You can't use all these points with all NAC solutions, nor do all enforcement-point vendors support the standards and APIs necessary to accomplish such a goal. But we introduce you to the possibilities before you proceed with a NAC deployment so that you can determine whether your organization's network and security goals, as set forth in your security policy, require a solution integrated with other security devices.

Some of these enforcement points come in different form factors. Multifunction network and security devices have become very popular in recent years — in many cases, encompassing all the enforcement models discussed in the following sections.

The descriptions in the following sections describe logical enforcement modules, rather than fully separate standalone devices and appliances.

Firewall enforcement

Your organization has, in all likelihood, already deployed many firewalls at various points throughout your network, such as

✔ The ingress and egress points to the network

✔ In front of datacenters

✔ Separating locations and departments

Because of their strategic placement, firewalls make logical sense as a point in which you can extend NAC enforcement.

In fact, some NAC solutions already use firewalls as enforcement points, as we describe in detail in Chapter 10. For other NAC solutions, however, extension of NAC to firewalls requires integration through available APIs and standards.

Firewalls also offer good NAC enforcement points because of the types of policies that the organization can potentially enact on a per-user or per-role basis. For example, a firewall placed in front of a corporate datacenter and integrated with a NAC solution can allow an organization to define very granular per-role policies for each group of users on the network. The organization might allow all employees access to features such as e-mail servers and certain file shares, but it can utilize firewall policies to allow only finance users to access sensitive financial data and applications.

This concept, increasingly referred to as *identity-aware firewalling,* is growing in popularity among organizations in all lines of business — including not only those that must meet the needs of compliance mandates such as Sarbanes-Oxley (SOX) and The Health Insurance Portability and Accountability Act (HIPAA), but also any organization that wants to segment their network by function and allow each user access to only the information that he or she needs to do his or her job. From a compliance perspective, the firewall now has visibility into the user, allowing organizations to not only enforce granular access control, but also to prove for audits and other reporting requirements that the organization has in fact enforced these policies.

In today's mobile world, users coming from multiple locations and multiple devices might show up anywhere on a corporate network at any particular point in time. As a result, some of the statically defined source and destination IP-address–based firewall policies are no longer relevant. By NAC-enabling firewall policies, you no longer have to rely on static firewall policies, allowing the firewall to essentially follow the user while he or she moves from one location and device to another. This strategy is much more aligned with the spirit of how and why these policies were first put together.

No longer do firewall security policies apply to users only when they physically plug into Ethernet ports by their office desks. The firewall now enforces its policy on a per-user or per-group basis.

IDP/IPS enforcement

You can use intrusion detection and prevention (IDP) or intrusion prevention system (IPS) devices as mechanisms to monitor end-user behavior on corporate networks, providing a feedback loop by which your NAC solution can change access control decisions based on end-user behavior.

These same systems have excellent visibility into all traffic that passes through them. In many cases, organizations have deployed IDP/IPS so that they can determine not only whether certain traffic is malicious, but also what application is involved in that traffic. These systems can restrict access to certain types of applications based on this technology. For example, an organization might not want users utilizing peer-to-peer applications on their network or non-approved instant-messaging applications, so well-positioned IDP/IPS systems can help accomplish this application level control by dropping any traffic that's not in compliance with these policies.

By extending this type of system to NAC, these policies can now become role-based. For example, certain groups of users might have a legitimate reason to use certain peer-to-peer applications. By extending NAC to IDP/IPS, you can allow those specific users to use these applications but fully restrict other users. Because end users bring so many of their own devices onto corporate networks, this type of policy enforcement can prevent access of unwanted applications — the same applications that you can restrict users from installing when they access the network from managed laptops and PCs.

Integration makes the NAC policies you now employ much more granular — at the application layer, rather than at the network layer — affording you a level of control that you can't get otherwise in many standard NAC solutions.

Table 14-1 lists only a few of the policies that you might put into place across your organization. In fact, if you have an IDP/IPS solution that has these capabilities, you might already have rolled out these kinds of policies. But when you include NAC with your IDP/IPS policies, you can alter or change the types of policies based on the specific user or user group, instead of setting the policies based on source and destination IP address. This type of policy applies well in situations in which you have mobile users in different roles across the organization.

Table 14-1	A Sample IDP/IPS Integration Policy			
Role	Application	Destination	Application Command	Action
Employees	P2P	Any	Any	Drop Log
Employees	FTP	External	FTP put file	Drop Log
Contractors	Instant messaging	Any	Any	Drop Log

Network antivirus enforcement

You may want to deploy NAC to ensure that the computers attached to corporate networks are running up-to-date antivirus applications. The goal is to do everything possible to minimize the potential for a virus outbreak on the corporate network. Although not 100 percent effective, antivirus software is extremely popular and has helped to stem the spread of viruses in recent years.

When you roll out NAC for endpoint integrity inspection and remediation, you need to decide what to do in the event that an end user's machine is out of compliance with antivirus policies and your NAC solution can't remediate it. The end user might be a guest or contractor who has no antivirus software installed on his or her laptop. In this case, remediation doesn't work unless it involves fully installing antivirus software on that end user's machine — an unlikely prospect in most scenarios. For example, the end user might not have the appropriate privileges to install new software on the machine, or your organization might not want to pay for licenses for these types of users.

Luckily, you can find network antivirus systems that you can use to help alleviate this issue, provided that you can integrate the antivirus system in question to extend your NAC solution. When performing this type of integration, you want to force all traffic from non-compliant systems through the antivirus gateway on the network. On the corporate network, you can use a configuration that includes switches, firewalls, and other network elements.

Thus, the antivirus gateway inspects all the user's traffic, so your organization doesn't have to face the always difficult decision of whether to actively quarantine or restrict access to users who aren't in compliance with the stated endpoint security policies.

REMEMBER

Maintain productivity without sacrificing security. If you can find a NAC solution that allows you to perform this antivirus integration, you can provide full access to required applications and data while maintaining the best possible security.

URL/Web-filtering enforcement

URL/Web filtering is a popular type of technology that restricts access to certain types of Web content and to specific sites. Often, these systems monitor all outbound Web traffic and consult categorization lists provided by the vendor to restrict users from browsing to Web sites that serve forbidden content. Restricting access to pornographic material on a business network is an often-cited example.

These systems have the potential to one day become a key part of the NAC solution. Now, instead of having simple blanket policies for URL/Web policing, the organization can roll out user and role-based policies that are more specific to each user's particular role or job function.

For example, your company might want to restrict access to employment Web sites to prevent employees from looking for other jobs while at work, as shown in one of the blocking policies in Figure 14-4. At the same time, you might have in-house recruiters or human resources professionals who require access to these sites as part of their jobs. By leveraging group membership records in the corporate LDAP directory, you can ensure that the people who require access to these sites have the appropriate level of access and the majority of your users are restricted. Of course, if a large number of your users are attempting to access employment sites while on the job, you probably have some bigger issues to worry about than simply restricting access!

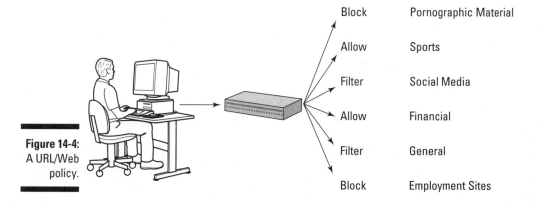

Figure 14-4:
A URL/Web
policy.

Block	Pornographic Material
Allow	Sports
Filter	Social Media
Allow	Financial
Filter	General
Block	Employment Sites

VPN enforcement

NAC shares many common types of concepts and policies with SSL VPNs.

A VPN solution — whether it's an SSL VPN, an IPSec VPN, or some other type of VPN — allows access to the corporate network, even though the user isn't physically located on the corporate network itself. Many organizations want to employ the same NAC policies for remote users that they employ for local users.

For example, if the NAC policy states that every user on the local network must authenticate with a one-time password from a machine that runs an up-to-date antivirus application, that policy really makes sense only if you can apply it globally. By allowing remote-access users to bypass these policies, the organization opens security holes and exposes itself to the exact threats that it wants to mitigate by designing these policies in the first place.

By integrating a VPN solution with NAC, you can extend your NAC deployment to ensure that it enforces the NAC policies for every user on the network, regardless of the user's physical location. This type of integration might take a number of forms, but in a generic case, you could use some of the same APIs and standards mentioned in the section "Learning from your Network," earlier in this chapter. For example, a couple of leading NAC solutions include native abilities to set and enforce IPSec VPN policies for both remote and local users.

This global enforcement of access control enables you to centrally manage all your access-control policies, ensuring that you consistently enforce every policy.

Application enforcement

No NAC vendor has announced or released a solution for integration of applications, but vendors will eventually create these types of NAC extensions allowing seamless integration of network policies (via NAC) and application policies (via the applications themselves).

Although most applications do (and will continue to) have authentication, NAC can provide additional information to each application so that the application can increase security and provide a better overall solution.

For example, if an IDP/IPS system senses an attack on the network and the NAC system detects that attack, NAC can provide that information to the application so that the application can determine whether the end user should have continued access to the application. Or, if the end user is allowed onto the network with restricted access because of a non-compliant endpoint machine, he or she might still need to gain access to certain applications. The application, however, can respond to this information by offering a more granular, intra-application control over that end user, such as by restricting certain functions within the application itself. The application might provide read-only access, rather than read/write access, for example.

Extending NAC on the Endpoint

NAC solutions are quickly driving towards a more complete integration across the entire network. The preceding sections focus on extending NAC into the traditional network and security infrastructure. But extending NAC to the endpoint also has some merits because all NAC solutions provide some form of endpoint integrity inspection by scanning endpoint devices to ensure that the appropriate antivirus, personal firewall, anti-malware, and other standard endpoint security suites are installed and running. Although most enterprises can meet all of their endpoint integrity needs by using this kind of inspection, you might have more specialized needs.

Client-side open standards and APIs allow the NAC vendor's endpoint integrity agents to fully scan the endpoint machine for endpoint software and posture assessment that the NAC solution from your vendor might not natively include. For example, although your NAC vendor might provide a native ability to scan for and remediate missing operating-system patches, your team might have already spent considerable time and money on your own chosen patch remediation solution. By using APIs (including the Trusted Computing Group's Trusted Network Connect and Microsoft's NAP SHA/SHV APIs), you can work with your patch vendor or on your own to successfully create scans that are fully integrated into the capabilities of the NAC endpoint-integrity inspection engine.

By extending NAC on the endpoint, you create a native solution that combines most of what you need and provides you with the ability to extend that solution further to address your specific needs.

Don't craft a security policy that's constrained to the limitations of available vendor solutions; instead, begin with a set of policies that meet the needs of your organization, and then choose the solution that best meets those needs.

Disk encryption integration

In a business environment that has increasingly mobile users accessing data from an ever-expanding range of devices, disk encryption becomes a great tool to help prevent data theft from lost or stolen machines.

Tens of thousands of laptops are lost or stolen each year in places such as airports, coffee shops, taxis, and other public areas. Those same laptops often contain a wealth of important information — many high profile cases have involved the loss of machines that contained credit card numbers, Social Security numbers, and other sensitive data. If the organizations involved had protected these machines by using encrypted disks, they could have greatly reduced the concerns over that data loss or theft.

While these solutions become more popular, NAC vendors will probably provide native checks to ensure that a machine has disk encryption software installed, which is actively encrypting.

In the meantime, the extensibility of NAC allows it to provide custom checks on the endpoint that ensure every applicable laptop complies with your disk encryption policies.

Data leakage prevention integration

The jury is still out on data leakage prevention (DLP) solutions. Vendors have come a long way in recent years in terms of their ability to effectively finger-print and identify sensitive corporate data without requiring each customer to maintain a team of people to keep the solution up to date and effective. Most of these solutions incorporate a network-based component, as well as an endpoint-based client component. By using NAC, you can ensure that your DLP solution is actively protecting each endpoint on the network, minimizing the risk of data leakage or data theft.

These types of solutions sometimes overlap with other solutions discussed in this chapter — including solutions such as disk encryption (which we talk about in the preceding section) and peripheral protection (as discussed in the following section). NAC can help you achieve your data loss and theft prevention goals, regardless of the approach that your organization takes.

Figure 14-5 illustrates some of the many ways that users can leak data from an organization, which should help explain why these types of solutions matter and how they can help to minimize the potential for data leakage. Most DLP solutions also include a network component that scans and fin-gerprints data while that data traverses the network, further expanding the scope and protection of the system.

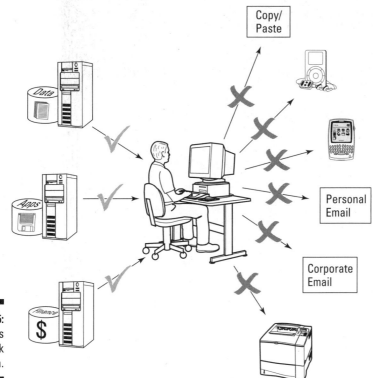

Figure 14-5:
How users
can leak
data.

Peripheral protection suite integration

USB drives provide very convenient ways to store and move data in a portable format. As a result, an enormous number of users rely on them not only for their personal data storage, but also for storing sensitive corporate data — a practice that most enterprises see as quite risky. This problem doesn't stop at USB drives, however.

Think about how many devices and media in a typical power user's arsenal have the capacity to remove data from the device:

- Many mobile phones, PDAs, and smartphones have storage media on which you can place data.

- Music players (iPods and other MP3 players, for example) have also become high-capacity mobile storage devices.

- Digital cameras are another great example. Beyond these types of devices, you can also find a variety of media cheaply available. CDs and DVDs are inexpensive and popular, and most computers sold today have the ability to write data to CDs or DVDs.

Printers are another source of potential data leakage from an organization.

The huge explosion of portable devices and media represents an increased potential for data to leak, or for someone to remove or steal that data, from your organization. As a result, you might already use some sort of endpoint software that provides you the ability to control usage of these types of devices and media. NAC vendors will likely respond to this market need by providing native integration if and when these peripheral protection suites become more popular.

In the meantime, you might consider extending your NAC implementation on the computers connecting to your network to provide greater value to your organization and ensure that you minimize your data leakage concerns.

Virtual sandbox desktop virtualization integration

The explosion of new types of devices into corporate networks has resulted in what some are calling the *consumerization of IT,* meaning that end users are demanding more choices than ever before in the type of devices that they use to complete their work. Control has gradually shifted away from the IT department and towards the end users in regards to managing these devices. Although many organizations have retained their control over managed machines, others have ceded some level of control over the purchase decision and the management of productivity devices to end users.

In these types of environments, an emerging kind of endpoint software is gaining in popularity. These software packages use virtualization technologies to create secure sandboxes on devices of the user's choice, and those sandboxes contain all corporate data and applications.

For example, a user purchases his or her own Microsoft Windows laptop, then installs a broad range of personal applications, in addition to those applications required for his or her job. By using these application or desktop virtualization technologies, the IT department can install on this machine a separate, virtualized machine that stores all work-related data and applications, and in which the user must perform all his or her work-related tasks. Virtualization software makes the virtual machine itself completely separate from the user's personal partition, typically encrypts or otherwise secures the virtual machine, and includes mechanisms that prevent data leakage or movement from one partition on the system to the other.

Organizations that deploy these types of solutions need to ensure that the user is really working from within the encrypted sandbox environment for the duration of his or her session, which you can do by extending your NAC deployment to perform the necessary scanning.

Don't confuse these computer-based desktop virtualization solutions with hosted virtual desktop environments, which have also become popular in recent years. In virtual desktop environment solutions, the data and applications remain in the datacenter, and the end user connects to the desktop via a connection such as Remote Desktop Protocol (RDP).

Patch management and remediation integration

NAC was first used to determine whether machines on the corporate network run the appropriate endpoint security products and whether those machines were patched with the latest critical operating system and application patches.

Most NAC vendors include these capabilities natively within their solutions, allowing you to scan various machines on the network for the presence (or absence) of any type of patch. NAC provides appropriate remediation if the endpoint does not have the necessary patches. But some NAC solutions don't provide this capability. Also, your company may have invested in its own patch management and remediation system, so you want to make use of that system in conjunction with your NAC deployment. In these cases, extending NAC allows you to integrate fully with your existing patch management and remediation system, and maintain use of the investment that your organization has already made in that technology.

For example, NAC allows a non-compliant machine on the network to have access to the remediation server, most likely through quarantine. The patch management client contacts the server for the appropriate patches, which is then automatically installed on the endpoint machine. After the machine is in compliance, the NAC solution reverses the access control decision to quarantine, and the end user gains the full level of access that he or she would have had from the beginning if the machine had initially passed all the endpoint integrity scans.

Backup software integration

Because NAC is extensible on the endpoint, you can even use NAC to scan for applications that might not seem like traditional endpoint-security applications. Backup clients, for example, aren't security applications, but you might have a policy that stipulates your organization's managed endpoints must have these applications installed and running.

By extending your NAC deployment on the endpoint, you have the ability to scan for these applications, ensuring that the backup software is backing up important corporate data appropriately.

If the client side of your backup software deployment has a tight integration with the server side, you might even set policies on the backup client, ensuring that it's appropriately configured to back up key corporate application data or other important items, such as a user's locally saved e-mail inbox.

Custom application integration

You can use many NAC solutions to scan for almost anything on an endpoint device.

Like with other software such as backup clients (as discussed in the preceding section), which don't necessarily relate to endpoint security, you might consider other applications on machines attached to your network necessary.

- ✔ For example, you might have mobile devices, such as Windows Mobile smartphones, that must have remote-wipe or device-reset software installed before you allow them to connect to the network and access corporate data. By using NAC, you can scan for this type of software, ensuring that you can remotely delete the device memory if the user loses that device.

- ✔ Or maybe you develop some of your own internal endpoint security, data protection, or productivity applications, and you want to ensure that every endpoint has installed these applications and has an up-to-date version running.

By using NAC, you can accomplish your goals beyond simple endpoint security. NAC gives you a fairly easy way to scan for just about any kind of software that you might need installed on an endpoint device. Although some of the ideas mentioned in this section may not fall into the realm of traditional security, you can use them to get more from your NAC investment.

By placing NAC on the endpoint, as well as across the network and security infrastructure, you gain many advantages because other technologies are simply more limited than NAC.

Part IV
The Part of Tens

By Rich Tennant

"They can predict earthquakes and seizures, why <u>not</u> server failures?"

In this part . . .

*T*his part offers quick references to the top-ten most helpful stuff on the planet about NAC. You can find help on topics ranging from key definitions, to planning your implementation, to where to go for more info.

Chapter 15

Ten Best Practices

*Y*ou face many challenges when you try to deploy NAC. But you can develop several practices that can help make your NAC deployment successful and productive.

You have to decide what you consider the success indicators for your deployment. This chapter gives you ten practices that can help you with your deployment, ranging from security best practices to organizational and operational best practices. When you use them together, you end up with a deployment that's functional, maintainable, and cost effective.

Have a Complete Plan for NAC

The most important step in planning what will ultimately become your NAC deployment is deciding what NAC means to you. You need to ask yourself several questions:

- ✔ Why do you want to roll out NAC?
- ✔ Where do you want to enable NAC?
- ✔ Who do you want to enable NAC for?

Your answers to these questions drive where you initially install NAC across your organization's network. Have an overall plan in your mind that you can use to determine when you complete your deployment. When you begin to think through the possibilities, you may find out that NAC can do even more for you than you originally thought, so keep an open mind to other solutions that NAC may provide.

Leverage Existing Authentication

Companies typically have one or more authentication sources available for users. The most common of these sources include Active Directory, LDAP, and RADIUS. To speed up your deployment, you can leverage your network's existing authentication, instead of creating a new authentication service.

Here are some of the users that you may want to authenticate:

- ✔ Guest users
- ✔ Corporate users
- ✔ Contractors
- ✔ Devices

If your authentication source is missing necessary access control information, such as groups, you can more easily add that role or group information to what you have than create an entirely new infrastructure.

If you're leveraging an existing authentication source, plan for the extra authentication load that NAC will add to your authentication servers.

Endpoint Compliance

If you're considering adding NAC to your network, you're most likely interested in some form of endpoint compliance. If you want to include endpoint compliance as a requirement for getting access to the network, you need to first decide what makes a device compliant.

Consider looking for antivirus software, anti-spyware software, firewall software, and operating system patches.

When you create this list of compliance requirements, make sure you consider the following devices:

- ✔ Guest machines
- ✔ Corporate machines
- ✔ Contractors' machines

Policy Enforcement

A lot of NAC solutions include optional enforcement. Even if you start out with an evaluate-only type of NAC deployment, you probably eventually want to enforce NAC policies in the network.

Look at the NAC solutions that you are evaluating to determine what methods of enforcement are included and how they fit with your organization's short and long-term goals for NAC. Several options for enforcement allow greater flexibility and more capabilities from NAC. These options include

- ✔ Switch-based enforcement
- ✔ Inline devices or appliances
- ✔ Endpoint or client-based enforcement

Try to leverage more that one option when you complete your deployment. For example, if you use endpoint enforcement, also set up a check-and-balance with network-based enforcement to enforce the policy so that you can protect yourself if the endpoint becomes compromised.

The closer to the endpoint you position enforcement, the more control you have over what the device can see. In a perfect world, you'd enforce policies everywhere possible:

- ✔ The endpoint itself
- ✔ The access layer switch
- ✔ An inline device in front of your protected resources

Management

If you can't successfully manage your NAC solution, you introduce a level of complexity on top of your network that can cause headaches when you move forward. Make sure that you're comfortable with the management flow of the NAC solution.

If possible, get a management system that allows you to manage all the parts of the NAC solution from one place. Look for a NAC management solution that can

- **Manage such important NAC components as the policy engine, switches, and the inline appliance from one location.** When thinking of management, think globally if you're a multi-national company.

- **Delegate administration in the management solution.** You can delegate tasks to different groups inside your company.

Logging, Reporting, and Auditing

If your NAC deployment experiences a problem, good logging and reporting alert you to the problem and help you identify a solution.

Look for a way to centralize all the log data to a single location, especially if your NAC deployment uses multiple policy engines. You can usually use a third-party management tool, such as a Syslog server, to accomplish the task, but some NAC solutions offer their own central logging and reporting engines. Most of the time, the built-in central logging and reporting engine gives you access to pre-canned reporting that can help you with the NAC solution deployment. You want a reporting tool that offers reports that help you with day-to-day operations and reports that help you when the NAC solution experiences a problem.

Audit trails are an important aspect of logging. If you need to meet some sort of regulatory compliance, auditing may have been a primary driver for your NAC deployment. Make sure that the log information includes as much detail as possible. You want to know who gained access to the network and when, what parts of the network they visited, what their devices looked like, and so on.

Helpdesk Support

The plan that you establish to deal with NAC deployment problems when they arise can dictate whether you successfully deploy NAC. Create a plan to help users if they can't get access to the network. You put NAC in place to control access to resources, but if a user can't log in or has problems, NAC's control limits the user's productivity.

Train your helpdesk personnel so that they can tell users how to get their machines on the network. Some problems to think about include

✔ The user's machine is out of compliance.

✔ The user's NAC agent or client does not allow them to connect to the network with appropriate access.

✔ The user can't authenticate.

Make sure that your helpdesk personnel have access to tools that they can use to identify and fix the problems that arise. These tools should include delegated admin privileges to the policy engine or management system, and centralized logging information.

Day-to-Day Operation

NAC needs to work continuously every day. Create a plan for how you tie NAC into ongoing processes. Some example events or processes to consider include

✔ New employees

✔ Employee termination

✔ Change of resource access

✔ Endpoint policy changes

Identify the people whom you want to manage each function and delegate the job function to them. For example, you probably want to make sure that new employees get access to the network, so you may want to make network access a part of your new-hire processes in HR.

Maintenance and Upgrades

After you roll out NAC in your network, your NAC deployment will undoubt-edly need some sort of maintenance and upgrades eventually. A few steps can save hours of headaches:

✔ **Set up a small lab that's a miniature version of your production NAC deployment.** Before you upgrade your production network, always test it in the lab to make sure that it's going to work and not introduce any problems. In other words, always test before rolling it out. Test such components as the endpoint software, policies, enforcement, and so on.

✔ **Do upgrades in phases.** Depending on your NAC solution, you may want to upgrade the endpoint clients first; then, you can try to upgrade the policy engine. Ask your NAC vendor for their recommendations on how you can successfully upgrade the various components of the NAC solution.

✔ **Have a rollback plan.** If the upgrade is unsuccessful, you need to roll back — and you need to have a plan for that rollback. Instead of allowing your network to block all productivity, you may want to roll back and do further tests in a lab before you try to upgrade again.

Future Expansion

NAC can provide solutions to many different problems that you'll identify over the years. When you identify new problems or challenges, see whether NAC can help you solve them. By keeping NAC in mind for future issues, you get more out of your NAC deployment. Ask the vendor that provides the solution to identify new technologies that they've added to the solution since you purchased because you may be able to leverage a new technology for some of these future issues as they arise.

Chapter 16

Ten Steps to Planning Your NAC Implementation

*W*e wrote this book to show you the way that many factors can lead to the ultimate success or failure of your NAC implementation. Because this solution spans multiple types of technology and, at the same time, many parts of your organization, you need to properly plan out every piece of the process and make those plans in the proper order.

If you haven't read through the rest of the book, this chapter actually provides a good introduction to the different phases of a successful deployment. Most of these topics are discussed in great detail throughout the various chapters of this book. Be sure to mark down topic areas that you and your organization might find difficult, and then study up on those areas — either by referring to the appropriate chapters of this book or by doing your own organizational and self-directed research.

Understand NAC

First, before proceeding with a NAC plan of any sort, you need to understand the technologies and the market. You don't need to take a deep-dive look at the different vendor technologies at this point, but rather a high-level review of marketing materials and data sheets from all the various vendors so that you can get a sense of the type of approach each vendor takes. Also, many analysts and trade journals track the NAC market closely, and these publications can provide an impartial view of all the primary competitors and approaches.

By the way, because you're holding this book in your hands, you've already taken the first step towards educating yourself, so read through this thoroughly and start thinking about how NAC can help your organization reach its short- and long-term security goals. Reach out to colleagues in the industry who have already deployed NAC, too. They can give you good insights into what to look out for and how NAC has helped them. You may find their input particularly valuable if they've already gone through the implementation process.

Create (or Revise) Your Corporate Security Policy

Your NAC implementation is only one piece in a broader corporate security policy that governs the types of technologies that are implemented to ensure proper security in your organization's network. This policy should provide guidelines that you can follow when planning for NAC in your network, and you and the other members of the implementation team can use this policy as an ongoing reference throughout your implementation. For example, a core set of endpoint security or authentication requirements might apply to all employees who want to access network resources. These requirements have a direct impact on the policies that you create while you roll out NAC. Chapter 6 covers this topic in detail, if you want to know more about corporate security policies.

Build a Cross-Functional Team

You absolutely must build this kind of team if you want a successful NAC implementation, and you absolutely must perform this step early in the process, rather than later. We have seen many NAC implementations stall because of internal politics or differences of opinion between the various groups involved. Identify everyone whom the NAC implementation will impact, and get them involved throughout the planning process. For example, if you're in the Security group and don't involve the Desktop team, you might choose a vendor's solution and only later realize that it doesn't integrate well with the software distribution solution that the Desktop team is rolling out. Avoid any bad blood or delays by getting everyone involved from the beginning. Chapter 7, about corporate cooperation, describes whom to get involved and when.

Seek Vendor Info and RFPs

After you educate yourself and identify your organization's core team, start looking at various vendors to come up with a short list of NAC vendors that you will invite in for further evaluation. Different organizations take different approaches to narrowing the list of vendors. Some organizations initiate design/sales meetings with interesting vendors to see how each vendor implementation fits with that organization's goals. Other organizations create Requests for Proposals (RFPs) that give each vendor a list of questions that they must respond to in a written fashion. Regardless of the approach, the goal of this step is to identify which vendors offer products that have sufficient functionality to meet the key goals of your NAC solution.

Test a Proof of Concept

This section and the two following sections are outlined more completely in Chapter 11. You can do proof of concept testing with one or more vendors, but if you do test with more than one vendor, you probably want to keep that list to a minimum because these tests, when executed properly, can take up a lot of both your and the vendor's time. The goal of this test is to deploy parts of the solution in a test environment so that you can ensure it works with your network and can deliver on the marketing that the vendor's sales organization has been feeding you.

Implement a Pilot

The pilot implementation is a lot like the proof of concept test, but the pilot involves actual end users. After you add end users to the equation, you start to get a really good sense of how seamless the NAC solution will be for users, how well your organization can deal with deployment problems, and whether the chosen vendor can meet your needs. At this point, don't deal with more than one vendor and treat the pilot implementation as the first step in a much larger rollout across the organization.

Rollout a Limited Production

After you successfully complete the pilot implementation, you need to move on to a limited product rollout. How you define "limited" can vary, depending on the size, complexity, and structure of your organization. Some organizations focus on specific locations as a starting point for their NAC deployment. Other organizations focus on specific user groups, independent of location.

Regardless of your approach, best practices dictate focusing on a specific subset of the whole organization as an extended trial. This limited rollout can help you work out any issues related to deployment — whether organizational or technical.

Try to focus on a subset of your environment that can give you the best possible cross section of devices, users, and network infrastructure equipment, allowing you to minimize the number of surprises when you move on to full production. Begin the limited rollout by only evaluating policies at first — so that you can correct issues before you end up limiting a user's access when he or she just wants to do his or her job.

Deploy the Full Production and Evaluate Policies

If you make it this far in the NAC evaluation and implementation process, you're well on your way to a successful deployment. Continue the rollout until it spans the full breadth of the intended implementation. Whether you take a location-by-location or user-group-by-user-group approach, plan the schedule so that you have sufficient buffer time to deal with any unforeseen circumstances while you move from one section of the deployment to the next.

During this phase, focus on evaluating policies, but don't enforce them. By evaluating policies only, you can make a widespread assessment of the health of the endpoints on your network and make any necessary corrective actions before you start enforcing policy. You never want to prevent your customers (the end users) from getting full network access. Aim for productivity without compromising security, which means that you should give users limited access only when necessary — such as after repeated attempts to correct a machine or when users purposely dodge security policies. Evaluation can give you a good sense of where things stand before you need to lock things down.

Deploy Full Production with Policy Enforcement

After you roll out NAC to a wide user group and ensure that you have an appropriate level of compliance with policies (as well as a proper machine-patching and software-distribution strategy), policy enforcement can move into full swing. Chapters 8 and 9 can give you a sense of which policies to enact, as well as when and how to enforce them. After you develop the appropriate policy approach, simply flip the switch and get things moving. Make sure that your helpdesk is ready to take on any additional calls in the first few weeks from end users who have issues that they can't correct on their own. If you do a sufficient job of evaluating policies, as discussed in the preceding section, you probably don't have to worry too much about this.

Assess and Re-Evaluate at Regular Intervals

Congratulations! You've successfully rolled out NAC across your organization, with full user authentication, endpoint integrity, network enforcement, and more. So, now what? Vacation? Retirement? Put your feet up on the desk? Not so fast — network, security, and user requirements evolve over time. While these changes happen, your NAC implementation strategy must also change. After you complete the rollout, ensure that your users are happy, your deployment team can efficiently manage the implementation, and the NAC rollout meets the needs and goals set forth in the very early stages of the implementation. Continual reassessment is a key part of any technology adoption, and you definitely need to make it a part of something as critical and visible as NAC.

Chapter 17

Ten Online Information Sources

*I*f you've already read through the rest of this book, you might be staring at the title of this chapter and thinking, "This book has provided so much valuable information and such a good understanding of NAC. Why would I need to go online for further assistance?" Although we certainly appreciate the implied compliment, you can find out much more about NAC. This chapter points you to various online information sources, including industry trade journals, vendor Web sites, standards organizations, and more.

Network World on NAC

Industry trade journals can be great sources of vendor-neutral information about these technologies, and in some cases, they offer comparisons or bake-offs of the various options. *Network World* has been tracking NAC from the early days, and its NAC portal has a lot of information on NAC, including some vendor comparisons.

```
www.networkworld.com/topics/nac.html
```

Trusted Computing Group

The Trusted Computing Group is a leader in developing standards for NAC and endpoint integrity. This portal includes links to the Trusted Network

Connect (TNC) standards, as well as case studies, white papers, and an up-to-date list of products and partners that support the TNC standards.

www.trustedcomputinggroup.org/groups/network

IETF NEA

The Internet Engineering Task Force (IETF) is a widely recognized and supported standards body that has developed a majority of the standards used on the Internet today. One of the emerging groups within the IETF is NEA — Network Endpoint Assessment. Although NEA hasn't yet published its official specifications as of the writing of this book, you can find draft publications at the IETF Web address in this section.

Although the NEA competes with Trusted Network Connect (which we talk about in the preceding section), the NEA drafts are based entirely on TNC specifications. Hopefully, everyone can get along in this crazy, mixed-up world!

http://tools.ietf.org/wg/nea

Gartner NAC Marketscope

The Gartner NAC Marketscope is an impartial review of the major vendors competing in the NAC space. Updated periodically (and likely to be replaced soon by a Gartner Magic Quadrant), this document describes the vendor approaches to NAC and assesses them both on their execution or current offerings, and on their future vision and roadmap, as provided by the vendors to Gartner.

Although you have to pay to access both this document and the Forrester Wave (discussed in the following section), they're well-respected industry publications used by many customers in a variety of industries. In addition, some vendors have gone through the expense of purchasing reprint rights for these publications, so you might be able to get a freebie!

www.gartner.com/displaydocument?id=500809

Forrester NAC Wave

The NAC Wave is a periodically refreshed assessment of the major vendors competing for your NAC dollars. Compiled by a well-known industry analyst, this document talks about approaches to NAC, in addition to major vendors.

www.forrester.com/go?docid=36450

Cisco NAC

You can look at the home page for the Cisco NAC solution. Depending on your system, use either

- ✔ **Cisco Clean Access:** www.cisco.com/en/US/products/ps6128
- ✔ **Cisco NAC Framework:** www.cisco.com/en/US/netsol/ns617/ networking_solutions_sub_solution_home.html

Juniper Networks UAC

The home page for the Juniper Networks Unified Access Control solution includes a variety of literature, including data sheets, white papers, case studies, and presentations.

www.juniper.net/products_and_services/unified_access_control

Microsoft NAP

This site, the home page for the Microsoft Network Access Protection (NAP) solution, describes the Microsoft native offering, as well as the extension of NAP through partnerships and the Microsoft APIs.

www.microsoft.com/technet/network/nap/napoverview.mspx

Symantec NAC

The home page for the Symantec network access control solution includes a wealth of information on the Symantec offering, including presentations, datasheets, and trialware.

www.symantec.com/business/network-access-control

Bradford Networks NAC

Bradford Networks, a strong player in the NAC space, has a Web site that includes marketing materials on the Bradford solution, whitepapers, case studies, and links to the reprint editions of some of the industry publications that we talk about in this chapter.

www.bradfordnetworks.com

Chapter 18

Ten Definitions

*T*hroughout this book, we introduce dozens of terms, along with an alphabet soup of acronyms! It's a lot to wrap your head around. You can find the ten most important definitions in this chapter.

802.1X

802.1X is the foundation for dynamic policy configuration and enforcement in many popular NAC architectures. It's the IEEE standard for port-based network access control. 802.1X was designed to securely authenticate users and devices when they attempt to attach to networks — it was initially designed for wired networks but was also adapted for use in wireless networks when they became more popular.

802.1X forces the user or device to authenticate before he, she, or it can transmit any packets on the network — in other words, 802.1X has to authenticate you before it assigns you an IP address and gives you a fully functional wired or wireless adapter.

The 802.1X protocols require three components:

✔ **Supplicant:** A client-side application with which the user or machine interacts in order to gather credentials and submit them to the authenticator

✔ **Authenticator:** Typically a switch or wireless access point that's responsible for performing the authentication and acting as the Policy Enforcement Point after granting a device or user access

✔ **Authentication server:** Responsible for validating the credentials provided by the authenticator — ensuring that the user has provided an appropriate user name and password, for example.

You can find a detailed definition of each of these components in Chapter 13.

AAA

AAA is an acronym for authentication, authorization, and accounting. Many NAC vendors use this terminology and concept. In most cases, the term describes the first two As in AAA, including the process of validating that users are who they say they are and then determining what level of access each user gets on the network, based on his or her credentials, as well as other pieces of information such as role in the organization. The three As are

- ✔ **Authentication:** Collecting some sort of identifying credential and verifying that information so that you can confirm, unequivocally, who the user is. Most NAC implementations support a variety of authentication mechanisms, ranging from user name and password to digital certificates and one-time passwords.

- ✔ **Authorization:** Determining what level of access a user can have on the network (or, more generally, which policies apply to that user) as a result of several factors. Authentication is usually part of the authorization that a user ends up with, but other authorization factors in many NAC implementations include endpoint integrity and attributes assigned to the user in the corporate directory (such as role or group).

- ✔ **Accounting:** Tracking what the user has done on the network. NAC solutions are generally equipped with granular logging capabilities that allow your organization to keep records of data and application access. These records can help you audit and perform other compliance tasks, or investigate network events after they occur.

Chapter 8 describes AAA in more detail.

Endpoint Integrity

Endpoint integrity is known by several marketing names — host checking, endpoint security, endpoint verification, and so on.

Despite the variety of names, most NAC solutions use a fairly similar feature set for endpoint integrity. *Endpoint integrity* is the process by which endpoint devices (such as PCs and laptops) are scanned to determine whether those devices have the appropriate endpoint security applications installed and running.

The requirements of a particular organization in this regard can range from simple scans, such as ensuring that a device has an antivirus application up to date and running, to more custom types of scans, such as ensuring that a device has a particular homegrown application installed and running.

Chapter 9 talks about endpoint integrity.

Policy Decision Point

In most NAC architectures, the *Policy Decision Point (PDP)* corresponds to the solution's main policy server. The PDP applies three basic steps:

1. Collect a full range of information about a user or machine's session — authentication and authorization information, endpoint integrity, location, time of day, and more.

2. Use this information to decide which resources (applications, data, and network segments) the user can access during that session.

3. Push this decision to the Policy Enforcement Point (PEP) in the form of a policy that the PEP implements until either

   • The session expires.

   • The PDP revises and refreshes the policy decision.

The PDP is the device or service that provides authorization to the Policy Enforcement Point(s) for every user and machine that attempts to access network resources.

Policy Enforcement Point

The *Policy Enforcement Point (PEP)* is the piece of network or security equipment that controls user access and ensures the authorization decision made by the Policy Decision Point (PDP).

In some NAC implementations, the PDP is a wired switch or wireless access point. In others, it's a firewall, IPS, server, or inline appliance. Depending on the implementation, the PEP and PDP can either be standalone devices or consolidated into a single device.

Statement of Health

The *Statement of Health (SoH)* is a protocol that allows Microsoft Windows machines on a network to report system health, or endpoint integrity, to a NAC policy server or Policy Decision Point (PDP) in a standards-based manner.

The SoH protocols were first released by Microsoft and supported on Windows XP Service Pack 3 and Windows Vista SP1.

Major NAC architectures, including Trusted Network Connect and Microsoft NAP, support these protocols and allow for the validation of a machine's integrity without requiring a vendor's custom-built endpoint integrity client, which can help simplify deployment tasks, in some cases.

Trusted Network Connect

Trusted Network Connect (TNC) is an open standard developed by the Trusted Computing Group (TCG). One of the first standards devoted exclusively to NAC, TNC ensures vendor interoperability across the large number of elements associated with any NAC solution. These standards focus mainly on endpoint integrity, although the TCG has recently released standards that expand TNC to a broader role in a NAC environment, including standards such as IF-MAP, which provides for a close coordination between many network and security devices.

We describe TNC in further detail in Chapter 13.

Juniper Networks Unified Access Control

Unified Access Control (UAC) is the Juniper Networks NAC architecture that authenticates users and scans for endpoint integrity. UAC relies on either

- ✔ The Juniper UAC agent installed on the endpoint
- ✔ The native Microsoft agent

Enforcement point choices range from any vendor's 802.1X wired switches and access points to a range of Juniper security devices, including all Juniper firewalls and IDP devices.

You can extend Juniper UAC to other endpoint and infrastructure products because it supports the Trusted Network Connect protocols.

Microsoft Network Access Protection

Network Access Protection (NAP) is Microsoft's version of their NAC architecture. NAP relies on a Microsoft NAP client installed on each endpoint and offers a variety of enforcement points. Enforcement includes 802.1X-enabled switching infrastructure, VPN servers, DHCP servers, and several other enforcement points.

NAP offers an extended ecosystem of partners and partner integrations that can increase the value of NAP to Microsoft's customers.

Cisco's Network Admission Control

Cisco's Network Admission Control (NAC) is Cisco's network access control product. Cisco offers two solutions:

- ✔ **Cisco NAC Appliance (Clean Access):** An inline appliance that's responsible for authenticating users, scanning endpoints, and enforcing access control policies
- ✔ **The Network Admission Control framework:** Allows integration and enforcement, typically via 802.1X, across existing network and security devices in the network

Index

• *B* •

• F •

BUSINESS, CAREERS & PERSONAL FINANCE

Accounting For Dummies, 4th Edition*
978-0-470-24600-9

Bookkeeping Workbook For Dummies†
978-0-470-16983-4

Commodities For Dummies
978-0-470-04928-0

Doing Business in China For Dummies
978-0-470-04929-7

E-Mail Marketing For Dummies
978-0-470-19087-6

Job Interviews For Dummies, 3rd Edition*†
978-0-470-17748-8

Personal Finance Workbook For Dummies*†
978-0-470-09933-9

Real Estate License Exams For Dummies
978-0-7645-7623-2

Six Sigma For Dummies
978-0-7645-6798-8

Small Business Kit For Dummies, 2nd Edition*†
978-0-7645-5984-6

Telephone Sales For Dummies
978-0-470-16836-3

BUSINESS PRODUCTIVITY & MICROSOFT OFFICE

Access 2007 For Dummies
978-0-470-03649-5

Excel 2007 For Dummies
978-0-470-03737-9

Office 2007 For Dummies
978-0-470-00923-9

Outlook 2007 For Dummies
978-0-470-03830-7

PowerPoint 2007 For Dummies
978-0-470-04059-1

Project 2007 For Dummies
978-0-470-03651-8

QuickBooks 2008 For Dummies
978-0-470-18470-7

Quicken 2008 For Dummies
978-0-470-17473-9

Salesforce.com For Dummies, 2nd Edition
978-0-470-04893-1

Word 2007 For Dummies
978-0-470-03658-7

EDUCATION, HISTORY, REFERENCE & TEST PREPARATION

African American History For Dummies
978-0-7645-5469-8

Algebra For Dummies
978-0-7645-5325-7

Algebra Workbook For Dummies
978-0-7645-8467-1

Art History For Dummies
978-0-470-09910-0

ASVAB For Dummies, 2nd Edition
978-0-470-10671-6

British Military History For Dummies
978-0-470-03213-8

Calculus For Dummies
978-0-7645-2498-1

Canadian History For Dummies, 2nd Edition
978-0-470-83656-9

Geometry Workbook For Dummies
978-0-471-79940-5

The SAT I For Dummies, 6th Edition
978-0-7645-7193-0

Series 7 Exam For Dummies
978-0-470-09932-2

World History For Dummies
978-0-7645-5242-7

FOOD, GARDEN, HOBBIES & HOME

Bridge For Dummies, 2nd Edition
978-0-471-92426-5

Coin Collecting For Dummies, 2nd Edition
978-0-470-22275-1

Cooking Basics For Dummies, 3rd Edition
978-0-7645-7206-7

Drawing For Dummies
978-0-7645-5476-6

Etiquette For Dummies, 2nd Edition
978-0-470-10672-3

Gardening Basics For Dummies*†
978-0-470-03749-2

Knitting Patterns For Dummies
978-0-470-04556-5

Living Gluten-Free For Dummies†
978-0-471-77383-2

Painting Do-It-Yourself For Dummies
978-0-470-17533-0

HEALTH, SELF HELP, PARENTING & PETS

Anger Management For Dummies
978-0-470-03715-7

Anxiety & Depression Workbook For Dummies
978-0-7645-9793-0

Dieting For Dummies, 2nd Edition
978-0-7645-4149-0

Dog Training For Dummies, 2nd Edition
978-0-7645-8418-3

Horseback Riding For Dummies
978-0-470-09719-9

Infertility For Dummies†
978-0-470-11518-3

Meditation For Dummies with CD-ROM, 2nd Edition
978-0-471-77774-8

Post-Traumatic Stress Disorder For Dummies
978-0-470-04922-8

Puppies For Dummies, 2nd Edition
978-0-470-03717-1

Thyroid For Dummies, 2nd Edition†
978-0-471-78755-6

Type 1 Diabetes For Dummies*†
978-0-470-17811-9

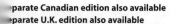

* Separate Canadian edition also available
† Separate U.K. edition also available

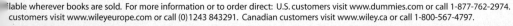
Available wherever books are sold. For more information or to order direct: U.S. customers visit www.dummies.com or call 1-877-762-2974.
U.K. customers visit www.wileyeurope.com or call (0)1243 843291. Canadian customers visit www.wiley.ca or call 1-800-567-4797.

WILEY

INTERNET & DIGITAL MEDIA

AdWords For Dummies
978-0-470-15252-2

Blogging For Dummies, 2nd Edition
978-0-470-23017-6

Digital Photography All-in-One Desk Reference For Dummies, 3rd Edition
978-0-470-03743-0

Digital Photography For Dummies, 5th Edition
978-0-7645-9802-9

Digital SLR Cameras & Photography For Dummies, 2nd Edition
978-0-470-14927-0

eBay Business All-in-One Desk Reference For Dummies
978-0-7645-8438-1

eBay For Dummies, 5th Edition*
978-0-470-04529-9

eBay Listings That Sell For Dummies
978-0-471-78912-3

Facebook For Dummies
978-0-470-26273-3

The Internet For Dummies, 11th Edition
978-0-470-12174-0

Investing Online For Dummies, 5th Edition
978-0-7645-8456-5

iPod & iTunes For Dummies, 5th Edition
978-0-470-17474-6

MySpace For Dummies
978-0-470-09529-4

Podcasting For Dummies
978-0-471-74898-4

Search Engine Optimization For Dummies, 2nd Edition
978-0-471-97998-2

Second Life For Dummies
978-0-470-18025-9

Starting an eBay Business For Dummies 3rd Edition†
978-0-470-14924-9

GRAPHICS, DESIGN & WEB DEVELOPMENT

Adobe Creative Suite 3 Design Premium All-in-One Desk Reference For Dummies
978-0-470-11724-8

Adobe Web Suite CS3 All-in-One Desk Reference For Dummies
978-0-470-12099-6

AutoCAD 2008 For Dummies
978-0-470-11650-0

Building a Web Site For Dummies, 3rd Edition
978-0-470-14928-7

Creating Web Pages All-in-One Desk Reference For Dummies, 3rd Edition
978-0-470-09629-1

Creating Web Pages For Dummies, 8th Edition
978-0-470-08030-6

Dreamweaver CS3 For Dummies
978-0-470-11490-2

Flash CS3 For Dummies
978-0-470-12100-9

Google SketchUp For Dummies
978-0-470-13744-4

InDesign CS3 For Dummies
978-0-470-11865-8

Photoshop CS3 All-in-One Desk Reference For Dummies
978-0-470-11195-6

Photoshop CS3 For Dummies
978-0-470-11193-2

Photoshop Elements 5 For Dummies
978-0-470-09810-3

SolidWorks For Dummies
978-0-7645-9555-4

Visio 2007 For Dummies
978-0-470-08983-5

Web Design For Dummies, 2nd Edition
978-0-471-78117-2

Web Sites Do-It-Yourself For Dummies
978-0-470-16903-2

Web Stores Do-It-Yourself For Dummies
978-0-470-17443-2

LANGUAGES, RELIGION & SPIRITUALITY

Arabic For Dummies
978-0-471-77270-5

Chinese For Dummies, Audio Set
978-0-470-12766-7

French For Dummies
978-0-7645-5193-2

German For Dummies
978-0-7645-5195-6

Hebrew For Dummies
978-0-7645-5489-6

Ingles Para Dummies
978-0-7645-5427-8

Italian For Dummies, Audio Set
978-0-470-09586-7

Italian Verbs For Dummies
978-0-471-77389-4

Japanese For Dummies
978-0-7645-5429-2

Latin For Dummies
978-0-7645-5431-5

Portuguese For Dummies
978-0-471-78738-9

Russian For Dummies
978-0-471-78001-4

Spanish Phrases For Dummies
978-0-7645-7204-3

Spanish For Dummies
978-0-7645-5194-9

Spanish For Dummies, Audio Set
978-0-470-09585-0

The Bible For Dummies
978-0-7645-5296-0

Catholicism For Dummies
978-0-7645-5391-2

The Historical Jesus For Dummies
978-0-470-16785-4

Islam For Dummies
978-0-7645-5503-9

Spirituality For Dummies, 2nd Edition
978-0-470-19142-2

NETWORKING AND PROGRAMMING

ASP.NET 3.5 For Dummies
978-0-470-19592-5

C# 2008 For Dummies
978-0-470-19109-5

Hacking For Dummies, 2nd Edition
978-0-470-05235-8

Home Networking For Dummies, 4th Edition
978-0-470-11806-1

Java For Dummies, 4th Edition
978-0-470-08716-9

Microsoft® SQL Server™ 2008 All-in-One Desk Reference For Dummies
978-0-470-17954-3

Networking All-in-One Desk Reference For Dummies, 2nd Edition
978-0-7645-9939-2

Networking For Dummies, 8th Edition
978-0-470-05620-2

SharePoint 2007 For Dummies
978-0-470-09941-4

Wireless Home Networking For Dummies, 2nd Edition
978-0-471-74940-0

OPERATING SYSTEMS & COMPUTER BASICS

Mac For Dummies, 5th Edition
78-0-7645-8458-9

Laptops For Dummies, 2nd Edition
78-0-470-05432-1

Linux For Dummies, 8th Edition
78-0-470-11649-4

MacBook For Dummies
78-0-470-04859-7

Mac OS X Leopard All-in-One
Desk Reference For Dummies
78-0-470-05434-5

Mac OS X Leopard For Dummies
978-0-470-05433-8

Macs For Dummies, 9th Edition
978-0-470-04849-8

PCs For Dummies, 11th Edition
978-0-470-13728-4

Windows® Home Server For Dummies
978-0-470-18592-6

Windows Server 2008 For Dummies
978-0-470-18043-3

Windows Vista All-in-One
Desk Reference For Dummies
978-0-471-74941-7

Windows Vista For Dummies
978-0-471-75421-3

Windows Vista Security For Dummies
978-0-470-11805-4

SPORTS, FITNESS & MUSIC

Coaching Hockey For Dummies
78-0-470-83685-9

Coaching Soccer For Dummies
78-0-471-77381-8

Fitness For Dummies, 3rd Edition
78-0-7645-7851-9

Football For Dummies, 3rd Edition
78-0-470-12536-6

GarageBand For Dummies
978-0-7645-7323-1

Golf For Dummies, 3rd Edition
978-0-471-76871-5

Guitar For Dummies, 2nd Edition
978-0-7645-9904-0

Home Recording For Musicians
For Dummies, 2nd Edition
978-0-7645-8884-6

iPod & iTunes For Dummies,
5th Edition
978-0-470-17474-6

Music Theory For Dummies
978-0-7645-7838-0

Stretching For Dummies
978-0-470-06741-3

Get smart @ dummies.com®

- **Find a full list of Dummies titles**
- **Look into loads of FREE on-site articles**
- **Sign up for FREE eTips e-mailed to you weekly**
- **See what other products carry the Dummies name**
- **Shop directly from the Dummies bookstore**
- **Enter to win new prizes every month!**

Separate Canadian edition also available
Separate U.K. edition also available

Available wherever books are sold. For more information or to order direct: U.S. customers visit www.dummies.com or call 1-877-762-2974.
U.K. customers visit www.wileyeurope.com or call (0) 1243 843291. Canadian customers visit www.wiley.ca or call 1-800-567-4797.

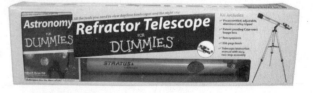